LATIN AMERICAN
POLITICAL YEARBOOK: 1997

LATIN AMERICAN POLITICAL YEARBOOK: 1997

Robert G. Breene, Jr.
Editor
United States

Alphonse Emanuiloff-Max
Associate Editor
Montevideo

Mario Rosenthal
Associate Editor
El Salvador

José Carlos Graça Wagner
Associate Editor
São Paulo

Routledge
Taylor & Francis Group

LONDON AND NEW YORK

First published 1998 by Transaction Publishers

2 Park Square, Milton Park, Abingdon, Oxfordshire OX14 4RN
711 Third Avenue, New York, NY 10017

Routledge is an imprint of the Taylor & Francis Group, an informa business

First issued in paperback 2017

ISSN: 1097-4997
ISBN 13: 978-1-56000-350-2 (hbk)
ISBN 13: 978-1-138-51151-4 (pbk)

Contents

1

Elections and Status of Political Forces (SPF) in Latin America

Although 1996 was not as rich with elections as was 1994 it still contained a number of important contests throughout the region, most of which require, and will be supplied with, that relevant background information necessary to an understanding of the "status of political forces" in the relevant country. Because Latin America is so well endowed with sovereign nations, coherency of description is aided by a system of subdivisions. That which is used here is Central America, MERCOSUR or, roughly, the Southern Cone, the Andean nations, and four of the Caribbean nations to include Mexico.

Before embarking on such a discussion, however, it is of some consequence to render definitive those vague general identifications of political positions (Left, Right) and proliferating sub-identifications ("center left," "center right," etc.) which "everybody" uses and nobody understands.

A Realistic Definition of the Political Left

In what follows the "Left" will be taken to mean the "political Left," the "Right" the "political Right." These were originally the extent of such descriptions, to be first "improved upon" by the addition of the term "Center." Further evolution of this lexicon produced "center left" and "center right," a scheme carried to its apparently ultimate stage of development with the introduction of "center center." Since nobody really knows the definition of these terms, an Alice-in-Wonderland situation results wherein "words mean what I say they mean" whoever "I" may be, but, as the Mad Hatter alone might understand, "I" seldom means the same thing on two consecutive occasions.

In the French National Assembly, the States General of 1789, the "privileged classes," the clergy[1] and the nobility, were seated on the right of this august body, the Right (physically) were therefore conservatives, those essentially wishing to maintain the status quo; those opposed to maintaining it were the Left. With which 143 years may be allowed to elapse, and the Reichstag is seated in Berlin, the representatives of the National Socialist German Workers Party (the Nazi party) seated on the right. These people certainly had no desire to maintain the status quo, but it was of quite specific benefit to the, by definition, Left MLs (Marxist-Leninists) to classify them as "rightists." As it was so to classify the fascists[2] of the socialist Mussolini, whose prewar "Mussoliniani" included the famous Italian communist, Gramsci.[3] Thus was perpetrated the great twentieth-century fraud which established the Nazis and Fascists on the Right, and the MLs on the Left.

As *Jerusalem Post* editor Louis Rapaport points out, even Nazi anti-Semitism was aped by the MLs: "The Soviet deportation figures after the Polish Jews were shipped east may not have been as impressive as the Nazi statistics, but they were staggering nevertheless: 382,000 Volga Germans in August-September 1941; 42,000 Balkars, 407,000 Chechens, and 92,000 Ingushi in February 1944; 202,000 Crimean Tatars in June 1944; 200,000 Meshketians in 1944; 200,000 Greeks in 1949."[4]

Harvard's Baird Professor of History, Richard Pipes, has shown in exquisite detail[5] that ML activities in Russia gave "rise to movements that assimilated their spirit and copied their methods to fight Communism...they do so not because they have contrary principles or aspirations but because they compete for the same constituencies..." ML, fascism, and nazism are therefore all appropriately lumped together into the Left. In Latin America the influence of these three Left ideologies has been strong in certain nations; Argentina and Bolivia will be used later in relevant examples of the triumvirate.

The Left therefore can be taken as the collectivist doctrine having little to no use for individual liberties and administered at the whim of its bureaucrats, frequently technocrats, not its citizens. For the purposes of this discussion the Right need not be defined. Finally, the military caudillos who arose in the 1970s in reaction to the lawlessness of the Left constitute special cases for which a place in the political spectrum need hardly be determined.

Elections and the SPF in Central America

COSTA RICA (WKLY 2.9, 10 OCTOBER 1996)[*]

José (Pepe) Figueres Ferrer (1906–1990) came to power in Costa Rica in 1948 thanks to the Caribbean Legion.[6] He was buried at his *finca*, La Lucha, which had been used for so long as a launching pad for his war against Nicaragua. Described by Under Secretary of State Sumner Welles as the "Costa Rican dictator" (*Washington Post*, 21 September 1948), he has received gentle, if confused, handling by the press. The last photo of Pepe in the LANS® archives, taken in 1986, shows him wrapped around the Sandinista boss of Nicaragua, President Daniel Ortega Saavedra, while the latter bestows "la maxima distinción nicaragüense," the Order of César Augusto Sandino,[7] on him.

Pepe's son, José María Figueres Olsen (b. 1954), West Point class of 1979, replaced his father as head of the National Liberation (social democrat) Party (PLN). Running on an anti-neoliberal platform, he won the presidential election of 6 February 1994 with 49.7 percent of the vote against the 47.5 percent polled by Miguel Angel Rodríguez Echeverria of the Social Christian Unity Party (PUSC). Miguel Salguero of the Democratic Force (FD)[8] received 1.9 percent of the vote. In the unicameral Legislative Assembly, Figueres's PLN won 28 of the 57 seats; PUSC, 25; and FD, 2.

On 30 December 1994 Figueres declared a day of national mourning on the death of Manuel Mora Valverde who had headed the Communist party (CP) since Romulo Betancourt, his brother-in-law, had bequeathed it to him in the 1930s. On 19 September 1996 Figueres was "the only head of state…who called Carlos Andres Pérez[9] to congratulate him on his liberation" (AFP[**], 20 September 1996). In early September 1996 the Costa Rican Central Bank announced that PIB (gross domestic product) growth would be between 0.5 percent and 1.5 percent, not the 3 percent forecast earlier. A July 1996 poll reported that 50.2 percent of Costa Ricans considered Figueres's work "bad to very bad," 35.7 percent "regular," and 12.7 percent "good." An August 1996 University of Costa Rica (UCR) poll reported that, inter alia, 79 percent think the country is not improving, 76 percent that the deputies legislate on their

---

[*] Wkly 2.9 refers to LANS Weekly Report, vol. 2, no. 9, wherein this article originally appeared. Spcl 2.9 would refer to LANS Special Report, vol. 2, no. 9.

[**] AFP is the French news agency, Agence France-Presse.

own behalf and 83 percent that the information released by the Figueres administration "deceives" the public.

The next elections are in February 1998, and the "thousands" of convicts in the newly formed Prisoners' Party (PPV) will apparently field a candidate. On 27 September 1996 PUSC proclaimed its presidential candidate for these elections as Miguel Angel Rodríguez.

EL SALVADOR (WKLY 2.9, 10 OCTOBER 1996)

With the Chapultepec Accords of 16 January 1992, the Farabundo Martí National Liberation Front (FMLN)[10] entered the political arena with a power which neither their military nor their political impotence would have gained for them. The FMLN did not field a political candidate in the 20 March 1994 elections, the Democratic Convergence (CD) having been little more than a front for them since their 1987 foundation. The CD was formed from, inter alia, the National Revolutionary Movement (MNR) and the Social Christian People's Movement (MPSC) which "remained" part of the FDR-FMLN, the Democratic Revolutionary Front (FDR) the "parallel political arm of the FMLN." All of this was, of course, "smoke and mirrors" to allow the FMLN terrorists a legal way to enter the political arena. In the runoff election of 24 April 1994 National Republican Alliance (ARENA) candidate Armando Calderón Sol won with 68.2 percent of the vote against CD candidate Ruben Zamora with 31.6 percent.

In the unicameral legislature ARENA picked up 39 of the 84 seats; the FMLN, 21; the Christian Democrat Party (PDC), 4; the CD, 1; and the evangelical Unity Movement (MU), 1.

In 1994 People's Revolutionary Army (ERP) chief Joaquín Villalobos allegedly "broke" with the FMLN to form the "moderate" Renovation Expression of the People (ERP). So allegedly did the National Resistance (RN) which joined the ERP under Villalobos to form the Democratic Party (PD) in 1995. Which allegedly left the FMLN with the People's Liberation Forces (FPL), the Central American Workers Party (PRTC) and the Salvadoran Communist party (PCES). All told there are over twenty political parties in the country.

On 6 October 1996 the FMLN held its national convention at the Francisco Menéndez National Institute in San Salvador, largely presided over by the coordinator general, Salvador Sánchez Cerén. It was decided to reduce the value-added tax (VAT) and stop privatizations, among other things, and preparations were made for the midterm elections.

The presidential elections will be held in March 2000, the midterm elections on 16 March 1997 where 84 National Assembly deputies and 262 mayors will be elected. Supreme Electoral Tribunal (TSE) president Jorge Díaz is expecting some 2.7 million voters to participate in these elections. According to the last Gallup Poll published in *Diario de Hoy* (San Salvador), 55 percent have no preference for any political party. On 29 September 1996 ARENA declared its presidential candidate to be Legislative Assembly president Gloria Salguero Gross who obligingly danced "La Macarena."

GUATEMALA (WKLY 2.9, 10 OCTOBER 1996)

Retired Guatemalan general and National Congress president Efraín Ríos Montt led the presidential polls during the spring of 1995 only to fall victim to a decision of the TSE the following summer. This case is deserving of a treatment which it will receive in a future Special Report. The result, however, was that, in the 12 November 1995 presidential election, National Advance Guard Party (PAN) candidate Alvaro Arzú Irigoyen gained 36.55 percent of the vote, Guatemalan Republican Front (FRG) candidate Alfonso Portillo 22.04 percent, National Alliance (AN) candidate Fernando Andrade 12.94 percent and New Guatemalan Democratic Front (FDNG) candidate Jorge Gonzales del Valle 7.71 percent. In the runoff election of 7 January 1996 Arzú won with 51.22 percent against Portillo's 48.78 percent. In the unicameral National Congress, PAN garnered 43 of the 80 seats; FRG, 21; AN, 9; FDNG, 6; and National Liberation Movement (MLN), 1.

Arzú has devoted himself largely to negotiating a "peace" with the Guatemalan National Revolutionary Union (URNG) which is also deserving of more discussion than can be provided here. All things being equal, the next presidential election should take place in November 2000.

HONDURAS (WKLY 2.8, 10 OCTOBER 1996)

On 6 August 1993 Honduran Liberal Party (PLH) presidential candidate Carlos Roberto Reina Idiaquez told *Prensa Libre* (Guatemala), "We do not agree with the economic methods of neoliberal cutting by the present government which has hit the people hard in favor of an elite…No, I believe we have an advantage over the neoliberalism of the Chicago boys of… [President] Callejas." As apparently he did.

On 28 November 1993 PL candidate Reina polled 52.36 percent of the vote, Honduran National Party (PNH), that of Callejas, candidate Osvaldo Ramos Soto 40.74 percent, Innovation and Unity Party (PINU) candidate Olban Valladares 2.96 percent, and Christian Democrat Party (PDC) candidate Marco Orlando Iriarte 1.07 percent. Reina was inaugurated on 27 January 1994. The PL captured 71 of the 128 seats in the unicameral National Assembly; PN taking 55; PINU, 2; and PDC none.

President Reina inherited a situation which was apparently "worse than he had thought" and was routinely unable to resist the blandishments of the money available from the International Monetary Fund (IMF), Inter-American Development Bank (IDB), and the like, as he had indicated that he would do. Although said in mid-1995 by a member of the opposition, there is some justification for "everybody knows there is chaos in Honduras, that anarchy reigns." This situation will be treated in an upcoming Special Report. The next general elections will be in November 1997.

THE 900 DAYS OF ROBERTO REINA (SPCL 2.10, 10 OCTOBER 1996)

On completing half (27 January 1996) of his four-year presidential term, President Carlos Roberto Reina of Honduras declared that he had "established the bases of a new republic." He went on to say that he had imposed a greater respect for the law and maintains an "implacable persecution of corruption." There does not appear to have been general agreement with this assessment.

Mr. Reina made the remarks about Callejas and the "Chicago boys" quoted above on 6 August 1993. After he was inaugurated president in 1994, however, he effectively joined the "Chicago boys."

Born in 1926, Reina experienced political puberty in the PLH, the older of the two parties still dominating the Honduran political scene. Although the framers of the 1824 constitution—Molina et al.—were versed in the eighteenth-century liberals from Voltaire to Rousseau, the nineteenth-century politicians were largely *caudillos* who "literally conceived [political campaigns] as wars, and on cessation of hostilities the various groups...liquidated all opposition."[11] President Reina appears to be from this school. In the late nineteenth century Celeo Arias's *My Ideas* vainly attempted to create a PLH doctrine, Policarpo Bonilla then further advancing the attempt.

The other major party, the PNH, was given its initial impetus in 1854 by President Trinidad Cabañas, a further boost in 1874 by General

Poinciano Leiva, the party finally emerging in 1915 under the supporters of Francisco Bertrand, its name assumed in 1923 (*Sufragio Libre* [Tegucigalpa], 8 July 1923). The PNH is important to Mr. Reina as his political life began in the "poorly organized parades and demonstrations...of the Liberal party in 1944" against the "continuismo" of President Tiburcio Carias whose PNH was replacing the "machetismo"[12] of the Honduran past.

An AFP dispatch of November 1993 describes Tiburcio Carias as "the dictator." But it was Carias who accepted defeat by the PLH candidate, Mejía Colindres, in 1928, then won the 1932 elections, only to face a PLH uprising which he was clearly obliged to put down. The pejorative label "dictator" is probably aimed at Carias's "continuismo" as introduced by article 202 of the 1936 constitution which allowed him to remain in power until 1943, Congress' unanimous vote extending this period to 1948.

President Reina originally threatened to "repudiate" the letter-of-intent which the Callejas government had signed with the IMF, his inference being that such arrangements with international lending agencies force countries such as Honduras into the rigors of *capitalismo salvaje* (savage capitalism). This appears to be largely political posturing, for within a year the IDB had arrived in Tegucigalpa as had, at least in spirit, the "Chicago boys."[13] Perhaps the reversal of the Reina government's position was due to the worsening of the Honduran economy during 1994, it being reported in March 1995 that the PIB had fallen 1.4 percent in 1994 as against a 6.1 percent rise in 1993. The details of Reina's retreat toward neoliberalism are more appropriate to chapter 2.

But there appears to be an interesting reversion to the caudillo governments which, "on cessation of hostilities," "liquidated all opposition." In particular, if the "opposition" (former President Callejas) is not guilty as charged, this appears to be such a reversion. This apparently remains to be determined.

In November 1994 former President Callejas and certain of his ministers were accused of "abuse of power and falsification of documents." This affair has thus been in progress for almost two years, but recent events can be used in summary.

On 11 September 1996 the attorney general brought charges against former Ministers Benjamin Villanueva and René Ardón for diversion of funds. Former President Callejas enjoys congressional immunity. The alleged diversion is of $22.5 million from the Petroleum Fund which is reported as having been established for use in lowering the cost of fuel. How the fund can be used is apparently in dispute. There are various deviations in the reports of the amounts involved. LANS was informed that the official report on the charges was leaked to the media and hence has only been able to obtain a partial list of allegations.

The list has ten items relating to allegedly illegitimate dispersion of funds: the first dispersal for life insurance for Callejas and his family at $150,000 to $200,000; the second for $130,000 to open the embassy of Egypt which was turned over to Callejas's cousin, Castillo; the fourth to an account in Callejas's name of $149,000; the tenth support in unspecified amount for a university rector whose son lost an eye; and so on. On 8 October 1996 Callejas maintained that all these distributions of funds were "legal and we are going to demonstrate this in the courts." A judgment based on the information available would appear to be premature.

But the Callejas camp, led by Johny Handal, minority leader in the National Congress, on 7 October 1996 accused the Reina administration of doing the same thing. Between 27 January 1994 and 30 June 1996, Handal said 700 million lempiras went into the Petroleum Adjustment Fund—he gave the bank account number—and, he claimed, this sum has been utilized for "specific and unknown purposes." Confirming the existence of the 700 million, the government claimed all its expenditures legal and legitimate.

It is not obvious what the outcome will be, but the battle itself has served to drive the woes of the Reina government off the front pages.

NICARAGUA

Elections were held on 25 February 1990 under the Sandinista Constitution of 1987. These are discussed below.

PANAMA (WKLY 2.9, 10 OCTOBER 1996)

Panama was not formerly considered a part of Central America, although it is often included at present.

The U.S. takeover of Panama on 20 December 1989 was not, under the DeConein amendment to the Carter-Torrijos Treaty, the "invasion" which President George Bush of the United States inexplicably called it. The operation was allegedly carried out to "bring democracy" and for other, hopefully, more cogent reasons and transferred caudillo Manuel Noriega to a U.S. prison. With a rare flash of humor Noriega had called Guillermo Endara Gallimany "that hunger-strike clown." Endara had been elected president on 7 May 1989, removed by Noriega and finally replaced by the United States to serve out his term of office. Some have asked if the United States really expected to "bring democracy" by the simple expedient of replacing Endara and walking away. As one Panamanian told the LANS editor in 1994: "The United States installed a new government which swore to respect the constitution written by Torrijos to support his dictatorship. A constitutional convention should have been held to write an appropriate constitution." With this Liberal Republican National Movement (MOLIRENA) candidate Carles agreed in a subsequent interview. In sum, the election was held, and Noriega's Democratic Revolutionary Party (PRD) resumed power.

In the 8 May 1994 elections PRD candidate Ernesto (Toro) Pérez Balladares won the presidency with 33.3 percent. Mireya Moscosa of the Democratic Alliance (AD) trailed with 29.1 percent, actor and salsa singer, Ruben Blades of the Papa Egoro (Mother Earth) Movement (MPE), got 17.1 percent, and Ruben Carles of Cambio 94 garnered 16.1 percent. The campaign had been rendered colorful by Blades, the boxer Roberto Duran, and outspoken First Lady Anna Mae de Endara; Toro had invited well-known U.S. "political scientists" Jesse Jackson and Oliver Stone to act as "election observers." The next election should be in 1999.

Various parties and alliances vied for the 72 seats in the Legislative Assembly, the results here simplified to: The PRD won 31 seats; the AD, 15; Papa Egoro, 6; MOLIRENA, 5; Solidarity Party, 2; and Christian Democrats, 1. On 29 September 1996 Mireya Moscosa was reelected president of the Arnulfista Party (PA), one of the parties of the AD.

The Political Situation in the MERCOSUR[14] Nations

ARGENTINA (WKLY 2.10, 17 OCTOBER 1996)

Carlos Saul Menem of the Justicialismo (Peronist)[15] Party (PJ) was sworn in as president of Argentina before the Legislative Assembly on 8 July 1989 for a term of six years. In August 1994 a Constituent Assembly replaced the 1853 constitution with a new constitution having thirty-four new articles and forty amendments to existing articles. The 1994 constitution, inter alia, reduced the presidential term of office from six years to four years and allowed reelection of the incumbent. In order to assure that the Assembly would approve the new constitution, former Argentine president Raul Alfonsín of the Radical Civic Union (UCR) had agreed to support such changes in the presidency in exchange for the creation of the post of cabinet chief. President Menem declared that such a post would not interfere with his conduct of affairs which appears to have been the case.

The elections were held on 14 June 1995, and President Menem won a second term with 50 percent of the vote as against National Solidarity Front (FREPASO) candidate José Otavio Bordón with about 36 percent and UCR candidate Horacio Massacesi with about 16 percent. Other parties included Alianza Sur (Southern Alliance), Movement Toward Socialism (MAS), Workers Socialist Movement (MST), Workers and Movement for Dignity and Independence Party (MODIN) and various additional ones.

Argentina has a federal district (Buenos Aires) and twenty-two provinces including Buenos Aires and the Territory of Tierra del Fuego. In the bicameral legislature of Argentina the old constitution gave each of the forty-eight members of the Senate a term of nine years with one-third of the members reelected every three years. Under the new constitution and beginning in 1995 there are three senators from each region, each with a six-year term. On 8 October 1995 the election for the first of these additional seats (in the federal district) was won by FREPASO candidate Graciela Fernández Meijide with 47.2 percent as against 24.2 percent for PJ candidate Antonio Erman González, and 23.3 percent for UCR candidate Jorge Vanossi. PJ candidate Eduardo Duhalde won the Buenos Aires gubernatorial election.

The Chamber of Deputies has 257 members elected for a four-year term, about one-half of them elected every two years. Following the legislative elections of 14 May 1995 the PJ held 137 seats; the UCR, 69; FREPASO, 26; and the remaining seats were distributed among a number of lesser parties.

There will be legislative elections in 1997, general elections in 1999, and the action for the midterm elections has begun. In general terms, the battle lines have long been drawn around the neoliberalism of President Menem. On 8 October 1996 Open Politic for Social Integrity (PAIS) held a plenary session of some 300 people from the sixteen departments of Cordova Province (northwest of Buenos Aires Province) and its capital (Cordova City). At this session an alliance with FREPASO for the 1997 elections was urged by Senator José Otavio Bordón. The next day FREPASO leader Carlos (Chacho) Alvarez stated that he would redouble his efforts to form a "common force" with the UCR because "the present crisis in the country moved the time when we want an alliance forward from 1999 to 1997" and because "the people are crying out that the opposition join together to defeat Menemism." On 10 October 1996 Constituent Assembly president and senator, Graciela Fernández, and Vice President Carlos Ruckauf dedicated the first constitution of the City of Buenos Aires, a move "toward full autonomy" supported, inter alia, by FREPASO, UCR, and New Direction (ND), and opposed by PJ. President Menem had not carried Buenos Aires in his second election as president.

On 12 October 1996 Domingo Cavallo announced his intention of running for a senate seat in the 1997 elections either in Gustavo Beliz's ND or in a party of his own creation. Cavallo was Menem's minister of economy from 1991 to July 1996. Finally, former President Alfonsín announced (13 October 1996) that he will make his final decision on a 1999 presidential run in 1998.

BRAZIL (WKLY 2.10, 17 OCTOBER 1996)

On 29 September 1992 President George Bush's "Indiana Jones" (Fernando Collor de Mello)[16] was impeached and resigned from the Brazilian presidency for a bacchanal of extortion and embezzlement on a truly grand scale. After an interim presidency by Vice President Itamar Franco, general elections were held on 3 October 1994. The presidency was won by Brazilian Social Democrat Party (PSDB) candidate Fernando Henrique Cardosa[17] with 54.28 percent of the vote over Workers Party (PT) candidate and Fidel Castro confidant, Luis Ignacio (Lula) da Silva[18] with 27.04 percent, National Order Rebuilding Party (PRONA) candidate Eneas Ferreira Carneiro with 7.38 percent, Brazilian Democratic Movement (PMDB) candidate Orestes Quercia with 4.38 percent, Democratic Workers Party (PDT) candidate Leonel Brizola with 3.18 percent, and other candidates with lesser percentages. President Cardosa took office 1 January 1995. By 17 January 1995 the new president's salary had been raised by 143.6 percent to $10,000 per month.

President Cardosa's popularity stood at 68 percent on 1 January 1995, then fell to 25 percent by late May 1996. Nevertheless, in September 1996 he first agreed to a run for reelection in the 1998 elections, this of course dependent on legislative approval of the second presidential term which is expected later this month (October 1996).

There are twenty-six states and the Federal District of Brasília in the nation. The Senate in the bicameral legislature has three senators from each of these political units, the term of office being eight years with a staggered reelection system whereby one-third of the members are elected in a given election, two-thirds in the next election. As a result of the general elections of 3 October 1994, 22 senators represented the PMDB, 19 the Liberal Front Party (PFL), 10 the PSDB, with about 9 other parties also represented. Former President José Sarney (1985–1990) was elected president of the Senate for a three-year term (1994–1997).

The Chamber of Deputies has 513 members all elected for four-year terms of office. After the 3 October 1994 elections the PMDB was represented by 108 deputies, the PFL by 89, the PSDB by 64, the PPR Reformed Progressive Party (PPPR) by 52, the PT by 49, the Progressive Party (PP) by 35, the PDT by 33, the Brazilian Workers Party (PTB) by 31, the Liberal Party (PL) and the Brazilian Socialist Party (PSB) by 14, and eight other parties by 10 or fewer deputies.

Municipal elections were held on 3 October 1996, there being 5507 mayoralties and 60,000 municipal council seats to be filled. According to a recent quota law, 20 percent of the candidates must be women. Only five mayors were elected in the first round, the remaining requiring a runoff election on 15 November 1996. The five were Juraci Magalhaes (PMDB) with 62 percent in Fortaleza (Caera); Raul Pont (PT) with 52 percent in Porto Alegre (Rio Grande do Sul); Cassio Taniguchi (PDT) with 48 percent in Curitaba (Parana); Robert Malhaes (PFL) with 47 percent in Recife (Pernambuco); and Antonio Imbassay (PFL) with 46 percent in Salvador (Baia). The results of the November runoffs will not be reproduced.

CHILE (WKLY 2.10, 17 OCTOBER 1996)

In 1964 Christian Democrat Party (PDC) candidate Eduardo Frei Montalvo won the Chilean presidency with 56.09 percent as against the 38.93 percent of "the Marxist physician,"[19] Salvador Allende Gossens, and the also-ran, Julio Duran, with 4.99 percent. It has been suggested that the impotent administration of Frei Montalvo led to Allende's 1970 victory because (1) Allende received fewer votes in victory (36.6 percent) than he had in defeat (38.9 percent), while the CD candidate, Radomiro Tomic, received half the votes (28.1 percent) that Frei had received (56.09 percent), and (3) most of the voters simply moved from the CD to the Independent candidate, Jorge Alessandri, giving the latter 28.1 percent. Whatever caused the shift, it paved the way for the "three years of Marxist rule in Chile (which) ended in the smoking ruins of his (Allende's) palace on 11 September 1973."[20] Out of these smoking ruins the government of General Augusto Pinochet Ugarte produced the true Latin American "economic miracle" by the simple expedient of introducing the country to the (almost) free market.

Pinochet's civilian successor, President Patricio Aylwin,[21] was elected in 1989 and more or less carried on his free-market policies. The last general election was on 11 December 1993 wherein the Democracy Parties Alliance (CPD) candidate Eduardo Frei Ruiz-Tagle, the son of Frei Montalvo, won the presidency with 58.01 percent[22] of the vote, he being trailed by Union for Chilean Progress (UPC) candidate Arturo Alessandri Besa with 24.39 percent, Independent candidate José Piñera with 6.18 percent, People's Unitary Action Coalition-Christian Left (MAPU-IC) candidate Max Neef with 5.55 percent, Allende Democratic Movement (MIDA) candidate Eugenio Pizarro with 4.69 percent, and others with less than 5 percent. A February 1994 amendment to the constitution provides a six-year presidential term.

In these elections 39 senators were elected to the bicameral legislature for eight-year terms, which, with those appointed for life in 1989, made a total of 47. Of those elected 13 were from the PDC, eleven from National Renovation (RN), 5 from the Socialist Party (PS), 3 from the Independent Democratic Union (UDI), 3 from Center Right Independents (ICR), 2 from Party for Democracy (PPD), and 1 each from two others.

The 1993 elections chose 120 deputies to serve a four-year term. Thirteen were from the PDC, 29 from the RN, 15 from the PS, 15 from the UDI, 15 from the PPD, 4 from the ICR, and fewer from three other parties.

CHILEAN MUNICIPAL ELECTIONS (WKLY 2.10, 17 OCTOBER 1996)

The Chilean municipal elections were held on 27 October 1996. The Chilean press reported that, with 97.4 percent of the vote counted, there were 30 percent more "right-wing" mayors elected than in 1992, a statement which is a function of the usually subjective definition of "right wing," "left wing," and "center" complicated by the almost meaningless "center right," "center left," and "center center." With these caveats, the "right" won 58.2 percent of the mayoral races, the "left" 59.1 percent of the council seats.

The Chilean Ministry of the Interior reported that, of the 6.175 million votes tallied in the councilmanic races, the PDC won 1.608 million; the RN, .844 million; the PPD, .762 million; the PSC, .655 million; Independent Lists–Independent Democratic Union (UDI), .594 million; Radical Social Democrat (PRS), .402 million; the Chilean Communist party (PCC), .315 million; and the remaining parties polling under 5 percent.

PARAGUAY (WKLY 2.10, 17 OCTOBER 1996)

General Alfredo Stroessner won the three-way presidential election of February 1988 with 88.64 percent of the vote which seemed to indicate the old caudillo's still firm grip on the political helm. And yet, a year later, Stroessner's fellow father-in-law, General Andres Rodríguez used his I Corps to end the thirty-four-year *stroñato*. The jockeying for succession had begun, a Colorado Party faction having arisen in support of Stroessner's son, Gustavo. Which may not have pleased the existing "heir apparent," Rodríguez, who led the 3 February 1989 coup to "bring democracy" which was followed by a 60 percent Rodríguez election victory in December 1989.

Under the 18 June 1992 constitution Colorado Reconciliation Movement (MRC) candidate Juan Carlos Wasmosy won the presidential elections of 9 May 1993 with 39.5 percent of the vote, as against Authentic Radical Liberal Party (Colorado faction) (PLRA) candidate Domingo Laino's 32 percent and Paraguayan National Encounter (PEN) candidate Guillermo Caballero Vargas's 27 percent. The term of office is five years. The "blessings of democracy" showered down the following year: (1) The first "general strike in thirty-six years" was called by the National Workers Central (CNT), the Unified Workers Central (CUT) and the Paraguayan Workers Central (CPT); (2) the Cuban People's Power Assembly president, Carlos Dotrea, and Secretary Sergio Pastrana "freely" entered the country; and (3) the military lost the right to vote.

In the nationally elected Senate of the bicameral legislature the MRC won 20 seats; the PLRA, 17; and the EN, 8. The Chamber of Deputies is elected by departmental constituencies, the MRC gaining 40 seats in the 1993 elections; the PLRA, 32; and the EN, 8.

PARAGUAYAN MUNICIPAL ELECTIONS (WKLY 2.15, 21 NOVEMBER 1996)

On 17 November 1996 mayors and municipal councils were elected in 220 Paraguayan municipalities. The pre-election violence in the country had been sufficient to place the military on permanent alert during the week before the elections were held. After the elections were held there was complaint, not about violence, but about the slowness of the election commission in tabulating the vote.

The National Republican Association (ANR), or Colorado Party, won the majority of municipalities, but the PLRA, or Liberal Party, increased its control from 43 to 55 municipalities. A Liberal coalition with PEN won the mayoral race with Martin Burt in the capital city of Asunción over the Colorado candidate Angel Ramón Barcini.

URUGUAY (WKLY 2.10, 17 OCTOBER 1996)

In the presidential elections of 27 November 1994 there was nearly a three-way tie, Colorado Party candidate Julio María Sanguinetti winning with 31.36 percent of the vote which was about 3.5 percent more than that garnered by Mariana Arana of Progressive Encounter and 2.5 percent more than that of Alberto Volonte of the National Party. Arana emerged as mayor of Montevideo, the "Brussels of South America." There were 16 other candidates with lesser percentages. The constitution provides that the members of the 30-member Senate and the 99-member Chamber of Deputies be proportionally elected under the same voting procedure which elects the president. The term of office in the bicameral legislature is five years.

This was Sanguinetti's second presidential election, his first in 1986 when the Army, having brought the National Liberation Front-Tupamaros (MLN-T) terrorists under control, handed the country back to the civilians. As LANS associate editor Dr. Emanuiloff-Max, a Montevideo resident, put it:

> His assumption of power (on 1 March 1995) coincides with the conflict between Ecuador and Peru, with the increasingly effective drive toward a durable economic-financial structure, and with the initiation of a functioning MERCOSUR...There is no alternative for a man of good faith. If Sanguinetti fails, in five years against this flow of a universal historical progression, a Marxist government, as already exists in the city of Montevideo, will be installed here in Uruguay for the first time.

THE AMENDED URUGUAYAN CONSTITUTION
(SPCL 2.16, 13 DECEMBER 1996)

In his 1994 election victory President Sanguinetti won with 31.36 percent of the vote in what was virtually a three-way tie. Under

Uruguay's newly amended constitution, such a result cannot be repeated.

The projected constitutional amendments had been approved by Uruguay's bicameral legislature on 15 October 1996, the Colorado, New Space (Social Democrat), and National Parties having voted in favor—save for Alem Garcia—the Broad Front (FA)[23] against. On 8 December 1996 the plebiscite was held on the proposed amendments, the citizenry deciding favorably by a vote of 50.2 percent against 46.41 percent. The amendments were primarily concerned with elections and municipal decentralization:

ELECTIONS AND POWERS OF THE PRESIDENT AND VICE PRESIDENT

1. The election of president and vice president will take place on the last Sunday of October every five years.
2. The president and vice president will be elected by an absolute majority (more than 50 percent of the votes cast). If, on the last Sunday in October, no presidential candidate receives more than 50 percent of the vote, there will be a second round between the two leading candidates on the last Sunday of November during the same calendar year. The same procedure will be followed for the vice presidential candidate.
3. If the Executive Power vetoes a legislative measure, a vote of three-fifths of the members of each legislative chamber will be required to override the veto.
4. The president is authorized to require of the (bicameral) General Assembly a vote of confidence in the Council of Ministers. The president can then declare that the Council lacks parliamentary support which authorizes replacement of the minister(s) declared "no confidence." The procedure also applies to directorates and decentralized services.
5. The national budget will be projected and approved in a form which will contain, inter alia, resources and estimates of their productivity with similar percentages for departmental governments.

NATIONAL LEGISLATURE AND LOCAL GOVERNING BODIES

1. Election of members of the Senate and Chamber of Deputies will take place on the last Sunday in October every five years.
2. Election of departmental and local governing bodies will take place on the second Sunday in May of the year following the national elections.
3. The accumulation of votes, for all effective offices save those of president and vice president, will take place under the symbol of the political party. Each party may field only one candidate for each elective office.
4. The municipal intendant will be the candidate receiving the most votes within the party which receives the most votes in the election.

5. The minimum age for members of the departmental juntas is lowered from twenty-three years to eighteen years.

REGULATIONS GOVERNING POLITICAL PARTIES

1. Political parties will nominate their candidates for president on the last Sunday in April of the election year.
2. Political parties will nominate their candidates for intendant at their convention of the Departmental Electoral College.
3. There will be a single nominee for intendant, who has received the most votes, unless the runner up has received more than 30 percent of the votes cast.

The Andean Nations Go to the Polls

BOLIVIA (WKLY 2.11, 24 OCTOBER 1996)

In the 6 June 1993 general elections National Revolutionary Movement (MNR)[24] presidential candidate Gonzalo Sánchez de Losada gained 36.2 percent of the vote, Patriotic Accord (AP)[25] candidate General Hugo Banzer 21 percent, Bolivian Solidarity Union (UCS) candidate Max Fernández 12 percent, National Conscience (CONDEPA)[26] candidate Carlos Palenque 12 percent, Free Bolivia Movement (MBL) candidate Antonio Aranibar 5 percent, and nine other parties 2 percent or less. Since no candidate won a majority, the selection would have rested with the National Congress, but General Banzer withdrew his candidacy, there was no runoff, and Sánchez de Losado was inaugurated on 6 August.

In the senatorial elections for the bicameral legislature MNR won 17 seats; AP, 8; UCS, 1; and CONDEPA, 1—for a total of 27. In the 130-seat Chamber of Deputies MNR received 52; AP, 35; UCS, 20; CONDEPA, 13; MBL, 7; and three other parties 1 seat each.

The next general election will be in June 1997 so that, although the maneuvering for position has begun, the competing forces have not really begun to take definitive shape. Much of the substance of the campaigns can be expected to revolve around the Hemispheric Left (HL) positions on AgRef (agrarian reform), coca-leaf production, and so on. While Bolivia completed the negotiations for its entry into MERCOSUR[27] on 10 October 1996 in Brasília, the signing to take place in Fortaleza, Brazil, on 17 December 1996, the campesinos—substantially *cocaleros*, or coca-leaf growers—were marching on La Paz, allegedly 200,000 strong, to "protest" the new

AgRef law. With whatever level of sincerity, President Sánchez de Losada recently told a German audience that he expected his MNR party—as is the case in most Latin American nations, Sánchez cannot succeed himself—to lose the 1997 elections because of the INRA (AgRef) law.

At least some of his fellow MNR militants do not feel as he does, Interior Minister Carlos Sánchez perhaps an example of this. On 12 September 1996 the MNR executive committee began meetings aimed at revising the party's rules governing qualifications for the various electoral offices among which is a requirement that a candidate for president have at least five years of militancy in the party. There is apparently considerable controversy on this provision which, inter alia, would disqualify Sánchez. Such a change is strongly opposed by La Paz prefect German Quiroga.

Two years ago former President Jaime Paz Zamora, accused by the FECLN (Special Anti-Narcotics Forces) of narcotrafficking activities, declared that he was retiring from public life and the leadership of the Left Revolutionary Movement (MIR).[28] Then in mid-1996, during a visit to jailed MIR vice chief Oscar Eid, he announced that he would run for president next year.

In September 1996 CONDEPA suffered a new schism which may demonstrate the aphorism that politicians do not make good bedfellows. The affair went public with the decision by the CONDEPA directors to expel Ricardo Paz Ballivian for "divisiveness" and for promoting a so-called successional project. Important to what follows is the fact that CONDEPA is led by Carlos Palenque Aviles, whose spouse and La Paz's former mayor, Monica Medina de Palenque, was a director. Rumor has it that the difficulties surfaced with the ouster of Paz and had their origin in some differences between Carlos and Doña Monica, both spouses denying any such thing. Perhaps relevant is the remark by Monica's father, Jorge Medina, also a director, that Paz had the power behind the throne which he abused with "absolute disloyalty." Monica has defended and continues to defend Paz while Carlos declares, with a catch in his throat, that "I am not going to speak of her who was my companion until yesterday..." Speculation is doubtless rampant, but, whatever the reality, this will probably not help CONDEPA. With what has been interpreted as an aside to Doña Monica, Sánchez de Losada remarked that the MNR has "open doors for the successional movement and for all youths, men and women..."

THE MONICAZO (WKLY 2.18, 12 DECEMBER 1996)

The schism in the Bolivian political party, CONDEPA, was brought about by a "difference" between the party leader, Carlos Palenque Avila, and his onetime spouse,[29] Monica Medina, the former mayor of La Paz and former CONDEPA director. Doña Monica launched her own party, Insurgent Bolivia (IB), at what was to have been the fiesta of the Monicazo. This took place in La Paz's Plaza San Francisco on the afternoon of 6 December 1996 and turned into a fine old donnybrook.

Before the fiesta could be gotten underway by the IB directors, a crowd erupted into the plaza with sticks, stones, and exploding petards which prevented the scheduled appearance of various musical groups and other entertainment with which the festivities were to begin. Nor was this all.

At about 1700 Bolivian Workers Central (COB) appeared to begin a new protest march. The affair quickly degenerated into serious confrontations with the participants throwing sticks and stones which left a number of injured and did considerable damage. The police were remarkable by their absence in spite of repeated calls for them. The IB militants claimed that the workers' group contained CONDEPA militants who were there to sabotage the Monicazo.

Vehicle traffic emptied into the plaza and Marscal Santa Cruz Avenue; petards were thrown by one group and the other. After 1900, a mob of demonstrators set fire to the stands prepared for the presentation of Doña Monica and her partisans, destroying the stage, the sound system, and almost everything which had been prepared for her.

Looking toward the general elections of June 1997,[30] an alliance had been announced among the IB, the Bolivian Solidarity Union (UCS) and the Patriotic Movement (MPP). What effect the brouhaha called the "Monicazo" will have on this coalition remains to be seen.

COLOMBIA (WKLY 2.11, 24 OCTOBER 1996)

The first presidential elections held under the 1991 constitution took place on 29 April 1994, Colombian Liberal Party (PLC) candidate Ernesto Samper Pizarro winning 48.9 percent of the vote, Social Conservative Party (PSC) candidate Andres Pastrana Arango 46.8 percent, Democratic Alliance M-19 (ADM-19)[31] candidate Antonio Navarro Wolff 3.96 percent, Unitarian Metapolitical Movement (MUM)[32] candidate Regina Betancourt de Liska 0.119 percent, and General Miguel

Alfredo Maza, former national security chief, 0.1 percent. Since no candidate received over 50 percent of the vote a runoff election was held on 19 June 1994 wherein Samper won with 50.9 percent of the vote against Pastrana's 49.1 percent.

Ten days after these presidential elections a recording of a conversation, alleged to be "among the Cali cocaine cartel chiefs," was reproduced in the Bogotá press.[33] The conversation related to the alleged injection of narcotrafficking money into the Samper and Pastrana campaigns. The charges against Pastrana do not appear to have amounted to anything, those against Samper have filled the communications media and, among other things, invoked U.S. refusal to issue a visa to the Colombian president. This situation will be treated separately; for now, one example must suffice.

In August 1995 President Samper's campaign manager and minister of defense, Fernando Botero, was jailed on narcotraffic-related charges. In January 1996, from prison, he told the press that Samper knew he had received six million dollars from the narcotraffickers, a statement which, according to an *El Tiempo* poll, 62 percent of the Colombians believed. Matters proceeded from there, but, to this time (October 1996), President Samper has not been removed from office. Congressional elections were held on 13 March 1994. In the Senate the PLC won 56 of the 102 seats; the PSC, 40; the ADM-19, 1; and various independent groups, 23. Two seats had been reserved for indigenous groups under the 1991 Constitution.

In the House of Representatives the PLC won 88 of the 165 seats; the PSC, 40; the ADM-19, 2; National Salvation Movement (MSN), 2; and various independent groups, 29. Under the terms of the "peace" accords two seats are reserved for the formerly terrorist Socialist Renovation Current (CRS) and, under the constitution, two are reserved for "ethnic and minority" groups.

The president is elected for a term of four years as are the members of the Senate and the House of Representatives. Which means that the next general elections will be held in 1997–1998.

ECUADOR (WKLY 2.11, 24 OCTOBER 1996)

The Ecuadoran general elections were held on 19 May 1996, there being nine presidential candidates in the race. There is some ambiguity as to the exact percentages attained by the various candidates, but there is no question as to relative placement. LANS carried out the elemental arithmetic calculations and was unable to match the reported results, one reason being that EFE*** (20 May 1996) reported, for example, Nebot with 1.3 million votes while AFP the next day reported the candidate having 1.043 million. If the 91.5 percent count of 4.468 million is taken, this is a spread of 5.8 percent. With this caveat in mind, the results were as follows:

Social Christian Party (PSC) candidate Jaime Nebot Saidi garnered 23.3 percent, Ecuadoran Roldosista Party (PRE) candidate Abdala Bucaram Ortiz 21.68 percent, New Country Movement-Pachakutik (MNP-P) candidate Freddy Ehlers 17.6 percent, People's Democracy (DP) candidate Rodrigo Paz 11.5 percent, and Ecuadoran Revolutionary Action Party (APRE) candidate Frank Vargas 3.7 percent. If "Blank Ballots" and "Disfigured Ballots" are considered as candidates, they polled fifth and sixth places between Ehlers and Vargas.[34] Since no candidate polled over 50 percent there was a runoff between the two leading candidates, Bucaram winning with 47.66 percent against Nebot's 39.9 percent.

Bucaram described himself as "the candidate of the poor," *El Comercio* (Quito) describing him as "entering political life as Quartermaster of Guayas (Province) police, later mayor of Guayaquil." After a "brief period of scandal" he was exiled to Panama. His running mate was Rosalia Arteaga Serrano, a doctor of laws, professor, and journalist, active in political affairs since 1986.

Mr. Bucaram hit his stride in early May, claiming that he was in danger of assassination as suffered by the Colombian publisher, Galán, and the Mexican presidential candidate, Colosio, this by the "Ecuadoran oligarchy." By June he had refined this claim, stating that three assassins—a professor, an executive, an aviator—had already landed in Ecuador to dispose of him. A few days later the Nebot camp reported "an explosive device" against a tree near the candidate's residence. "Bah," said Mr. Bucaram, "The outrage against me was real. His is only a Chinese rocket." Both candidates survived the ordeal.

In the May elections for the unicameral National Congress the PSC won 26 seats, a loss of one from its bloc in the previous congress. The PRE won 19, a gain of 8. The DP won 12. Thus, as Jijon points out (*Vistazo* [Quito] 23 May 1996), there are three medium-sized blocs which will render it almost impossible to establish a governing consen-

---

*** EFE is the Spanish news agency, Efemerides.

sus or alliance in this 77-seat legislature. Jijon's article articulately covers the successes and failures of the various parties by province. Suffice it to say here that the Democratic Left (ID) and the NP won 5 seats each, the MPD 4, and the other three groupings 2 or less.

PRESIDENT BUCARAM, LOS IRACUNDOS, AND SEÑORA DE BOBBITT (WKLY 2.13, 7 NOVEMBER 1996)

"The French don't care what you do, really, so long as you pronounce it properly," according to Professor Henry Higgins. Whether the Ecuadorans care about the curious behavior of their chief executive or how he pronounces it has apparently not been seriously investigated (7 November 1996).

But President Bucaram's "pop" singing has been well publicized since his inauguration. Perhaps the most remarkable example of his lyrical efforts surfaced in September 1996 with the record by "Los Iracundos" (The Infuriated), a singing group whose most noteworthy performer is the Ecuadoran chief executive, Abdala Bucaram. Indeed, the front of the record is graced with a photograph of President Bucaram in his presidential sash.

Lorena Gallo de Bobbitt, an Ecuadoran lady, gained international fame by amputating what Petronius Arbiter would have called the "member" of her husband. A U.S. court in essence then declared such activity legal. In latter October 1996 President Bucaram appeared prominently with the *gentil dama*, Lorena, pretty and pink, at the baptism of Amar Pacheco. Psychologist Cecilia Jaramillo hurried into print to tell readers how normally President Bucaram was behaving. The description of the affair by certain of the president's political enemies must, as Gibbon remarked of the Empress Theodora's peccadillos, "remain veiled in the obscurity of a learned language."

PERU (WKLY 2.11, 24 OCTOBER 1996)

On 28 July 1990 President Alberto Fujimori was inaugurated succeeding the avowed Marxist and admirer of Senderista "principles," President Alan Garcia. President Fujimori's "autogolpe," which led to the Peruvian constitution of 29 December 1993, is described elsewhere.[35]

Alberto Kenyo Fujimori Fujimori has shaken up whatever "traditional" political structure there may have been in Peru. In 1990 he defeated a coalition which had been put together to support Mario Vargas

Llosa, a Peruvian writer resident in England who has since spent much of his time attacking Fujimori with his pen. In the elections of 9 April 1995 President Fujimori, running under the banner of Movimiento Cambio 90 (Movement for Change 1990) which he had formed five years before, was reelected with 64.42 percent. The retired Organization of American States (OAS) chief Javier Pérez de Cuellar, running as the Union for Peru (UP) candidate, received 21.82 percent. People's American Revolutionary Alliance (APRA)[36] candidate Mercedes Cabanillas received 4.11 percent, Democratic Coordination-Possible Peru (C-PP)[37] candidate Alejandro Toledoa 3.24 percent, and Civic Works Movement (MOC) candidate Ricardo Belmont 2.58 percent.

In the elections for the unicameral Congress Cambio 90 won 67 of the 120 seats; UP, 17; APRA, 8; Independent Moralizing Front (FIM) 6; C-PP, 5; and People's Action (AP), 4. The Congress is completed with two parties having 3 seats each and three parties having 1.

Under the 1993 Constitution both the president and the Congress are elected for five-year terms, the next election thus due in 2000. Two vice presidents are elected, Ricardo Marquez Flores and César Paredes Canto receiving these posts in 1995.

A PROPHET IS NOT WITHOUT HONOR SAVE IN HIS OWN KITCHEN
(WKLY 2.14, 14 NOVEMBER 1996)

When President Fujimori first entered the Presidential Palace in 1990 he was accompanied by his First Lady, Doña Susana Higuchi de Fujimori. All was apparently not well with the First Family, as appeared to be the case with the abrupt departure of Señora de Fujimori from the Presidential Palace after accusing her husband of "corruption and insensibility to the poor." The inscrutable President Fujimori made no comment save perhaps that inferred by his withdrawal of the title, "First Lady," from Señora de Fujimori which he bestowed on his eldest daughter, Doña Sofia Keiko.

The former First Lady then launched herself into politics, appearing in the first position on the list of candidates for an alliance which need not be described. But the National Election Commission (JNE) declared her ineligible which led to her "hunger strike" which apparently failed to move the members of the commission. By February 1996 Ms. Higuchi had, of course, written a book and was seeking a publisher through her lawyer who, in turn, was seeking a divorce for her which he obtained, as she wished, on the anniversary of her nuptials.

Two weeks ago (early November 1996) President Fujimori created a new ministry, the Ministry for Promotion of the Woman and Human Development. Ms. Higuchi was in the press a few days later with a denunciation which may have considerable merit. "This," she said, "is a purely bureaucratic creation and will probably constitute a political electioneering entity."

VENEZUELA (WKLY 2.11, 24 OCTOBER 1996)

For the malversation of $17.3 million, some part of which ended in his foreign bank accounts, Carlos Andres Pérez completed twenty-eight months of house (over seventy years of age) arrest in September. Various individuals have since volunteered to serve more rigorous sentences for $8 million per year. Of more direct concern, Pérez was removed from the Venezuelan presidency in May 1993[38] for these peccadillos. Which led to the general elections of 5 December 1993.

There was a seventeen-candidate field in these presidential elections, National Convergence (CN) perhaps the most important. This coalition included Independent Elections Commission-Christian Socialist (COPEI) "dissidents," Movement Toward Socialism (MAS), the Venezuelan Communist party (PCV), and a dozen "chiripero" (lucky gambler) parties. CN candidate Rafael Caldera Rodríguez won the presidency with 30.46 percent of the vote, followed by Democratic Action (AD) candidate Claudio Fermin with 23.60 percent, COPEI candidate Oswaldo Alvarez Pérez Paz with 22.73 percent, and Causa R (Radical Cause) candidate Andres Velásquez with 21.96 percent. The next general elections will be in 1998.

In the Senate of the bicameral legislature, AD won 16 of the 49 seats; COPEI, 14; Revolutionary Left Movement (CN-MAS-MIR), 10; and Causa R, 9. In the Chamber of Deputies AD won 55 of the 199, COPEI, 54, CN-MAS-MIR, 50, and Causa R, 40. Certain aspects of the Caldera Program are discussed in chapter 2.

FROM THE BEAUTY PAGEANT TO THE PRESIDENTIAL PALACE
(WKLY 2.17, 5 DECEMBER 1996)

The comely Irene Saez, Miss Universe of 1981, is presently the mayor of Chacao, Venezuela. A late September poll shows Ms. Saez preferred in the presidential elections of 1998 by 40.9 percent of the electorate while the incumbent, President Caldera, is considered a poor administrator by 80 percent. [Doña Irene has carried her commanding lead into the New Year—Ed.]

Caribbean Nations: Dominican Republic, Haiti, Puerto Rico, Mexico

DOMINICAN REPUBLIC (WKLY 1.1, 9 MAY 1996)

Meanwhile, the eastern two-thirds of the Island of Hispaniola (Dominican Republic) face a 1996 election forced on it when the United States pressured incumbent President Balaguer to cut his term in half. The runner-up in the 1994 election, the Castroite and Sandinista supporter, Peña Gómez, appears well positioned for these elections.

ELECTIONS IN THE DOMINICAN REPUBLIC (WKLY 1.2, 16 MAY 1996)

Today (16 May 1996) U.S.-imposed presidential elections are taking place in the Dominican Republic, these pitting Lacinto Peynado of the Social Christian Reform Party (PRSC) against the Social Democrat party's Francisco Peña Gómez, and Dominican Liberation Party (PLD) candidate Leonel Fernández. Peña was the runner-up in the 1994 elections, a Castroite who appeared prominently on the platform at the January 1995 FSLN rally in Managua.

THE DOMINICAN ELECTIONS (WKLY 1.3, 23 MAY 1996)

In the 16 May elections SD candidate Peña received 45.48 percent of the vote, PLD candidate Fernández 38.85 percent, and PRSC candidate Peynado 15.17 percent. There will therefore be a June runoff.

DOMINICAN RUNOFF ELECTIONS (WKLY 1.9, 4 JULY 1996)

On 30 June 1996 the presidential runoff election was won by the PLD candidate, Leonel Fernández, with 51.25 percent over the SD and Castroite candidate, Peña Gómez, with 48.75 percent. Since these percentages are almost exactly those predicted by the last Gallup Poll, it appears unlikely that President-elect Fernández can be pressured by the United States into halving his term of office as was President Balaguer.

During the run-off campaign Peña played a curious "race card" against his opponent (EFE, 10 May 1996; AFP, 5 June 1996), in effect claiming to be the "blacker" of the two. The photos demonstrate the literal truth of this, but, in this well-integrated nation, the importance hardly follows.

HAITI (WKLY 1.1, 9 MAY 1996)

In Hispaniola's western third (Haiti) the defrocked (1988) Salesian, Castroite, Marxist, Jean-Bertrand Aristide, was choppered to the presidential throne by the United States in 1994. This year his "dauphin" (René Garcia Preval), having allegedly won the election with 85 percent of the vote, replaced him, Mr. Aristide wedding Mildred Trouillot.

PUERTO RICAN GENERAL ELECTIONS
(WKLY 2.13, 7 NOVEMBER 1996)

The constitution of the Commonwealth of Puerto Rico was ratified by the people of the island and the U.S. Congress in 1952, the Commonwealth coming into existence on 25 July 1952. The head of state (governor) and the members of the bicameral legislature are elected every four years.

In the general elections of 3 November 1992 New Progressive Party (PNP) gubernatorial candidate Pedro Rosello won with 49.9 percent of the vote, Popular Democratic Party (PPD) candidate Victoria Muñoz gaining 45.9 percent, and Puerto Rican Independence Party (PIP) candidate Fernando Martin 4.1 percent.

In the elections for the 27-member Senate the PNP won 20 seats; the PPD, 6; and the PIP, 1. In the 53-member House of Representatives the PNP won 36; the PPD, 16; and the PIP, 1.

PNP candidate Pedro Rosello won the 5 November 1996 gubernatorial race with 51.8 percent, followed by PPD candidate Hector Luis Acevedo with 44.2 percent, and PIP candidate David Noriega Rodríguez with 3.81 percent.

The figures do not appear (6 November 1996) to be complete on the legislative races, but a qualitative idea may be obtained from the numbers being reported in the Senate races late Wednesday (5 November). At that time the PNP candidates had 47.54 percent of the vote, the PPD 40.57 percent, the PIP 8.18 percent, the Independent candidate 3.41 percent with "other" parties holding less than 1 percent of the vote. The Constitution guarantees the minority parties additional representation in the legislature in numbers which may vary from one-quarter to one-third of the seats. The makeup of both houses could be similar to that emerging from the 1992 elections.

An obvious conclusion from both the 1992 and the 1996 elections is that Puerto Rican independence as represented by the PIP does not particularly appeal to the voters.

PRI FOLLOWS THE MEXICAN ELECTIONS WITH "COUNTERREFORM" (SPCL 2.13, 15 NOVEMBER 1996)

On 10 November 1996 municipal elections were held in the Mexican States of Mexico, Coahuila, and Hidalgo which, by yesterday (14 November), the Institutional Revolutionary Party (PRI) appeared to be winning. For example, with the conclusion of the recount in 62 of the 122 municipalities in the State of Mexico, PRI was declared the winner in 40 of the races, Revolutionary Democratic Party (PRD) the winner in 14 with National Action Party (PAN) taking 6.

As a reference it may be recalled that, in the elections of 21 August 1994 for the Federal Chamber of Deputies in the bicameral legislature, PRI obtained a total of 300 (277 by direct election, 23 by proportional representation); PAN, 119 (18 direct, 101 proportional); PRD total 59 (5 direct, 64 proportional); and PT (Labor Party), 12 (all proportional).

On 31 October 1996 the Mexican Executive and the political parties agreed on a number of reforms of COFIPE (Federal Election Procedures and Institutions Code), a move generally hailed as a solid advance toward "real democracy." Yesterday the PRI-controlled Chamber of Deputies threw out "at least sixteen" of these accords, these relating to campaign financing and various other election campaign affairs and procedures.

A typical, and generally remarked, example of this "counterreform" is the elimination of political coalitions: each party must now field its own candidate. Although an oversimplified example, if PAN and PRD could have formed a functional coalition for the 1994 elections which obtained the percentages of both (42.54 percent), they would have threatened President Zedillo's 48.77 percent and, in the legislative elections, might have threatened the PRI majority position.

By a vote of 282 to 142 the accords were thrown out. The opposition—PAN, PRD, PT—maintained that PRI "was afraid" to sustain the accords after the "defeats which they sustained in Mexico, Coahuila, and Hidalgo."

A Special Case: Nicaragua

THE SECOND "FREE" NICARAGUAN ELECTIONS (WKLY 1.3, 23 MAY 1996)

Costa Rican president Oscar Arias is credited with—his advisor, John Biehl, probably responsible for—the creation of the Esquipulas Accords, signed in Guatemala in August 1987 "to bring peace and democracy" to a Nicaragua ruled by the Soviet- and Cuban-backed Sandinista National Liberation Front (FSLN). In the 25 February 1990 elections which followed the FSLN was opposed by the United National Opposition (UNO), a coalition of fourteen political parties, two "centrist" unions, and the Private Enterprise Council (COSEP), its logical presidential candidate COSEP head Enrique Bolaños Geyer. But Bolaños was informed in the fall of 1989 that President George Bush had chosen Violeta Barrios de Chamorro, the widow of the fiery *La Prensa* (Managua) publisher and a member of the first FSLN junta. UNO won the elections with 57.4 percent of the vote as against 40.8 percent for the FSLN. Ranking Nicaraguan politicians told the LANS editor that the FSLN vote would have been closer to 20 percent save for the ineptitude of the election observers. For example, a *La Prensa* account had FSLN Managua mayor Carlos Carrion telling his superiors that only 150,000 to 170,000 votes were assured the Sandinistas (13 percent of the voters).

After the elections, outgoing president and FSLN secretary general Daniel Ortega Saavedra (b. 1945, La Libertad) declared that the FSLN would "govern from below." Their chief lever of power would be the Sandinista People's Army (EPS)[39] commanded by Daniel's brother, Humberto (b. 1946, Juigalpa). An arrangement, struck just before Doña Violeta's inauguration and described to the LANS editor by a participant, left Humberto in EPS command, forcing Vice President-elect Virgilio Godoy and Jaime Cuarda, the minister of agriculture, into ostracism and resignation, respectively. In addition, the Sandinistas maintained command of the National Police and the General Directorate of State Security (DGSE), the latter the domain of the "red-diaper baby," Lenín Cerna. After two years UNO lost even its control of the National Assembly.

The forty-eight-year-old Antonio Lacayo Oyanguren, Doña Violeta's son-in-law, emerged from a murky background in 1989 to become her campaign manager, with her inauguration moving into a power-behind-the-throne position as minister of government in what Cardinal Obando calls a "co-government with the Sandinistas." Lacayo sought Sandinista support for 1996.

In the meantime Humberto, ensconced in an immense "liberated" living compound on the Masaya Road,[40] kept unfettered command of the EPS until he decided to retire in 1995, then turning command over to his Sandinista chief of staff, Joaquín Cuadra. That spring, either (a) a "split" occurred in the FSLN or (b) "Sandinista Theater" began when the "moderate" Sandinista, Sergio Ramírez Mercado, formed the Sandinista Renovation Movement (MRS). Ramírez had been playing the "moderate" role since the 1970s, albeit, he was "orthodox" President Ortega's vice president, recently justifying that regime.[41] [That Villalobos was doing the same "split" thing in the Salvadoran FMLN is relevant—Ed.]

Therefore, the 20 October 1996 elections, under a supreme election commission (CSE) run by a Sandinista, perhaps have two parties of Sandinista "tendency." Which means that now (May 1996) there are forty-three other parties seeking the presidency. Of the many interesting situations represented, probably only the Liberal parties and Lacayo warrant discussion.

Nicaraguan liberalism came to power with the revolution of General José Santos Zelaya (1893), the party founded as the Nationalist Liberal Party (PLN) (1913). In 1944 the Independent Liberal Party (PLI) branched off, further branching forming the Constitutional Liberal Party (PLC) (1974). With the Sandinistas (1979) the PLN was outlawed. With the 1990s the Neo-Liberal Party (PALIC) and the Liberal Party of National Liberation (PLUIN) arose.

In 1990 two politicians rose to prominence from these parties, Arnaldo Alemán Lacayo, elected mayor of Managua, and Virgilio Godoy, elected vice president of Nicaragua (1990) and nominated for president by the PLI (1995). Alemán is a forty-nine-year-old lawyer and former president of the Nicaragua Coffee Growers whose courage in facing the Sandinistas as Managua mayor has made him the country's most powerful politician. He emerged from a Sandinista prison to head the PLC. With the incorporation of the PLN members and the 1995 victory on the Atlantic Coast, this new Liberal Alliance (AL) became the most important Nicaraguan political grouping. The PLC convention (11 July 1995) nominated Alemán the presidential candidate of a AL including PLN, PALIC, and PLIUN. In October 1995 Enrique Bolaños became Alemán's campaign manager which should bring the Nicaraguan Conservative Party (PCN) and some contra Nicaraguan Resistance Party (PRN) support.

Antonio Lacayo has consistently supported the Sandinistas, working closely with DGSE chief Cerna whose intelligence reports on Toño's enemies appeared daily on Lacayo's desk. He signed the Protocols of Transition for the Chamorro government which set the stage for the Sandinistas to "govern from below." He soon appeared at the FSLN Party Congress in 1991, escorted by Humberto, where he delivered the closing address. The next year he delivered the National Assembly to the Sandinistas.

Ybarra Rojas was Lacayo's vice minister of government until, fearing that Toño was preparing to shift the blame for his own activities to him, he fled the country. He described Lacayo's bribery of the National Assembly in a deposition which he gave in Cochabamba, Bolivia, in February-March 1993. The LANS editor verified this deposition in a Managua interview with Nicaraguan comptroller general Guillermo Potoy. In brief, Lacayo allegedly used funds from narcotrafficking and certain charities in order to bribe a Center Group (GC) of 8 deputies out of the disparate 51 of UNO. These 8, with the 39 Sandinista deputies, gave the Sandinistas 47 against the 43 remaining UNO deputies plus Moisés Hassan. The 47 boycotted the plenary session of 28 July 1992, and the now "moderate" Ramírez took the matter to the Sandinista Supreme Court which declared the session illegal. Toño then used the Sandinista National Police to restructure the National Assembly.

Lacayo opponents finally succeeded in amending the 1987 Sandinista Constitution—under which the 1990 elections were held—so that Toño, as the president's son-in-law, is ineligible for the presidency. It now (May 1996) appears that a Sandinista Supreme Court and a Sandinista CSE may have voided the amendment. In April 1995, 2000 delegates named Lacayo the presidential candidate of a new political alliance, National Project (PRONAL). Former Sandinista minister of tourism Fernando Guzman read the PRONAL platform while Lamumba-trained[42] Nicaraguan Socialist Party (PSN) president Gustavo Tablado assured the delegates that the PN would "guarantee continuing democratic forces."

The Democratic Action Party (PAD) of "the Counterfeit Contra" (Edén Pastora Gómez) is amusing, the Arriba Nicaragua (AN) of the international financier, Alvaro Robelo, is fascinating in the accusations against its candidates, but neither appears a serious contender. A 6 May poll shows Alemán with 35 percent, Ortega with 21 percent, Robelo with 6 percent, and Lacayo with 5 percent.

NICARAGUAN ELECTIONS (WKLY 1.9, 4 JULY 1996)

The registration of candidates with the CSE having been closed, on 12 June 1996 the three-day period of formal opposition began. Presidential candidate and National Assembly deputy Moisés Hassan formally introduced opposition to Sandinista presidential candidate Daniel Ortega for initiating the "piñata,"[43] to Lacayo because his candidacy is unlawful under the constitution and to Robelo because "we do not want an Italian president." It appears to be correct that Robelo became an Italian citizen, although the allegations about the banker's involvement in a $12.5 billion money-laundering scheme, largely arising from Aosta, Italy's prosecutor David Monti's references to him, are apparently too tenuous for Hassan. Several others, to include front-runner Alemán, were formally opposed. CSE president Zelaya announced that the decision on who may run will be announced on 6 July 1996. Meanwhile *Del Noticiero Nicaragüense* (DNN)[44] announced that "twenty-three men who aspire to govern…are totally unknown to the Nicaraguans…"

THE SECOND "FREE" NICARAGUAN ELECTIONS
(WKLY 2.3, 29 AUGUST 1996)

The election campaigns were to have begun on 2 August and concluded on 16 October, the general elections to follow on 20 October. However, FSLN presidential candidate Ortega, who was in Managua (between visits to Castro's Havana) on 17 July to celebrate the seventeenth anniversary of Sandinista "victory,"[45] declared that his campaign opened with the rally that day. There is agitation in some quarters to delay the final Sunday of voting beyond 20 October, and it appears wise to remain flexible on 16 October. Enough has happened since LANS preliminary report (Wkly 1.3 above) to justify further consideration, beginning with the disqualification of potential candidates.

Sandinista Rosa Marina Zelaya is president of the CSE which is overseeing these elections, which has a majority of Sandinistas and which has as its "legal advisor" the Sandinista Orlando Tardencilla. The CSE must decide which ones, among the candidates who have filed for president, are eligible to run. A few hours before the 12 June deadline for filing charges of ineligibility, Reform Action Movement (MAR) presidential candidate Moisés Hassan Morales challenged the qualification of FSLN presidential candidate Daniel Ortega, PRONAL presidential candidate Antonio Lacayo, and AN presidential candidate

Alvaro Robelo. Ortega was challenged for "enriching himself excessively and illicitly" while Nicaraguan head of state from 1979 to 1990, Lacayo for being constitutionally disqualified as President Chamorro's son-in-law. Robelo was challenged on the basis of "allegations...that accuse him of being connected with mafia groups in foreign countries."[46]

More telling would be Hassan's challenge based on Robelo's Italian citizenship. National Justice Party (PJN) presidential candidate A. Díaz Cruz further challenged LA presidential candidate Arnaldo Alemán while Nicaraguan Democratic Alliance Party (PADENIC) challenged MRS presidential candidate Ramírez. Nor would this be the grand total: Pastora[47] would be challenged on the basis of his Costa Rican citizenship, Montealegre for his alleged U.S. citizenship, PADENIC presidential candidate Mayorga by the "Conservative La Passionaria"[48] for failure to pay for her campaign hats. When the dust settled, Lacayo was out of the race as Doña Violeta's son-in-law, Robelo, Montealegre, and Pastora out because of their citizenship. The Sandinista CSE dismissed the charges against the "orthodox" Sandinista Ortega and the "moderate" Sandinista Ramírez for "lack of evidence" which, since the Chamorro government never investigated the "piñata," was technically correct.

Perhaps the most bizarre comment on the disqualifications was made by Doña Violeta's daughter, Cristina Chamorro de Lacayo, who described the disqualification of her husband as "political assassination" and compared it to "the physical...assassination of my father (*La Prensa* publisher, Pedro Joaquín Chamorro), a tragedy which cost the country instability, wars...and a (Sandinista) dictatorship." Her husband was to suffer further indignity.

When the smoke had cleared there were presidential candidates from nineteen parties and four alliances of parties, each with his retinue of candidates for the National Assembly. For example. PADENIC candidate Mayorga occupies slot no. 9 on the ballot as do his party's National Assembly candidates, these arranged in order of importance as determined by the party. If PADENIC receives something like 20,000 votes, the first of its candidates gets an Assembly seat; if 40,000, the first two, and so on. Lacayo anticipated being given the no. 1 position among the Assembly candidates, but "his" party vetoed this, putting him in third place, a real blow.

A 6 May poll had given Alemán 35 percent, Ortega 21 percent, Robelo 6 percent, and Lacayo 5 percent. With Robelo and Lacayo out of the race an August poll narrowed this separation of the front-runners to about 10 percent. The Ortega campaign appears to have resurrected the Somoza bugbear as its principal plank. Said the FSLN spokesman in Miami in August: "All of those who are with him (Alemán) are Somocistas, ex-National Guard." The U.S. press appears to be buying into this misrepresentation, but it seems unlikely that the Nicaraguans will do so.

There have been registration problems in the northern part of the country, controversy over the printing of the ballots and the distribution of campaign funding, and a donnybrook in the ranks of the PRN. Meanwhile the Chamorro government floats serenely above the "low-intensity peace" (Mayorga) over which it has allegedly presided for nearly six years, Doña Violeta issuing a statement (2 August) that her government "would guarantee free and transparent elections," saying that on 10 January 1997 she is "going to turn over a nation reconciled, in full reconstruction, with individual liberties," this with a 60 percent unemployment rate.

In twenty-six municipalities of northern Nicaragua there is "a general disorder" in the preparations for the coming elections which is attributed to the armed bands of former members of the Sandinista military, former anti-Sandinista guerrillas, and common criminals, a figure of 400 such being estimated. In certain quarters the 5,000 troops which Sandinista general Joaquín Cuadra has sent to the region are likewise viewed with some misgiving. The region was supportive of the Contras and sympathetic to those former Contras who feel themselves defrauded by the reconciliation process. Earlier this summer the Agency for International Development (AID) election observer, Cindy Gerson, was briefly kidnapped there. Voter registration is not being conducted in this region as elsewhere, and there is a continuing conflict between a Sandinista mayor, for example, and the residents who claim their registration rights to be restricted.

Mr. Arthur Estopiñan, chief of staff to U.S. Congresswoman Ileana Ros-Lehtinen, spent about a week in the "trouble zone" of northern Nicaragua as an election observer connected with the International Republican Institute observing the registration process in those remote mountain-jungle areas.

"These campesinos," Mr. Estopiñan told LANS in a 26 August 1996 interview, "have deeply held convictions on political principles and possess a strong desire to vote, to engage in the electoral process. They also feel that the Chamorro government has not been open to their concerns, basically paying little attention to them and providing little if any of that financial support which they desperately need." The method of registration, for this area dubbed "ad hoc," was for them to trek for several hours over difficult terrain to one of a number of registration tables, then wait for several hours in line. There were various obstacles put in the way of this largely anti-Sandinista population, one being the restriction to two weekends. Did this adversely affect registration?

"It would have," Mr. Estopiñan replied, "but the pressure put on by the international observers got the two weekends increased to four. We now believe that over 90 percent of the eligible voters are registered, some 380,000 to 400,000." Mr. Estopiñan will be returning to Nicaragua for the October elections.

The PRN hoped to rally the votes of over 20,000 former members of the resistance (Contras: Nicaraguan Democratic Force [FDN], etc.) to their banner. Such was not to be, the problem arising when the president of the party, Fabeo Gadea, lost the presidential nomination to Enrique Quiñones by three votes. In June "Cmdte. Chispero" and a band of ex-Contras occupied the Radio Corporation transmitter allegedly in order to pressure the CSE to approve presidential candidate Quiñones. Of those stations which Chispero might have chosen as his target, this one has, as a co-owner, Fabeo Gadea. PRN president Gadea now maintains that his party will support Alemán.

NICARAGUAN ELECTIONS OF 20 OCTOBER 1996
(SPCL 2.11, 18 OCTOBER 1996)

In the first of these articles on the 1996 elections in Nicaragua (Wkly 1.3 above) the Esquipulas Accords background of the 1990 elections and the Sandinista "governing-from-below" strategy have been discussed. After almost six years of this strategy a new president is to be elected, President Violeta de Chamorro unable to succeed herself.

By spring 1996 there were forty-odd parties seeking CSE sanction to run in the fall elections, a figure which was reduced to nineteen parties and four alliances of parties by disqualification. Of these, only PADENIC (Democratic Alliance Party [Liberal]) presidential candidate Arnoldo Alemán and FSLN candidate Daniel Ortega appear to have any realistic chance of winning in a first round, such a win predicated on the victor receiving more than 45 percent of the vote.

The Transmogrification of Daniel Ortega

At a Sandinista rally in Ocotal, Nicaragua, in latter September 1996 the slogan "Después de Dios, Daniel Ortega" (After God, Daniel Ortega) appeared on a blanket and typifies the bizarre (alleged) metamorphosis or transmogrification of Daniel Ortega which began as the summer of 1996 was coming to an end. The atheist ML (Marxist-Leninist) Sandinista in the battle-fatigue uniform is now allegedly a God-fearing free marketeer in cowboy trousers and white shirt with a proclivity for throwing white flowers in the air. A few days ago the lifelong ML and only surviving FSLN founder, Tomás Borge, told Nicaraguan television that times have changed to the extreme, that Daniel Ortega "now believes in God." Nor is that all.

In the Sandinista "Hymn"—to the melody of Beethoven's "Ode to Joy"—"Yankees" are referred to as the "enemies of mankind." Ortega is now calling for the establishment of "relations of mutual respect and cooperation with the United States" (AFP, 21 September 1996) and has abandoned the "Hymn." Perhaps in keeping with his newfound religious belief, he no longer considers Cardinal Obando y Bravo "the spiritual chief of the counterrevolution" and has offered him the Ministry of Education in his new government if he wins. In line with his new "government for all" Ortega signed an alliance in latter September with (some) former Contras of the Nicaraguan Resistance (RN) in which he promised the Ministries of Interior, Agrarian Reform, and Natural Resources for them.

Last week AFP collected a series of eight important areas on which Ortega has come around to near perfect agreement with Alemán. Perhaps the most bizarre is the one relating to the "piñata" (conflict over confiscated property) wherein Alemán repeats what he has been saying, "The solution of this problem will be a priority in order to restore confidence in justice and the respect for the property right." Ortega's new position is "I will have no confiscations [his government had carried them all out, and he lives in a "liberated" mansion]. Titles will be given to beneficiaries of the expropriations [himself?] and indemnization to those affected."

The Ortega government has openly confronted the Catholic hierarchy, driving more than a score of clerics out of the country for "counterrevolutionary activities" (AFP, 9 October 1996). Which prompted the vicar of "education in the faith" Monseñor Silvio Fonseca to reply to Ortega's "change of heart" with "It is not enough that they have good intentions…true peace and reconciliation cannot be given without repentance and atonement for the evil wrought."

Polls have been conducted, in the main, by CID-Gallup and Borge and Associates, although the Communications Investigation Center

(CINCO), run by Doña Violeta's Sandinista son, Carlos Fernando, conducted one poll which was within about 1 percent of the Borge results at the time. The polls consistently showed there to be only Alemán and Ortega in the race, the remainder of the field trailing far behind. Whatever else may be happening, however, preparations are underway for another great poll-watching event.

On 15 October 1996 Nicaraguan ambassador Tijerino pointed out that the OAS was fielding ninety-seven observers among whom will be the peripatetic former U.S. president James Carter with thirty-five from his "Carter Center" to include Costa Rican Oscar Arias and Ecuadoran Osvaldo Hurtado. The U.S. Republican Institute for International Affairs is sending twenty-seven observers under State Secretary of California William Jones and the Clinton administration, three led by AID chief J. Brian Atwood.

U.S. Congresswoman Ileana Ros-Lehtinen recently expressed her concern that the slowness in the voting-card distribution by the CSE might stop as many as 15 percent of the 2.4 million eligible voters from voting. Whatever inefficiency or skullduggery characterizes the second free Nicaraguan election, it is to be hoped that one of the observers will stumble over it.

NICARAGUAN ELECTIONS OF 20 OCTOBER
(WKLY 2.11, 24 OCTOBER 1996)

During 1996 the polls have been consistently correct in predicting victory for Liberal Alliance candidate Arnaldo Alemán over Sandinista candidate Daniel Ortega in the presidential elections, although they apparently never indicated a first-round victory for Alemán with over 45 percent of the vote. In the spring Alemán enjoyed a 14 percent lead which shrunk to 10 percent in the summer and then to between 4 percent and 8 percent in the fall.

Alemán appears to be on the way to a victory of about 9.8 percent over Ortega, this advantage having held from the beginning of the count, Nicaraguans for Free Democracy reporting at 0225 on 21 October that, with 39,809 votes counted Alemán enjoyed a 9.8 percent lead, this dropping slightly to 9.58 percent with "over one million" counted, then rising to 9.82 percent when 62.57 percent of the about 2.4 million votes had been tabulated. The verdict would appear well assured.

"These elections provide a real test of the Nicaraguans' desire for democracy and freedom," Mr. Arthur Estopiñan (Wkly 2.3) told LANS in a 23 October 1996 interview.

"Particularly in northern Nicaragua," Mr. Estopiñan went on, "many arrived at the polling places at five in the morning, then had to wait until twelve or one in the afternoon before they could vote. This on top of a two- to three-hour walk to the polling place proved the depth of their interest."

Mr. Estopiñan is convinced that the foreign investment which can correct the country's economic malaise will now recommence, many potential investors having waited to see if another economically disastrous Sandinista regime was to be installed.

Particularly important is President-elect Alemán's statement that there will be no "protocols of transition" this time around as there were under the Chamorro government and which were largely responsible for what Cardinal Obando called the "co-government with the Sandinistas."

MAYORAL AND LEGISLATIVE RESULTS IN THE NICARAGUAN ELECTIONS (SPCL 2.12, 2 NOVEMBER 1996)

The following mayoral elections were projected when one race allegedly had over 90 percent vote count, six over 80 percent, nine over 70 percent, 13 over 60 percent, 16 over 50 percent, one at 45 percent: The Liberal Alliance won Chinandega (Chinandega Department), Managua (Managua Department), Masaya (Masaya Department), Matagalpa (Matagalpa Department), Granada (Granada Department), Rivas (Rivas Department), Juigalpa (Chontales Department), Jinotega (Jinotega Department), Bluefield (RAAS [Zelaya Department]), San Carlos (Rio San Juan Department). The FSLN won Ocotal (Nueva Segovia Department), Somoto (Madriz Department), Esteli (Esteli Department), Leon (Leon Department), Jinotepe (Carazo Department), and Puerto Cabezas (RAAN).

LANS' sources in Nicaragua are doubtful about the magnitude of the presidential vote which the FSLN received. They have also told the LANS editor that, while Alemán and his running mate, Bolaños, had no doubt about their presidential victory, they were clearly concerned about vote fraud in the elections for the National Assembly. LANS reproduces below the results in the National Assembly race projected by *La Prensa* (Managua) with the caveat that these are not final and are felt in some quarters to result from successful Sandinista fraud.

The Liberal Alliance is projected to seat 44 delegates; the FSLN, 37; the Nicaraguan Christian Road Party (PCC), 6; the Nicaraguan Conservative Party (PCN), 3; PRONAL, 2; and Sandanista Renovation (MRS), 1 (maybe). The PCC appears to have an "arrangement" with the FSLN which, if correct, bodes ill for the Assembly. PRONAL's two seats means Lacayo has no seat.

One Nicaraguan source told LANS that, following Alemán's victory, many of the much-ballyhooed "observers" packed up and left, this when the most dubious part of the election—the National Assembly count—was hardly underway.

THE SANDINISTAS CLAIM VOTE FRAUD (SPCL 2.13, 15 NOVEMBER 1996)

The polls in Nicaragua had scarcely closed on 20 October 1996 when a Sandinista chorus, led by Secretary General Daniel Ortega, began to claim vote fraud against the FSLN, embellishing these charges with those of a now meaningless "Somocista" fraud. Dispassionately viewed, there are several reasons for dismissing these charges. First, international observers were stumbling over each other in an attempt to assure "free and fair elections." Next, from certain of these observers LANS has learned that the only possibility of vote fraud was thought by many to have existed, not in the presidential election which Alemán won handily, but in the congressional elections in which the FSLN picked up what some consider to be a suspiciously large number of Assembly seats. Finally, the CSE, the president of which is Sandinista Rosa Marina Zelaya, is in charge of the electoral machinery, and, if the group errs, it will probably be in favor of the FSLN and not their opponents.

Indeed, by the end of October the CSE had made no final reports on the election, declaring at that time that it would be the middle of November before any final results would be officially announced. Which, if anything, compounded the general state of confusion that prevailed. Also to be factored into this bizarre performance is the fact that the forces of public order in Nicaragua, the police and the army, are still under Sandinista control, and the ability of these organizations to "look the other way" in situations which might favorably affect the Sandinistas has been frequently claimed with what appears to be considerable justification.

In early November the FSLN petitioned the CSE to declare the elections in Managua Department null and void and to hold new elections. Ortega claimed various frauds which the serried ranks of foreign and local election observers had missed. By this time Sandinista mayoral candidate Carlos Guadamuz was proclaiming himself mayor of Managua. Nor have matters observably improved in this battered land to the present time.

From the afternoon of 6 November to the morning of 12 November, the losing mayoral candidate in Matagalpa and fifteen of his "fanatic" supporters illegally occupied the Red Cross installations in that city. Local Red Cross president Mario Benevides had been receiving death threats. As *La Prensa* (Managua, 13 November 1996) commented, "The physical aggression against Channel 2 TV News journalists and our editorial associate Xavier Araquistain by FSLN partisans are making it clear that the Sandinista Front has returned to the culture of violence which has characterized it."

NICARAGUAN ELECTIONS (WKLY 2.15, 21 NOVEMBER 1996)

The Nicaraguan CSE has officially announced the victory of Arnaldo Alemán in the presidential elections of 20 October 1996. CSE president Rosa Maria Zelaya announced that, contrary to the Sandinista claim of irregularities in the elections, of the 8,900 voting places in the 170 municipalities, only 11 had problems.

Of the 1,773,401 votes cast, 92,432 were declared null. The AL received 904,880 votes; the FSLN, 669,443; the CC, 76,621; the PCCN, 40,096; PRONAL, 9,323; MRN, 7,724; and sixteen other parties received lesser totals. With the support of the PCN, President Alemán could have a majority in the National Assembly.

FSLN secretary general Daniel Ortega continued his protest against, among others, the Nicaraguan Catholic Church which he now claims to have used "ponzona, veneno y odio" (poison, venom, and hate) to prevent his electoral triumph.

NICARAGUAN ELECTIONS AGAIN (WKLY 2.17, 5 DECEMBER 1996)

By the time the CSE declared Alemán the winner the widowed new president-elect had already designated his eldest daughter, María Dolores, age twenty-four, as First Lady. At the same time the CSE declared Alemán the winner it also rejected Daniel Ortega's demand that election results in Managua and Matagalpa Departments be annulled.

But many of the other elections, in particular, the confused situation along the nation's northern border, appear to remain in a state of flux. And reports have come in of National Assembly seats won by candidates with as few as 5000 votes whereas something of the order of 20,000 votes in these slate-oriented elections appear to be required.

The best estimate as to the makeup of the National Assembly now appears to be as follows: Alianza Liberal, 42 seats; FSLN, 37; PCCN, 4; PCN and PRONAL, 2 each. One seat has tentatively been assigned to each of the following: Independent Liberal, PRN, MRS, Unity Alliance, and UNO-96 Alliance.

The PCCN is headed by Reverend Guillermo Osorno. Osorno was in the Sandinista customs service for a number of years until, apparently finding religion, he became a minister. Before the October elections he had tentatively been chosen by Daniel Ortega as a running mate, then, apparently with mutual agreement, he ran under the PCCN banner. During the election, a possible FSLN-PCCN alliance was discussed, an alliance which, with the present numbers, would bring the Sandinista bloc within one seat of the Alemán bloc in the National Assembly.

When recently asked his intentions Reverend Osorno said he hoped to be the "pastor of the National Assembly." When asked if he would support the Sandinista, Bayardo Arce, or the Liberal, Ivan Escobar Fornos, for president of the Parliament, he refused to name his choice.

THE DEPARTING PRESIDENT WRITES HER AUTOBIOGRAPHY
(SPCL 2.11, 18 OCTOBER 1996)

Dreams of the Heart: The Autobiography of President Violeta Barrios de Chamorro of Nicaragua. Violeta Barrios de Chamorro (with Sonia Cruz de Baltadano and Guido Fernández). Simon and Schuster. New York. 23 September 1996. 352p. Index. Reviewed by the editor, LANS.

The title is apt: this is a book of dreams wherein the facts are seldom allowed to interfere with the dreams. But it is an important book by a lady whose ancestors were important in Nicaraguan society, Nicaraguan affairs, and the Nicaraguan Conservative Party and whose reminiscences, like those of de Talleyrand and the ancién régime, portray a Nicaragua which no longer exists.

The book begins with an ex-post facto dream, "...from the time I met Pedro, the risen specters of our forefathers seemed intent on cutting a path for us in the history of our country." In reality, the murder of Doña Violeta's husband, the fiery *La Prensa* publisher, Pedro Joaquín Chamorro, cut the path and catapulted her into a fame which she would probably not otherwise have enjoyed and without which she assuredly would not have been offered a place on the first Sandinista junta and, ten years later, the nomination for the Nicaraguan presidency. In her Epilogue she concludes with another dream, that of the Nicaragua she would like to be leaving to her people which differs considerably from that which she is leaving.

But these matters of detail are not important to this book. What is important is the portrait of the seventh-generation—in 1762 "Don Francisco Sacasa...arrived in Nicaragua" from Spain—upper-class Nicaraguan lady of the Conservative Party (PC), her distinguished background, her marriage to a publisher of world renown, her devotion to him and to their offspring. More concisely, it is an account of how an upper-class, Nicaraguan, PC lady of her background should react to various situations, albeit, many of them on a grand scale. And somehow, what should have happened is woven into the account as if it did happen. Well, perhaps it did. Agriculture Minister Jaime Cuadra told the LANS editor that he had to resign his ministry when Doña Violeta left Humberto Ortega in command of the Sandinista Army, Vice President Godoy's party chief told him of a "back-room" oil deal with Pérez's Venezuela. But perhaps all that is simply fantasy, and everything happened as Doña Violeta says: she did simply "refuse to fall into the old pattern of an eye for an eye."

Whether her discussion relates to her son-in-law, Lacayo, or to a Sandinista offspring, her attitude is consistently what that of an upper-class Nicaraguan lady should be. And in that lies the significance of the book. It might also account for some of the disappointments which certain quarters have felt in her regime, but it is nonetheless must reading for those interested in more nearly understanding the chaos which is Nicaragua of six years of the Chamorro government.

Notes

1. One of the most remarkable occurrences of the nineteenth century was the transformation of the hierarchy of the Roman Catholic Church from the First to the Third Estate, a rare glimpse of true political acumen.
2. The name was taken from the Fasces, a bundle of elm or birch rods bound around an axe with a penetrating head by a red strap, the emblem of official authority (strength). They were carried on the left shoulder with the left hand of the lictors who escorted the highest Roman magistrates. They were probably of Etruscan origin.
3. Antonio Gramsci is described by Carl Boggs (*The Impasse of European Communism*, Westview Press, 1982) as the originator of the "gradual building toward proletarian-socialist hegemony within the political infrastructure of bourgeois society."

4. Louis Rapaport (*Stalin's War against the Jews: The Doctor's Plot and the Soviet Solution*, Free Press, 1990), p.75.
5. Richard Pipes, "Communism, Fascism and National Socialism," chapter 5 of *Russia under the Bolshevik Regime* (Knopf, 1993).
6. The Caribbean Legion is discussed in chapter 3.
7. Augusto Calderón Sandino was the illegitimate son of Gregorio Sandino and Margarita Calderón, an Indian servant (spcl 2.12).
8. This coalition included the Humanist Ecological Movement (MHE), the Patriotic Union Party (PUP), the People's Union (PU), the Costa Rican People's Party Partido del Pueblo Costarricense [PPC]), and the Workers Party (PT).
9. Carlos Andres Pérez (spcl 1.5) will be discussed further in chapter 2, "Venezuela."
10. The Farabundis will be discussed in chapter 3, "El Salvador."
11. William S. Stokes, *Honduras*, University of Wisconsin Press, 1950.
12. *Machetismo* consists in reducing one's opponent to pieces using the machete. *Machete* is of course the diminutive of *macho*, an axe or hammer.
13. This contemptuous pejorative refers to the scholarly economic school of Nobel Laureate Milton Friedman and his associates at the University of Chicago. Professor Friedman was given carte blanche by Chilean head of state, General Pinochet Ugarte, to set up a program for the Chilean economy, the result being the first and as yet unequalled Latin American "economic miracle."
14. MERCOSUR is the acronym "Common Market of the Southern Cone" which will be discussed in chapter 5, "Trade and Tariff Associations."
15. *Justicialismo* derives from the Spanish word, *justicia* (justice). However, *justicialismo* is shorthand for the intricate web of Peronism, a statist doctrine aimed at "social justice" for which cf. William F. Stokes (*Latin American Politics*, Crowell, 1959).
16. In late 1995 Collor de Mello declared his intention of reentering the political arena.
17. President Cardosa (b. 18 June 1931), a socialist whose prolific writings harshly criticized capitalism, was asked by a journalist why his politic differed from his books. "Forget my books," was the reply, a remark reversely reminiscent of U.S. president Richard Nixon's "We're all Keynesians now." Cardosa was the father of what Mexican economist Luís Pazos calls the "much discredited theory of dependency" which blames Latin American poverty on "exploitation" by the industrialized nations. Now Cardosa calls these "nostalgic socialists" who cling to his theories the "widowers of socialism."
18. By mid-August 1995, Lula had been replaced by José Dirceu as head of the PT which he had founded; he then said that he was withdrawing from politics permanently.
19. Mark Falcoff, *Modern Chile, 1970–1989: A Critical History*, Transaction Publishers, 1989.
20. Robert Moss, *Chile's Marxist Experiment*, Newton Abbot, 1973.
21. Aylwin ran on the Concert of Democratic Parties (PDC) ticket.
22. Two percent more than his father—name recognition?
23. The grouping, reminiscent of the 1930s, is made up of socialists, "former" communists, "former" terrorists, independents, and dissidents of the traditional collectivist parties.
24. The turbulent history of the MNR will be discussed in chapter 2, "Bolivia."
25. AP was a coalition of the Nationalist Democratic Action (ADN) and the Revolutionary Left Movement (MIR).
26. The rather complex process of selecting a mayor left the comely wife of the CONDEPA chief, Monica Medina de Palenque, mayor of La Paz. Doña Monica came in second in the popular vote, but her tally delivered only five of the thir-

teen city-council seats to her party. When she received the one ADN vote and the one MIR vote it was sufficient for a majority.

27. For Bolivia's entry into MERCOSUR see chapter 2.

28. For further information on MIR see chapter 2.

29. On 10 December 1996 Carlos Palenque submitted eighty pages and two videos to the Fifth Family Court in his counterdemand against Doña Monica.

30. At the end of November 1996 these general elections were officially called for 4 June 1997.

31. This is the allegedly peaceful version of the terrorist M-19 (Nineteenth of November Movement).

32. This is the "populist-occultist" party.

33. The question of President Samper's relation to narcotrafficking has not been definitively answered, although there are some further details in chapter 3.

34. The field was rounded out with two independent candidates, Liberal Party-Alfaro Radical Front (PL-FRA) candidate Ricardo Noboa and Democratic Movement (MPD) candidate Juan José Costello. The FRA is the successor to the allegedly formerly terrorist Alfaro Vive, the MPD described as "Maoist." In early 1992 the Alfaristas threatened to "return to clandestinity" if the "right oligarchy" of Jaime Nesbet won the elections, a remark relevant to Bucaram.

35. The "autogolpe" of President Fujimori is discussed in chapter 3, "Peruvian Terrorism."

36. APRA was founded by Victor Raul Haya de la Torre who is usually treated with more deference than he may merit. Eudocio Ravines (*The Yenan Way*, Scribners, 1951), who knew him well, describes him as "A fighter who began with liberal and leftist tendencies...and came to use all the methods of nazism and stalinism." In January 1995 Augustin Haya de la Torre was announced as the candidate of the United Left (IU).

37. This was formed in 1992 by "dissident" APRA members.

38. For further information on Pérez's peccadillos see chapter 2, "Venezuela."

39. The name of this party army was not changed until 1995.

40. Roger Miranda and William Ratliff, *The Civil War in Nicaragua: Inside the Sandinistas*, Transaction Publishers, 1993.

41. Sergio Ramírez Mercado, *Hatful of Tigers*, Curbstone Press, 1995.

42. The Patrice Lamumba Friendship University was established in Moscow in 1960 by Khrushchev and staffed by the KGB. KGB Major General Pavl Erzin was its first vice rector. Its mission was to educate Third World students as nuclei for pro-Soviet activities in their homelands.

43. A "piñata" is a fragile figure which, when broken, rains presents on the guests at a fiesta. This is the nickname given to Sandinista "liberation" of property, private or commercial, which they then bestowed on themselves and their cronies.

44. *Del Noticiero Nicaragüense* is the excellent Nicaraguan news service run by *La Prensa* editor Horacio Ruiz.

45. The Castroite, Foro São Paulo member, and loser of the recent Dominican runoff election, José Francisco Peña Gómez, appeared on the platform at this celebration as the most prominent international visitor.

46. Here the reference is to newspaper accounts of an Italian prosecutor linking the banker, Robelo, to a bank group which is alleged to have carried out a $12.5 billion money-laundering scheme. An EFE dispatch of 23 July 1997 alleged that, on 1 July 1996, Aosta's (Italy) prosecutor David Monti solicited the Nicaraguan government to investigate these charges.

47. Edén Pastora Gómez was taken to the bosom of the international press which continues to refer to him as the "legendary" Comandante Cero. Since the reality

of this "counterfeit Contra" appears to have been generally unknown, chapter 3, "Nicaragua," is devoted partly to him.

48. This somewhat satirical *nom de guerre* of course refers to the Spanish communist Dolores Iburruri who figuratively "knitted by the guillotine" until the Spanish War ended, then spent most of her remaining days in Moscow.

2

Politico-Economic Backgrounds in Latin America

"We're like Robin Hood. We take from the Rich and give to the Poor," said Pierrot. "What Poor?" asked Pierrette. "Us Poor," replied Pierrot. This can be taken as a definition of "corruption." "From each according to his ability, to each according to his need," said Heinrich Karl Marx in what can be taken as a definition of "collectivism." Specific study of Latin American economies appears to demonstrate that corruption and collectivism, not necessarily in order of importance, have been responsible for most, if not all, of the economic woes of the region. This is the same as saying that the political and economic woes of a given nation cannot usually be separated. Which is worth saying in introduction to the following politico-economic updates.

Argentina

CAN THE "ARGENTINE ECONOMIC MIRACLE" SURVIVE?
(WKLY 2.4, 5 SEPTEMBER 1996)

On 4 January 1995 the Argentine minister of economy, Domingo Cavallo, proudly announced that Argentine inflation had been only 3.9 percent in 1994, the lowest in forty-one years, this without the price controls of 1953. But the Argentine Stock Exchange fell 3 percent that day and another 3 percent the next. Capital, the propellant of free market and statist economies alike, was fleeing the country, $2.5 billion of it Cavallo announced in early March, a figure doubled in a few days to $5 billion. The flight was generally attributed to the "tequila effect," a reverberation from the Mexican economic debacle of December 1994. There were a few who asked why, if the Argentine economy was as sound as supposed, some of the capital fleeing Mexico might not have alighted in Buenos Aires. And then in March the Menem government announced its return[1] to the IMF for a loan of $2.4 billion, an additional $6.3 billion to be obtained from "multinational financial organizations and commercial banks." What, if anything, had happened to the "Argentine financial miracle"? Asking why such a miracle had been demanded conjures up the specter of Juan Domingo Perón.

Juan Domingo Perón

The apparently "natural" child[2] Juan was born in Lobos (Buenos Aires Province) into an Argentina which had been evolving toward his particular brand of caudillismo since the establishment by Juan de Garay of (Santa María de) Buenos Aires in 1590. Argentina to the mid-nineteenth century was the battlefield of the port (Buenos Aires) versus the provinces, a situation allegedly settled by the constitution of 1853 which was supposedly modeled on that of the United States. In reality there was sufficient variance—state of siege, power of the executive, and so forth—to allow full play to the clever caudillo.

Entering the Colegio Militar in 1911, Perón was a lieutenant colonel by 1939 when he began a year in Italy as an observer with Italian Alpine units as an assistant attache in Rome. In Italy he developed an admiration for the methods of Hitler and Mussolini,[3] particularly for the latter's "corporate state." While accusations of Axis support by Argentines in general and Perón in particular were probably exaggerated, Mussolini's system would be copied by Perón.[4]

The Perón mystique has been irrationally enhanced by his proclivity for the ladies and the theater. Eva Duarte was a middling actress who, in 1943, replaced María Inez in the Perón apartment. When Colonel Perón was elected president in 1946, Evita received her promotion to second wife; she died in 1952, having contributed immensely as "spiritual chief of the nation" to her master's aura. In early 1956, María Estela Martínez Cartas (Isabel), an exotic dancer at the Happy Land Club in Panama, moved into the apartment of the now exiled "conductor," to be advanced to the rank of third wife five years later.

Perón was thus a lover of considerable scope and a soldier whose military ability was never tested. But, above all, he was a politician who, according to one of his laudatory biographers, "set a strategy that had as its aim the capture of political power."[5] The vehicles for this strategy were primarily the General Confederation of Labor (CGT) and the military via the United Officers Group (GOU). In creating what a generally admiring Rock[6] calls "his veneer of monolithic, unassailable strength," he built on his inheritance from previous regimes to create a quite reasonable imitation of Mussolini's corporate state. Agriculture had been to some extent nationalized; commerce, banking, and industry were further nationalized. The press was "restrained" by newsprint restriction, by government purchase of radio broadcasting through Argentine Institute of Trade Production (IAPA), and by the purchase of most Buenos Aires newspapers by Alea SA (Sociedad Anónima) whose stockholders apparently included Evita.[7]

Perón's First Five-Year Plan (FYP) was introduced in 1946, failed, and was followed by a second in 1952. Those who admire the Conductor's statist policies blame the failure on the "economic crisis of 1949–1952"; their opponents blame statist inability to adapt to, or even to understand, the basic economic transformations which produce such crises. On 10 November 1954 Perón crossed his rubicon, shattering his fragile alliance with the church with his attack on "some bishops," "some priests," and "some Catholics." The Second FYP having done little to halt the Argentine economic malaise, the Conductor's labor unions had begun to defect. In a frantic effort to retrieve his unraveling corporate state, he delivered his "Cinco por Uno" (five dead enemies for every dead Peronist) speech on 31 August 1955 which led to the alienation of the military.

On 20 September 1955 Perón fled into the Paraguayan embassy and an exile from which he would return in 1973 as Argentina's newly elected president. His death in July 1974 seated his vice president, third wife and former exotic dancer, Isabel, on the presidential throne. Her inability to deal with the escalating anarchy resulted in her removal by the military two years later, Perón's legacy having all but assured this.

As Professor Stokes points out, "no Latin American country ever had such an extensively planned economy as Argentina from 1943 to 1955 [the Perón era]...less than half the economy...in private hands as compared to 80 percent under British socialism,"[8] Stokes then enumerates that government control of a broad spectrum of industries from petroleum to steel, of commerce through its exchange monopoly, of banking. An Argentine commission in 1955 concluded that the state-owned railroads were "virtually inoperative." Rock[9] admits to the immense railroad featherbedding, rates falling 32 percent on static volume (1947–1953), as the workforce grew 60 percent (1943–1957). And, finally, there was *justicialismo* (social "justice"), a program of government (1) intervention in and control of employer-employee relations and (2) resource transfer among societal segments.

That Argentina's economic woes were the fruit of Perón's corporate state was well known: in 1977 President Jorge Videla announced his intention of selling 370–400 state-owned companies. But announcements were about as far as such programs went until the flamboyant son of Syrian immigrants, Carlos Saul Menem, appeared on the scene. As the prominent author and economist, Dr. Alejandro A. Chafuen, told LANS, "Menem's great contribution was to interpret Peronism as a sentiment rather than a doctrine; Peronism made the Argentines aware of their true identity, more diverse, less 'European' than they had felt."

"A prominent Argentine businessman spoke at one of our meetings a few years ago," Dr. Chafuen continued. "He told us that, instead of the leader we expected for the transformation to the free market, we got a caudillo from the provinces, with a marriage in shambles, dark menacing sideburns"—the mutton chops are gone now—"and a frightening past."

Menem was greeted on election day (14 May 1989) with interest rates about 100 percent per month, inflation forecast at 50 percent in May. On 9 July 1989, five months before President Alfonsín was to have stepped down, he turned over his office to Menem, one more government "solution," the Primavera Plan, having just exacerbated the economic chaos. Within two weeks Menem's program began to emerge with Senate legislation authorizing him to privatize state enterprises. In spite of carping by such as *The Economist*—"Menem...has no idea what to do next" (3 March 1990); maybe he knows but he is a "confidence man" (24 July 1993)—a program unfolded which was described by Union Democratic Center (UCD) presidential candidate Alvaro Alsogary (minister of economy, 1956–1958):

> What we are seeking...is a complete transformation of the economic system which has existed in Argentina during the last forty years. Menem calls the program one thing, Roberto Campos another, but it is all the same thing, it is the philosophy of free enterprise, of a market economy to finish with the failed directed, inflationary economy. (*Diario las Americas*, 22 September, 1989)

This is the "neoliberalism" which is the target of the "crusade" by the Hemispheric Left, of the Chiapas Encounter (see chapter 3, "Fidel Ruz Castro"). By the end of 1993 Menem's transition from the statist to the free market economy appeared to be working insofar as inflation was concerned:

Inflation had fallen from 4000 percent per year in the latter 1980s to 17.5 percent in 1992, 7.4 percent in 1993 and the 3.9 percent mentioned above in 1994. But the balance of payments and tax-collection indicators were not what could have been desired, and privatizations were encountering difficulties. In early August 1994 the Congress of Argentine Workers (CTA) and the Argentine Workers Movement (MTA) were calling a general strike against Menem's "neoliberal" policies, the still "peronista" CGT opposing the CTA and the MTA. Attempts to bring government expenses for retirees under control have, however, been blocked by the CGT from the beginning. The fiscal problems of early 1995 were adumbrated in that fall of 1994, and attacks on Cavallo as the father of "neoliberalism" heated up as the Association of State Workers (ATE) presented congress with 600,000 signatures opposing the privatization of nuclear power. In a word, the opposition to that privatization, reduction of government expenditures and the other measures which might lead to fiscal solvency were increasing in a way which should have delighted Cuba's Castro.

And then on 26 July 1996 President Menem dismissed Economy Minister Cavallo, an action that has been interpreted as a sop to the forces of anti-neoliberalism. Although it is too early for meaningful recounting of the programs of Cavallos's successor, Roque Fernández, he appears to be garnering unpopularity from various sectors. And the "peronist" CGT refused (13 August 1996) to call off its planned general strike. The anti-neoliberal crusade of the Hemispheric Left is in full swing while the weaknesses in Menem's attempted move to a free economy, which the economist, Alejandro Tagliavini, pointed out in the spring of 1995, are at least to some extent still present (partial presentation):

> The basic problem is that Argentina has neither deregulated or privatized as much as was believed and still must support a great and interventionist government...a debt of $60 billion remains...the 10 percent unemployment rate has its origin...[in a] labor market [which] is severely regulated by antiquated socialist labor legislation...the economy is not deregulated...Finally, as a consequence of the lack of deregulation the bureaucratic apparatus of the State has not been seriously diminished.

An IMF team arrived in Buenos Aires two weeks ago (August 1996) to demand an austerity in the handling of the Argentine deficit to be brought about by reduced government spending and "even" increased payroll taxes. With unemployment "bordering on 20 percent," according to UCLA professor and former World Bank chief economist Sebastian Edwards, "such a course would further distort an already inefficient labor market."[10] Of the other policies which Edwards advocates to "encourage private-sector growth," space allows only the specifics of his "visionary labor-market reform" to combat "rigid labor legislation."

As Edwards points out, an "array of taxes and regulations has served well a small group of privileged workers but has greatly hurt the economy...slowed job creation and reduced the international competitiveness of Argentine exports." Edwards suggests a "comprehensive labor-market reform" which would substantially reduce unemployment, boost investor confidence, and renew the "Argentine economic miracle." The realities of such reform remain to be implemented, their effects to be demonstrated.

Bolivia

THE BOLIVIAN NATIONAL REVOLUTIONARY MOVEMENT
(SPCL 1.9, 31 JULY 1996)

Crucial to any account of contemporary Bolivian political affairs is an understanding of the twentieth-century history of the National Revolutionary Movement (MNR). But no discussion of that classic High Andes nation is comprehensible without a word on the mythologized Inca who had hardly established himself in the region before Hernando and Gonzalo Pizarro displaced him in the early sixteenth century.

The Inca mythology is largely the work of the half-Inca, half-Spanish Garcilaso de la Vega[11] who wanted good press for his Quechua-speaking forebears. In reality, the Inca Empire had conquered Upper Peru (Bolivia) about a century before the Spaniards arrived, adding its peasants to those it had dominated previously.

The Inca god was the Sun who sent two of his children, Manco Copac and Mama Oello Huaca, to teach the Peruvians the arts of civilized life. From these children of the god allegedly descended the extensive family known as the Incas, one of whom was supreme. To the Incas, everything—"Science was not intended for the people" (non-Incas), Garcilaso tells us—to the people, nothing: they had neither the right to change their dress, their abode, their profession, nor to own anything, only the duty to serve the god's descendants, the Incas. If you choose to believe Garcilaso, however, this happy peasant lived in utopian bliss, all his earthly needs allegedly provided to him. In reality he may have suffered less under the Spanish than under the Incas.

Sucre's establishment of Bolivian independence and the War of the Pacific, which landlocked Bolivia in the latter nineteenth century, are discussed briefly in Weekly 1.12 (below). The woes of the twentieth century, in Bolivia as elsewhere on earth, have been largely the result of that communism-fascism-nazism trichotomy which constitutes the Left in spite of those historical non sequiturs discussed in chapter 1 (see "A Realistic Definition of the Political Left").

The disastrous Chaco War with Paraguay (1932–1935) left a bitterness and disillusion among Bolivians from which arose two groups, (1) the Marshal Santa Cruz Lodge or RADEPA (Cause of the Fatherland), modeled on the Black-Dragon type Japanese secret societies and bent on taking over the government, and (2) the Bolivian Leftist Front (FIB) from which the MNR would emerge.

General Enrique Peñaranda was elected president in 1940, his unknown opponent in the race, José Arze, running on the FIB ticket and garnering 10,000 of the 58,000 votes cast. From this FIB ticket would emerge the "Trotskyite" Revolutionary Workers Party (POR), the "Soviet-line" Left Revolutionary Party (PIR) and the MNR. The MNR's revolutionary spirit was encouraged by the nazi-fascist fifth column through the German Legation, the Transocean Agency, and the German Club. In 1941, when the Axis was victorious everywhere, the MNR adopted its name. On 7 June 1942 the Movement announced its official program which was largely, as Ostria G. demonstrates,[12] an echo of the German National Socialist program. The MNR founder was Victor Paz Estensorro.

In latter 1943 RADEPA aligned itself with the MNR and carried out a successful coup, putting the unknown Major Gualberto Villaroel in the presidency. Terror was a part of the Villaroel regime, perhaps typified by the murders at the "Balcony" and was, to some extent, responsible for its demise. On 14 July 1946 Villaroel ended his days hanging from a lamppost.

During the next forty years the MNR evolved from the fascist far Left through the communist far Left into what approximates the free-market Right, albeit, presently under siege.

Three days before the elections of 3 May 1951 three Bolivians met in Santiago, Chile, to sign an agreement, a photostat of which Jules Dubois[13] obtained. The Bolivians were José Fellman Velarde, representing the MNR, José Quiroga Vargas of the Bolivian Communist party's central committee, and Juan Lechín Oquendo, head of the POR and the Bolivian Mine Workers Federation (FSTMB). The document that they signed laid out a program of (1) farmland and industry expropriation, (2) support for Communist party activities and (3) support for the U.S.S.R. The Bolivian CP had endorsed the Paz-Lechín ticket, Lechín withdrawing in favor of Siles Zuazo.

Paz received a plurality in the six-way presidential race that should have thrown the election into the Congress. Instead (cf. Ostria, ibid.), President Urriolagoitia turned the government over to a military junta and left the country. The junta head, Seleme, refuged in the Chilean embassy and Paz was put into the presidency by a short-lived revolution carried out by his MNR, remnants of RADEPA, the FSTMB, and the Bolivian CP.

In April 1952 Paz E. entered the "Palacio Quemado" (Burned Palace) and began implementing the far-Left program: (1) Lechín, heading the newly created "people's militias," told President Ibañez of Chile that "55,000 guns are in the hands of the people..." (*Ercilla*, 1956); (2) By 1953 the communist El Pueblo admitted that, under farmland expropriation, "the farms lie abandoned...";[14] (3) The failure was admitted by Paz as he turned to aid from the "imperialists." The Left hewed to its line, the MNR's Hernan Siles Zuazo succeeding to the presidency on 16 June 1956, later admitting that his government faced a collapse "which could lead to communist rule" (NYT,[*] 2 October 1958).

In the fall of that year the Bolívar was devalued to B 11,000/US $1. Paz E. succeeded Siles in uncontested elections in 1964, fleeing into Peruvian exile (November 1964), to be replaced by a military junta. During the turmoil of the next seven years the far Left seemed to have solidified its position when a new force under the MNR's Paz and the Socialist Falange's Gutiérrez arose in Santa Cruz. With Paz's support, the rebels dispersed the opposition and installed Col. Hugo Banzer Suárez in the presidency, this in spite of aid offered the Bolivian "liberation forces" by Castro.

A Paz E., prophetically described as conservative in a UPI[**] dispatch, ran second to Banzer but was inaugurated president in 1985. The remainder of the unique tale of changing MNR colors will be told in Wkly 1.12 below. Toward the end of the MNR's long, if interrupted, reign the remarkable change of the MNR from the far Left to the free market took place. This change was accompanied by "the most impressive" economic turnaround (*Economist*, 20 October 1990].

---

[*] Here and hereinafter NYT will be used to reference the *New York Times*.

[**] UPI will hereinafter refer to the United Press International News Agency.

By 1989, for example, inflation was 17 percent (versus 24,000 percent), growth was approaching 3 percent, and 14 percent (versus 1 percent) of GDP was being collected in taxes. Since Sánchez de Losado's presidency began, the left has again struck out at "neoliberalism" with considerable success, leaving the economic future of Bolivia somewhat in doubt.

THE PUZZLE THAT IS BOLIVIA (WKLY 1.12, 1 AUGUST 1996)

In 1993 the landlocked Andean nation of Bolivia—named for the Great Liberator, Simón Bolívar—thought it had finally won its "Window on the Sea," the event immortalized by an AFP wire photo of the Peruvian and Bolivian presidents frolicking in the surf at a beach called Sea Bolivia. In March 1995 Bolivian Naval Force (FNB) Admiral Miguel Alvarez and various of his subordinates were arrested for money laundering (AFP, 19 March 1995), and in April 1996 still landlocked Bolivia celebrated the thirty-third anniversary of the Naval Academy of La Paz, Bolivia (EFE, 26 April 1996).

Bolivia boasts the ultimate *altiplano* (high plane), this averaging 13,000 feet in altitude, lying between two *cordilleros* (ranges) of the Andes, southeast of Lake Titicaca and making up the historically important portion of that nation, Upper Peru, or Charcas (Bolivia). A half-century after Sucre's declaration of independence (1825), difficulties with Chile led President Adolfo Ballivian to sign a treaty with Peru (6 February 1873). A series of increasingly acrimonious claims led to a declaration of the War of the Pacific by Bolivia against Chile (1 March 1879). Bolivia was joined by Peru, these two allies being decisively, if not immediately, defeated by Chile. Before the war, Bolivia had held some 200 miles of seacoast south of the Lao River. The treaty of 11 December 1883 left a landlocked Bolivia, its border nowhere much closer than 100 miles from the Pacific.

On 6 June 1993 Gonzalo Sánchez de Losada of the MNR gained 36.2 percent of the presidential vote; General Hugo Banzer of the AP 21 percent;[15] Max Fernández of the UCS 12 percent; Carlos Palenque of CONDEPA 12 percent; Antonio Aranibar of MBL 5 percent; and nine other parties 2 percent or less. Banzer withdrew, there was no runoff, and Sánchez de Losada was inaugurated 6 August 1993 succeeding President Jaime Paz Zamora. The next three years would be devoted to (1) the by now typical Latin American battle between neoliberalism and the anti-free market Left and (2) the coca puzzle.

The 7 May 1989 elections had brought Jaime Paz Zamora, the leader of the Revolutionary Left Movement (MIR) and nephew of the MNR godfather, Victor Paz Estensorro, to the presidency with the assistance of Banzer. It soon became clear why Banzer had thrown his support to the "European-trained marxist," Jaime, the former having clearly (*Diario las Américas* [Miami], 22 September 1985; 1 July 1989] drawn the latter toward the free market. Gonzalo de Losada became Paz Z.'s minister of planning, a "cigar-chomping businessman" who "oversaw the most impressive" (*Economist*, 20 October 1990) economic turnaround in recent history. Paz Z. could not constitutionally succeed himself, but it seemed (1993) that the economic future was promising under the new president.

The anti-neoliberalism of the Hemispheric Left (HL) manifests itself in opposition, inter alia, to (1) privatization of government enterprises, (2) reduction of government payrolls and in demands (3) for higher minimum wages, (4) more government "services," and so on. The privatization aspect may be used here as an example.

An incomplete list of government "enterprises" for which privatization was being planned in 1995 included ENDE (electricity), ENTEL (telecommunications), YPFB (oilfields), ENFE (railroads), LAB (airline), and COMIBOL (minerals). On 15 October 1995 the State of Siege—to be discussed—was raised, and, less than two weeks later Bolivian Workers Central (COB) organized a 10,000-man La Paz march "in repudiation of privatization, the savage increase in the cost of living and the forced eradication of coca cultivation." Executive Secretary Oscar Salas announced a "civil resistance front against government economic policy" two days later.

COB's activities continued into 1996, general strikes, with the disorders routinely accompanying them, being the order of the day. As an example of the success of these anti-neoliberal tactics, the privatization of the petroleum industry was postponed for the sixth time in late June 1996, this time until 26 September 1996. During it all, IMF president Michel Camdessus, IDB president Enrique Iglesias et al. continued pumping money, largely for charitable projects, into a nation which, had it paid its debt service in 1994, would have used 35 percent of its $1 billion export income to do so. No predictions will be made. The coca-leaf situation does appear to be unique.[16]

It has recently been reported (AFP, 23 July 1996) that 40,000 campesino families are engaged in the production of coca leaves. By Bolivian law, legal coca-leaf production is restricted to 12,000 hectares (30,000 acres). Thus, legal coca-leaf production would involve less than one acre per family, a figure which has apparently not been approached. Numbers vary somewhat, but a figure of 45,000 hectares (111,000 acres) for 1993 coca production is apparently reasonable. Each of the 40,000 families would thus be cultivating three acres, more or less. Assuming the 12,000 hectares are for "licit" use, this would leave some 33,000 hectares for the lucrative narcotrade.

The *cocaleros* have their own union headed by Executive Secretary Evo Morales and belonging to COB. By the end of August 1994 President Sánchez was encouraging the coca producers to dialog with his government but maintaining that "we are not going to permit marches and mobilizations" (EFE, 1 September 1994). He warned that his government would use the military and police as necessary to reestablish peace in El Chapare, the central region of the country and principal coca-leaf-production area. He expressed his concern over "foreigners" among the campesinos and reports of "paramilitary and parapolice," the latter being organized by Morales.

In the meantime, FECLN had accused former President Paz Z. (EFE, 28 March 1994) of receiving and carrying out the instructions of narcotrafficker Isaac "Osa" (Bear) Echeverria. "Not true," said Paz, then recognized his "errors." Osa was just a personal friend, and he, Paz, had been "naïve." He then announced his retirement from public life, from leadership of MIR, and his withdrawal from the 1997 presidential race (EFE, 11 April 1994). Two years later Paz had changed his mind.

The vice chief of MIR, Oscar Eid, was locked up on charges of narcotrafficking. Paz visited his cell to "salute" him. He took advantage of this occasion to announce that he was coming out of retirement; he was going to run for the presidency in 1997 after all (AFP, 1 June 1996). Other MIR stalwarts have been involved in narcotrafficking, but none of the importance of Paz and Eid.

These various developments overlap in time, President Sánchez's declaration of a State of Siege coming midway through former President Paz's "retirement." At midnight in mid-April 1995 and after the arrest of some 300 directors of COB and *cocalero* boss Evo Morales, Minister of Government Sánchez Berzain announced the imposition of the State of Siege to "guard our national integrity." Sánchez went on to say that these union chiefs had disturbed the public order and the peace of the nation with "strikes, marches, blockades and violence against persons and property." As has been remarked, when the State of Siege was lifted the disturbances began again.

BOLIVIA JOINS MERCOSUR (WKLY 2.18, 12 DECEMBER 1996)

Bolivia's entry into MERCOSUR (see chapter 5, "Trade and Tariff Associations") will be officially compacted in Fortaleza, Brazil, on 17 December 1996. Bolivia, which will join MERCOSUR on 1 January 1997, will be the second nation—Chile was the first—to join this grouping since it was formed by Argentina, Brazil, Paraguay, and Uruguay.

Brazil

THE "ECONOMICS" OF COLLOR DE MELLO AND HIS PREDECESSORS
(SPCL 1.10, 8 AUGUST 1996)

Neither former President Collor de Mello's woes[17] nor his economic "plan" for Brazil, requisite to an understanding of the present conditions in that country, can intelligibly be taken out of the brief historical context which is here first introduced.

Contemporary "political thought" appears to maintain that "democracy" is a "good thing"[18] and PC so that monarchy is, ipso facto, a "bad thing" and PIC. Nevertheless, Brazil waited until 1889 to follow "the vogue of becoming a republic" and may have been the better for it. The Portuguese Royal Court and much of its nobility descended on Río de Janeiro in 1808 and transferred the headquarters of the Portuguese Empire[19] to Brazil. This paved the way for Brazilian independence from Europe without that "enlightened" democracy which had filtered from the Paris of the Cowardly Lion of Lucerne, through Bourbon Madrid, to the Spanish Empire in the Americas and shattered it. In 1821, after a fainting spell induced by visions of Louis XVI's guillotine, King João accepted the Spanish Constitution of 1812, then sailed for Portugal leaving Prince Pedro in Río as regent after telling Pedro to place himself at the head of any irresistible separatist movement. Prince Pedro did just this with the *grito*[20] of Ypiranga in answer to a summons to return to Portugal. And the empire of Brazil and Emperor Pedro I emerged.

In November 1889 Dom Pedro II sailed for Europe ending the three-quarters of a century of the Brazilian empire. About a century later Collor's election victory would be widely acclaimed as Brazil's transition to "full democracy," an hyperbole justifying the choice of 1964 as a starting point for this report on the background against which President Bush's "Indiana Jones" Collor would operate.

In early 1963 retired Admiral Carlos Penna Botto detailed to the LANS editor the efforts of then President João (Jango) Goulart to bring the "giant of the South" into alignment with the U.S.S.R., with the well-known Cuban journalist, Carlos Todd, supplying the details of Castro's contribution. These details are well documented by Prof. John W. Foster Dulles[21] who describes the countercoup which, in the spring of 1964, placed Army Chief of Staff Branco in the presidency. U.S. press and presidents have simplified this complex affair into a military coup; Dulles takes the position that the military takeover was in reality an action preventing a Goulart coup. The sequence of events leading to the Goulart ouster may be begun with the unsuccessful 1930 presidential campaign wherein the political position of the Brazilian military[22] began to dissolve before the assaults of the Left.

On 30 October 1930 a group of young officers, allied to Vargas's Aliança Liberal, put their man in the presidency. Branco opposed this rebellion as he would oppose the 1932 rebellion aimed at Vargas himself. The latter was delighted with his new job, making the necessary arrangements in 1937 to guarantee its permanence, only giving it up in 1945 at the insistence of the military.

Vargas was president again in 1950, the successful candidate of the Brazilian Workers Party (PTB), his secretary of labor a Goulart whom the former COMINTERN agent, Eudocio Ravines,[23] described in 1955 as "the fondest hope of the Kremlin." Then in August 1955 Major Rubens Vaz was assassinated in an attempt on Carlos Lacerda, opposition politician and journalist, which had been ordered by Gregorio Fortunato, head of Vargas's personal guard. The ensuing crisis precipitated Vargas's resignation and suicide on 24 August 1955, the succession of Vice President Café Filho. In the chaotic aftermath and with the support of the Brazilian Communist party (PCB), Juscelino Kubitschek was elected president, Jango Goulart vice president.

Jango was again elected vice president in 1960, this time under Janio Quadros. On 25 August 1961 Goulart was in the People's Republic of China when Quadros "relinquished" the presidency, advising the Armed Forces to establish a junta. They did not, although the Third Army (Río Grande do Sul) rebelled in favor of Jango who was inaugurated 8 September 1961 and who kept Almino Alfonso, advocate of a "Cuban regime," as his PTB leader in the congressional House.

During the next two years chaos compounded until, in January 1964, Goulart came down on the side of the PCB, intervening in the National Confederation of Industrial Workers (CNTI) election to assure communist control and calling for PCB legislation. Then came the Goulart rally of 13 March 1964 which PCB chief Luís Carlos Prestes claimed to have organized and at which PCB central committeeman Osvaldo Pacheco was at Goulart's right hand, "sometimes prompting him."

The first reaction to the call for an overthrow of the existing order was that of the women of São Paulo, some half million attending a "March for God and Liberty." By 25 March the Goulart supporter and General Workers Command (CGT) head, Leonel Brizola, had orchestrated a navy rebellion which backfired and sealed the president's fate. By 2 April 1964 Jango was on his way to Uruguay, and the days of the generals had begun.

In 1984 they ended when the Brazilian military arranged the return of government to civilian control. Assistant Secretary of State Motley of the United States was "excited" over this "return to democracy," President Reagan "applauded," and José Sarney, age fifty-five, was inaugurated on 15 March 1985. At this time the economic failure of the generals had bequeathed an annual inflation rate between 200 percent and 250 percent; neither Motley nor Reagan, neither prince nor pauper, had an inkling of the economic chaos which the civilian statesmen would compound during the next eight years.

Sarney rode into office on a wave of press euphoria and introduced his "Cruzado plan" which was to pump new life into the economy. In 1986 even the normally free-market journal, *Barrons* (New York), endorsed this plan of price freezes, wage hikes, and government intervention. Sarney created two new currencies, the *cruzado* and the *cruzado novo*, and increased the federal payroll by 30 percent. Sarney's "plan" exacerbated Brazil's economic plight to the point that he left office generally reviled and bequeathing a 1,760 percent inflation rate to his successor, Collor de Mello. An index of consumer prices, established at 100 in March 1986, had reached 3,041,400 in February 1991 when Collor discontinued it.

Collor's "slick" (*Economist*) and expertly stage-managed campaign surprised even himself with his victory. He claimed his program would "get the government off the backs of the people," put the corrupt in jail, reduce government, make the rich pay, all to resuscitate the Brazilian economy. Arriving in office he unveiled his solution. It included the price-control nostrum which had just failed under Sarney, privatization of government enterprises, reduction of government payrolls and expenditures, tax collection, and a new measure which *Business Week*'s Prof. P.C. Roberts accurately described as a "one-way ticket to Disasterville," a raid on the nation's bank accounts.

Economy Minister Zélia Cardosa de Mello "and two young economists" devised the plan whereby Collor reached into the nation's private and corporate accounts, withdrawing $80 billion, two-thirds of the country's ready cash; Collor was implementing marxist Lula da Silva's plan. Collor's bank raid was a disaster. Unable to pay its employees, unable to sell its products, by mid-May 1990, for example, auto production, Brazil's "industrial backbone" (*Business Week*), fell to zero, other industrial activities suffering severe, if not such ultimate, shocks. A year later, with the resignation of Minister Cardosa, *The Economist* announced that "the party was over," one more government "economic solution" had gone the way of its predecessors. The year 1992 ended with the oft-restructured foreign debt overhanging an economy struggling under a 1,500 percent inflation rate.

But young Lochinvar from Alagoas escaped blame for his economic failures; immense embezzlement charges removed him from the presidency before these could really be noticed. A brief caretaker government was headed by Collor de Mello's vice president, Itamar Franco, and was followed by the Cardosa government and its economic solution, which requires individual treatment. Unlike the government of Pinochet Ugarte in Chile, the Brazilian military had proven themselves anything but economic experts, but their "democratic" successors had invoked true economic chaos.

THE BRAZILIAN *REAL* ECONOMIC PLAN (SPCL 2.16, 13 DECEMBER 1996)

In conjunction with Brazilian president José Sarney's "Cruzado plan" an index of consumer prices was established in March 1986. In less than five years, by February 1991, this index had reached 3,041,400 and the plan was interred beside its failed predecessors. When the bacchanal of President Bush's "Indiana Jones," Collor de Mello, ended with the latter's expulsion from the Brazilian Presidential Palace, Vice President Itamar Franco assumed the presidency. From April 1993 to April 1994 President Franco's minister of finance was the sociologist and prolific author, Fernando Henrique Cardosa, the progenitor of the *plano real*, who would be elected Brazilian president on 3 October 1994.

The first stage of this plan consisted of a combination of spending cuts and an increase in tax rates and collections intended to eliminate a budget deficit originally projected at $22 billion. After a favorable November 1993 federal Supreme Court decision on COFINS (Social Security contributions), the so-called "centerpiece"[24] of this first phase, the ESF (emergency social fund), was created in 1994 by constitutional amendment. Congress did adopt the amendment that allowed the government to deposit 20 percent of those government revenues specifically earmarked for particular purposes in the ESF and thus assure financing of social welfare spending in 1994 and 1995. But, at the same time, the legislative body did not change the requirements whereby the government shared a significant portion of its revenue with the states and municipalities.

The second stage of the *plano real* was initiated on 1 March 1994 with the creation of the "unit of real value" (URV), Minister Cardosa quipping at the time, "Reading the newspapers, I don't understand what I'm about to do." LANS is indebted, for the description that follows, to various sources, in particular, to interviews with Brazilian finance counselor José Ricardo Alves and economist William Sweet of Río de Janeiro.

The URV has been described as the "consolidation of three inflation indices, these compiled by (1) the Brazilian Institute of Geography and Statistics (IBGE), (2) the Getulio Vargas[25] Foundation (FGV), and (3) the Economic Research Foundation of the University of São Paulo (FIPE)." The idea behind its creation was the elimination of the indexing of prices to prior inflation, providing instead this URV to which such indexing could be linked.

1. The IBGE is a Brazilian federal government organization. It maintains a record of the inflation in the price of a "basic basket" of thirty-one goods and services, the basket appropriate to a family with an income equivalent to five minimum wages. At that time (1994), the minimum wage was about $100 per month, so this relates to a family income of some $500 per month. The calculation covers the period from the fifteenth of one month to the fifteenth of the next, for example, it provides an inflation figure for 15 June–15 July.

2. The FGV has been putting out its General Index of Market Prices (IGPM) inflation index for some thirty years. It is more general than the IBGE and was being used at that time by the financial markets. This index was calculated on a calendar monthly basis.

3. The FIPE index was calculated on a weekly basis, using the four weeks previous to the calculation. Here, as in (1), a basket of consumer goods and services was utilized to make the calculation, but this basket differed from (1) by being appropriate to families with twenty minimum wages, that is, with monthly incomes of about $2000.

A familiar example of the dampening effects of the URV on inflation is given by the price behavior of a product, say bread, in the basket. If bread represented 10 percent of the basket, its price inflation of 10 percent would only amount to an inflation of the URV by (10 percent)(10 percent)=1 percent.

According to Mr. Alves, in practice it was found that the three inflation indices correlate rather well and render their joint utilization to establish the URV straightforward. On introduction, the URV was to function as a stable index which, on 1 July 1994, would become the unit of Brazilian currency, the real, in value equal to the U.S. dollar. What the URV did was wean the public consciousness away from inertial inflation. Such inertial inflation engenders a sort of domino effect whereby the increase in the price of one commodity is followed by a built-in increase in the prices of other commodities.

This effect was heightened by the requirement in the spring of 1994 that salaries, for example, be expressed in URVs. Since the URV per se was not going to inflate as was the cruzeiro, this had the widespread effect of subliminally convincing the public that inflation had fallen from a monthly rate of 40 percent to 1 percent—or so. At the same time, the Brazilian federal budget was balanced for 1994 by a temporary expedient: The constitution was amended for the imposition of a 0.25 percent tax on checks which raised something like R$5 billion, but this tax ran out at year's end. On 1 July 1994 then:

The third stage of the *plano real* was initiated. A new currency was introduced, the real, which, for bookkeeping purposes, replaced the URV, not only in the offices of the Ministry of Finance, but also throughout the country. As Counselor Alves told LANS, "On 1 July 1994, the basic basket corresponded to R$106.41; yesterday, 3 December (1996), the same basket corresponded to US$106.74."[26] This is a truly remarkable accomplishment and demands answers to two questions: (1) How did this happen? and (2) Can this level of performance continue? Neither of these questions can be ultimately and definitively answered, but there are obvious contributing factors.

The answer to (1) is partly specific—in 1994 at least, inflationary pressures were assuredly relieved by a balanced federal budget—and partly ethereal: during the spring of 1994 the populace in general was indoctrinated with the stability of the URV through a wage measured in these stable units which purchased as much at the beginning of a given month as it did at the end. Thus indoctrinated, the public was psychologically prepared to accept the stability of the new currency. And did so. The real was no more backed by gold, silver, or some other stable guarantee of value than the cruzeiro had been.

With regard to (2) certain economists have used the expression "built on sand" in referring to Brazil's *plano real*. This is not an unreasonable description given the fact that the continued stability of the currency unit depends on factors such as (a) continued balanced federal budgets; (b) rational state budgets; (c) recasting of irrational retirement and health laws; (d) rationalization of the tax structure; (e) collection of something more than 50 percent of the taxes due; (f) encouragement of sound economic growth; (g) privatization; and, since no review as sketchy as this can expect completeness, (h) so on. This list is aimed at those factors from which inflationary pressures may be expected to arise; that is to say, those situations wherein Brazil does not collect enough in taxes from its citizens to provide for whatever largesse its politicians wish to shower on those citizens.

Most of this short list (a-h) requires no explanation, for example, (g) privatization of government enterprises[27] being a by now familiar procedure in Latin America. However, others deserve what little anecdotal illustration can be given here:

(b): Under the 1988 constitution 30 percent of the 1994 federal tax receipts went to the states, 5 percent to the municipalities.

(c): Retirement[28]: Men could retire on full pension after thirty-five years, women after thirty. (The average number of years spent in retirement is 17.5.) Retired congressional employees are receiving R$1,753 per month, those still working R$1,018. In Parana, ministers of the Tribune of Accounts are credited with fifteen years service on the day they take office. Health: One hospital claimed and received Authorization of Hospital Internment (AIHO) for hospitalization of over 50 percent of the residents of one small town in one year.

(d) and (f): Stockholders of companies with income greater than R$780,000 pay 60.7 percent on dividend income discouraging capital formation. Only Bangladesh and Burkina Faso tax exports as does Brazil. In 1995 there were fifty-seven different taxes and "contributions." For each R$100 of payroll employers pay over 100 percent in taxes, "contributions" and "worker benefits."

For most, if not all, of these possible disaster areas the Cardosa government is apparently seeking to introduce the requisite corrective action, by constitutional amendment or ordinary legislation. Whether or not President Cardosa is reelected may have an important effect on the conclusion of this program of correction. To this point, however, the most serious "economic indicator," inflation, appears to be behaving remarkably well.

BRAZILIAN MURDER: THE LADY OR THE TIGER
(WKLY 1.13, 8 AUGUST 1996)

[Since Wkly 1.13 was distributed in August 1996, the Brazilian government has produced a special commission which decided that the lady did it. Since the first of the year (1997), however, such a conclusion has been disputed, the most recent development being an order for the exhumation of Farias's body—Ed.]

On 24 June 1996, the bodies of Paulo César ("P.C.") Farias, age fifty, and his "namorada," Susana Marcolina, 28, were found on their backs in the "matrimonial bed" (EFE, 25 June 1996). They were quite dead of heart-shots from what was originally reported as a Brazilian Taurus .38, also found on the bed. The bed was in P.C.'s luxurious compound on Ipioca Beach, eight kilometers from Maceió, the capital of Alagoas State, Brazil. The pair had died the day before, Sunday, 23 June.

That this was a "crime of passion" wherein Susana shot P.C., then herself, was initially maintained by the family and hurriedly supported by the Alagoas State authorities, prominent among whom was director of the Legal Medicine Institute, Dr. Marco Peixoto. Peixoto carried out an autopsy and reported, inter alia, that (1) P.C. died first, (2) Susana was the only one with "powder marks" on her hands, and (3) she died of a heart shot. Alagoas, which is the home state of the deposed former President Collor de Mello and his "treasurer," P.C. Farias, appeared to be on the way to closing the case as a "passionate" murder-suicide when Brazilian federal authorities intervened. In order to understand why they intervened, it is necessary to recount recent Brazilian history.

On 15 March 1990 the Brazilian presidency was assumed by Fernando Collor de Mello, then Latin America's most charismatic (a black-belt, jet-pilot "Indiana Jones" according to President George Bush), young (age forty) political figure and his glamorous, young wife, Roseane, age twenty-six. In his election campaign this scion of a "media-empire" family and governor of the minuscule State of Alagoas, pledged himself to do various things, most relevant here, the jailing of corrupt politicians. In less than three years Collor had been impeached as a "corrupt politician" and was former President Collor.

The first small black cloud appeared on Collor's horizon with some remarks by state petroleum company president, Motta Vega, in October 1990 when he was fired for not being a "team player." Then in May 1992, Pedro, Fernando Collor's brother, began talking to *Vega*, the world's fifth-largest news magazine, and what "Abel," of what came to be known as "Cane and Abel," had to say would bring his brother down. Perhaps Pedro talked because Fernando and his *eminence grise*, P.C., were putting millions into an Alagoas media conglomerate in order to drive Pedro out of his media empire. A few months later, the Brazilian Congress would agree that the outline of Fernando's gigantic extortion scheme had been sketched by Pedro. It allegedly went like this.

With the cooperation of government officials highly placed by Collor, P.C. would arrange for important business leaders to obtain government concessions after paying huge fees to dummy corporations. These fees then made their tortuous way to Fernando and P.C., congressional investigators concluding that the pair had collected $32 million, 70 percent to Fernando, 30 percent to PC. They estimated this amount to represent only some 20 percent to 30 percent of the total embezzled.

Collor, one of *People* magazine's "50 most beautiful people," on taking office, said that he would live in his family's modest Brasilia ranch home to exemplify the austerity he preached for Brazilians. At this time, P.C. was carrying out a $2.5 million renovation of this "modest" abode and removing $250,000 from his and Fernando's bank accounts in anticipation of the latter's coming "bank freeze."

The alleged methods of extortion were simple: P.C. set up certain corporations—Brasil Jet and EPC (Empresa de Participaçoes e Construçoes) the most important—and was provided with cooperative ministers. Examples: Cetenco, a construction company, paid EPC $206,000 for "verbal advice on tax issues." Emirio Morães, a prominent São Paulo industrialist, paid EPC $239,000 because "Farias (P.C.) presented himself as an intimate friend of President Collor." Three cane planters paid Brasil Jet $350,000 the day before Collor signed a decree exempting the planters in the region from a value added tax.

President Collor's salary was $30,000 per year. Clearly the millions flowing from this operation enabled him to buy such things as a $1.7 million Paris apartment and a Mercedes 500SL, renovate his Maceió apartment for $165,000 and provide Roseane with a $20,000 monthly allowance for jewelry and clothing, among other things. Economy Minister Zélia Cardosa de Mello, age thirty-seven, she of the kiss-and-tell affair with Justice Minister Bernardo Cabral, age fifty-eight, and her associates received $500,000 from P.C. Even Roseane's secretary, María Teixeira, was able to buy a $250,000 apartment in Brasilia.

The millions washed through the lives of the Fernando-P.C. inner circle, leaving a paper trail which investigators apparently found easy to follow—40,000 checks, for example—if prosecutors have so far had a strange inability to utilize. The bacchanal ended on 29 September 1992 with Collor's impeachment and resignation. In the intervening four years P.C. fled Brazil, only to be picked up in Thailand in November 1993 and brought back to be condemned to seven years for "fiscal fraud" (EFE, 24 December 1994). By 28 December 1995 he had completed less than one-third of this sentence, but the remainder was forgiven by the "traditional Christmas pardon." Nobody knows the amount of the embezzlement, but it was recently reported (AFP, 26 June 1996) that $400 million in "secret bank accounts will disappear" with his death.

Collor has thus far fared even better, he having been cleared of "passive corruption" by five of the eight Brazilian Supreme Court justices in December 1994, the five declaring that there was "insufficient proof," this in spite of a forty-volume "charging document" (AFP, 1 December 1995). The prosecutor stated that he was preparing a charge of embezzlement, but nothing has occurred as yet. Following his Supreme Court acquittal Collor, after telling *Vega* that he was going to settle in Miami, went abroad in April 1995. He returned in December telling *Zero Hora* (Porto Alegre) that his return to politics was "inexorable, only a question of time," a statement which he followed with a polemic against the Cardosa government. Two months later an obstacle to such plans may have arisen in Maceió.

P.C. was writing his memoirs of "Collorgate" as the P.C.-Collor affair has been dubbed by the press. It has been claimed that P.C.'s brother, Luíz Romero, discovered that these memoirs were being written. Whether or not such is the case, the press learned of the project, and, a month after the news appeared in the press, P.C. was dead. In taking over the PC murder case, the Brazilian federal authorities inferred that the Alagoas State authorities were more interested in protecting the Collor de Mello interests than in finding the murderer(s).

Once the Feds took over it was reported that the "authorities of Alagoas" spread the tale of murder-suicide (EFE, 13 July 1996). Federal Police Chief Pedro Berwanger declared that "the lies have short legs," dismissing the (shot-through-the heart) suicide theory and all but accusing four ex-police guards of at least complicity. The gun was the police Taurus,[29] and the "bodyguards," although apparently certain to have heard the shots, did not find the body until the next day. And P.C.'s relations with the Alagoas police appear to have been longer lasting and more intimate than originally thought.

In September 1991—Collor was president then—the Alagoas police designated twelve of their agents to act "at the disposition of Paulo César Farias" even though he was not a government functionary. Proctor Delegate Luís Barbosa has stated (EFE, 13 July 1996) that these police were apparently the same ones who were transferred on the day after imprisonment was ordered for P.C. (31 June 1993), "apparently in order to cover the flight" of Collor's "treasurer." Alagoas police chief Loão Evarista dos Santos explained that these police were "released to seek other employment." Which, as P.C.'s bodyguards, four of them found.

Motive and opportunity therefore existed for the murder of P.C. and his "namorada." Brazilian authorities all but supported this scenario when they entered the investigation. And the case dropped out of the headlines until last week when *Vega* carried a leaked account of a report which Badan Palhares (University of Campinas) and the "Alagoas experts" are to present to the public on 9 August and which allegedly demonstrate that Susana shot herself. The weapon has changed from a .38 Taurus to a .38 Rossi, both revolvers of Brazilian manufacture. Intricate trajectory arguments, illustrated with a computer-enhanced trajectory photograph, allegedly back up this viewpoint.

Nonsense, inferred Professor of Legal Medicine George Sanguinetti (Federal University of Alagoas) with "The distance between the weapon and the hand of Susana, at more than two meters, could not allow suicide...That body was put there!"

If Badan is correct, what would have been an important political crime will be reduced to a trivial "crime of passion." Or is Sanguinetti correct? The question may well remain: The Lady or the Tiger?

Ecuador

THE PERU-ECUADOR BORDER SKIRMISH OF 1995
(WKLY 1.10, 11 JULY 1996)

On the night of 26–27 January 1995 Peru reported an attack on a frontier position by an Ecuadoran helicopter, this leading to a "full" Peruvian mobilization in the region. By 7 February, Peru reported that it had retaken Tiwintza Base, the last of three bases in their territory occupied by the Ecuadoran military. At this point President Fujimori of Peru declared a unilateral cease fire which appears to have generally held. This skirmish occurred in the 78-kilometer region that is still unmarked along the 1,700-kilometer border shared by the two nations. This was not the "war" proclaimed by the press, it was a border skirmish, but it has received sufficient attention to justify careful consideration to include (1) the location of the disputed territory, (2) the historical background of the dispute, and (3) the shipment of Argentine arms to Ecuador.

Location of the Disputed Territory

Three ranges of the Andes coalesce into one as they flow south-southwest out of Colombia and into Ecuador (Equator), then bend to the east and flow south out of Ecuador into Peru. The southernmost extension of Ecuador is in Loja Province. The frontier then bends to the northeast, striking the Condor Range (Cordillera del Condor) some twenty-five kilometers northeast, then following the San Francisco Gorge on the western slope of the range some eighty kilometers northeast to the vicinity of Yaupi, Ecuador, and the confluence of the Zamora and Santiago Rivers. The terrain is jungle mountain.

Historical Background of the Dispute

On 23–26 July 1941 Peru, with land, sea and air forces, advanced on Ecuador through El Oro, Loja, and El Oriente Provinces. In spite of what Oscar Reyes calls a "brave resistance,"[30] Ecuador was powerless, Peru occupying most of El Oro and advancing on Guayaquil when the ABC powers[31] and the United States intervened and with reason. This period marked almost the zenith of the Axis powers' successes, and the threat of Axis exploitation of this South American war was real.

The Third Conference of American Foreign Ministers convened in Río de Janeiro that fall for "study and resolution" of continental unity. With the Japanese Pearl Harbor attack, the Peru-Ecuador war took center stage at this conference. The pressure was sufficient to force agreement on Ecuador, and the Protocol of Peace, Friendship and Limits was signed in Río on 29 January 1942, the congresses of the two nations ratifying the treaty a few months later. As Reyes points out:

> The Republic of Ecuador now [1949] has a territorial extension of 260,205 km². When it was the Royal Audiencia[32] of Quito [c. sixteenth century]…it had a territory of about 1,037,890 km.²..

As the Audiencia (29 August 1563) its territories extended south along the coast to Paita, ninety-five kilometers south of the present border, east to include Piura, southeast to Cajamarca, then northeast to include Chachapovas and Moyabamba. The border then swung further northeast to include most of what is now Peru to the Yavari River which was the boundary between Spanish and Portuguese territory. In 1793 the Spanish Crown reestablished the Viceroyalty of New Granada, including the Quito Audiencia therein. The Audiencia was more precisely established with its southern boundary at Tumbes, about where it has remained, now Piura, Cajamarca, Moyabamba, and Mortilones within Peru (Viceroyalty of Lima), but Quito still including most of the Amazon headwater region in Spanish territory on the eastern slope of the Andes.

Ecuador defined its independence (15 February 1812) with its constitution wherein it declared that this presidency of Quito would include the territories of the Audiencia, but the Congress of Cucuta (1819), controlled by Venezuela and Colombia, left Ecuador in pieces. The Peru-Colombia war (1828) ended with the defeat of the Peruvians, the Treaty of Guayaquil, and the theoretical erasure of Ecuador. By 1830 the Ecuadorans, at their national assembly in Riobamba, had written a constitution in which Ecuador was given the lands of the Kingdom of Quito. By the Treaty of Pando-Noboa (12 July 1832) between Ecuador and Peru it was agreed that "they will recognize and respect the present" frontiers. But these boundaries had never been defined so the next 100 years were open to Peru to state, with military force, just what the boundaries might be.

Twice Peru invaded Ecuador by the coast, the first time in 1858, the second in 1941. The 1995 skirmish was hardly comparable to these earlier operations and appears not to have been initiated by Peru. Further, the evidence appears to indicate that Ecuador began beefing up its military almost a year before the outbreak of hostilities.

Argentine Arms Shipments to Ecuador

On 27 September 1995 Fine Airlines, Inc., a U.S. firm, filed a discrimination complaint against the Government of Peru for having adopted a resolution on 7 March 1995 prohibiting Fine from operating to, from, or over Peru. On 3 July 1996 the U.S. Department of Transportation (DOT) dismissed the complaint. Peru responded with an account of arms smuggling based on documents provided by the Argentine government. These documents described the shipment by FM (Fabricaciones Militar) of 6324 packages of "secret military material," these weighing 167,700.5 pounds (p. 2) and made up of 8,000 FAL rifles; eighteen 155-millimeter field pieces; 10,000 nine-millimeter pistols; 350 mortars; 50 heavy MGs; 58,000,000 rounds of ammunition; 45,000 artillery rounds; 9,000 grenades; and twenty tons of explosive.[33]

Fine was listed as the carrier, FM as the consignor, and Restor Metals as the consignee. While admitting that it had operated several flights between Argentina and Ecuador in February 1995 and not denying that the cargo was munitions, Fine stated that "on all occasions, the entire aircraft was chartered by a third party...a Texas firm (AES [Airline Equipment Specialists]) that has now disappeared." Further, Fine claimed that "all documents which might conceivably indicate the nature of the cargo were presented to, and carried by, the crew in a sealed pouch" so they had no idea of its nature.

These are the "bare bones" of a smuggling operation in which, in mid-1995 AAN[34] (10 April 1995) later described a 100-ton missile cargo on a Bulgarian aircraft stopped at Cabo Verde, a similar shipment stopped in the Azores three weeks earlier.

If there is any wider involvement than that of Argentina and Ecuador, it has apparently not surfaced with reasonable supporting evidence. This is not a routine HL operation or HL Support—Mothers of Disappeareds, and so forth—would be demonstrating.

PERU-ECUADOR: NO REAL CONFLICT (WKLY 2.17, 5 DECEMBER 1996)

In the closing days of November there was a brief uproar over Peru's purchase of eighteen MiG-29s from Byelorussia. The Ecuadoran minister of defense expressed public concern over the purchase; the U.S. National Security Council talked of "denunciation" to be made before the Mission of Military Observers Ecuador-Peru (MOMEP); and the chief of U.S. Southern Command, General Wesley Clark, declared himself "concerned with the impact of the arms purchase on the peace process between Ecuador and Peru."[35]

The Chilean Air Force chief, General Fernando Rojas Bender, brought rationality to the discussion with his remark that this was nothing but the "routine process of material replacement." This appeared to satisfy President Bucaram of Ecuador who referred to his close friendship with his Peruvian colleague and said that "we will surely converse at the Summit of the Americas in Bolivia."

Honduras

THE 900 DAYS OF ROBERTO REINA (SPCL 2.10, 10 OCTOBER 1996)

On 6 August 1993 PLH presidential candidate Roberto Reina told *Prensa Libre* (Guatemala), "We do not agree with the economic methods of neoliberal cutting by the present government...we have an advantage over the neoliberalism of the Chicago boys." He was inaugurated president of Honduras on 27 January 1994, only to join the "Chicago boys" somewhat later.

President Reina originally threatened to "repudiate" the letter-of-intent which the Callejas government had signed with the IMF, his inference being that such arrangements with international lending agencies—the IMF, the WB, the IDB, and so forth—force countries such as Honduras into the rigors of *capitalismo salvaje* (savage capitalism). This appears to have been largely political posturing, for within a year the IDB had arrived in Tegucigalpa as had, at least in spirit, the "Chicago boys." Perhaps this reversal of the Reina government's position was due to the worsening of the Honduran economy during 1994, it being reported in March 1995 that the GDP had fallen 1.4 percent in 1994 as against a 6.1 percent rise in 1993. A few examples illustrate this change from an anti-neoliberal administration to a neoliberal one with a "human face": (1) the international lending agency loans; (2) reduction of government payrolls; and (3) privatization.

International Lending-Agency Loans

In January 1995 an IDB mission arrived in Honduras to begin negotiations for a forty-year loan,[36] ten years at 1 percent, thirty years at 2 percent.[37] By late July IDB president Enrique Iglesias had arrived in Tegucigalpa. He ratified a $700 million letter of credit and arranged a $40 million loan for "works in the areas of health, education and potable water" and $25 million for a tourist and environmental "project" in the Bahía Islands. ($27.4 million in AID money would be forthcoming in September for "various development projects," but only the IDB project is considered here as an example.)

Reduction of Government Payrolls

Another aspect of neoliberalism—or "savage capitalism" as Colombia's Samper has called it—is the reduction of government payrolls (featherbedding). By mid-April, responding to WB pressures, the Reina government had discharged "at least 5000" bureaucrats from its "over 70,000" in various ministries. In April it agreed to the discharge of some 2500 more for a grand total of something like 10 percent.

Privatization

Encouraged by various international lending agencies, President Reina announced the formation of the Public Administration Reform Program (PRAP) in August 1995. His government proposed to accomplish this reform through a reorganization which will consist, perhaps most importantly, of the liquidation of various state entities and the privatization of services such as telecommunications, airports, and electricity.

The loan money will probably be spent whether or not this neoliberal program is indeed carried out. But the Reina government appears to have transmogrified itself from an anti-neoliberal entity to a neoliberal one although claiming its "neoliberalism" to have a "human face."

Paraguay

PARAGUAY: THE UNICULTURAL SOCIETY (SPCL 1.1, 20 MAY 1996)

Paraguay is a historical accident, the residue of a foredoomed attempt to open communications between the mines of the Andes and the Atlantic, but it is an accident which would not have survived save for the immense courage of its uniquely homogeneous people. To this Arcadia, Voltaire sent his Candide in 1759 to find "happiness" of the "noble savage" variety. This double land to the southeast of Bolivia includes the arcadian Parana Plateau—a modest 1,000 to 2,000 feet in altitude—to the east of the Paraguay River, the dry and forbidding Chaco to its west. The plateau is the extension of that of southern Brazil, the Chaco a land of stoneless sand and clays brought from the Andes by the great rivers.

In Spanish America the realities of existence usually produced a three-tiered people. The first of these, the criollos, were the descendants of the conquistadors mothered by women of Spanish extraction, the second, the mestizos, conquistador descendants mothered by women of Indian extraction; the third were Indians. The Guaranies inhabiting the area cordially welcomed the handful of Spaniards who assisted them against the surrounding hostile tribes, then ethnically swamped them to produce a homogeneous mestizo society. The "father of the nation" was the first Spanish governor, Martínez de Arala, whose six Guarani women blessed him with, according to his will, eight children, four of whom married captains.

The capital (Nuestra Señora de Asunción) was established on the left bank of the Paraguay river in August 1537 by Juan de Salazar y Espinoza. The following month Asunción was designated the headquarters of all Spanish colonies in southern South America, a distinction it lost in the next century to its offspring, Buenos Aires, when it was decided that the route through Paraguay to the Peruvian mines was ultimately impractical. From this point its history is a valiant tale of struggle for survival, first, as a Spanish outpost against Portuguese expansion from Brazil, then as a solitary outpost against Brazil, Argentina, Uruguay, and Bolivia. A century ahead of other Spanish colonies in seeking independence, it deposed its last Spanish governor in 1811, to be ruled for thirty tranquil, if oppressive, years by El Supremo (Dr. Francia), for about thirty more by the López, father and son. The kaleidoscope then picked up speed, and, between 1870 and 1932, the nation had one triumvirate and thirty-two presidents.

From a club formed by Paraguayan exiles in the Buenos Aires of 1850 arose Paraguay's Liberal Party. (Here we ignore the factions created by time and temperament.) In 1874 General Bernardino Caballero founded the other major political party, the Colorado. Three decades of Liberal rule ended on 17 February 1936 with the fall of President Eusebio Ayala at the end of that Chaco War wherein Paraguay again demonstrated its immense cohesive courage. As in Bolivia, the man on the white horse, Colonel Rafael Franco, led a mixed bag, a far Left in which were included fascists and communists.

And chaos succeeded chaos, compounded by the Civil War of 1947. Finally, on 4 May 1954, order was restored when the war hero, General Alfredo Stroessner, gave President Federico Chaves his marching orders. The energetic and serious Stroessner[38] would give Paraguay almost four decades of order and substantial economic growth, in the 1980s bringing the country into the same free-market arena which Bolivia was entering after almost five decades of disastrous upheavals under the far Left.

But as 1989 opened the caudillo was an aging seventy-nine and soon to be displaced as has been discussed in chapter 1, as have the blessings of that democracy which descended on the country. Privatizations, a critical component of neoliberalism, began in 1994, these furnishing fodder for the guns of the Left as they have throughout Latin America.[39] Another important facet of the HL campaign is AgRef which has become important in Paraguay.

It has been suggested that the Oviedo-Wasmosy conflict, as well as Wasmosy's earlier actions against the military, arose out of President

Wasmosy's feared rapprochement with Castro, although the evidence for this is not conclusive.

PARAGUAYAN ENIGMA (WKLY 1.2, 16 MAY 1996)

Unlike the Ecuador-Peru border skirmish of 1995, the HL and HL Support may have important involvement in the developing Paraguayan situation.

Juan Carlos Wasmosy won the May 1993 elections, telling *ABC Color* that his (ANR-Colorado) party would govern "for decades and centuries" backed by the Armed Forces, a quotation from General Lino César Oviedo who was largely responsible for the 1989 overthrow of General Stroessner. The honeymoon was short; under the pressure of left agitation (anti-neoliberal, pro-AgRef) Wasmosy arrested, inter alia, Generals Bernal Ocampos and Benítez in 1994, dismissed General Ayala in 1995 and, on 22 April 1996, General Oviedo. Apparently claiming some suzerainty over Latin America, (1) the United States sent a communiqué classifying "anti-constitutional" action as "totally unacceptable," (2) U.S. Ambassador Robert Service "accompanied" Wasmosy to the presidential palace and (3) U.S.-chosen[40] OAS secretary general Gaviria "departed immediately" for Asunción.

Venezuela

THE FINE ITALIAN HAND OF CARLOS ANDRES PÉREZ (SPCL 1.5, 19 JUNE 1996)

In May 1993 the Venezuelan Senate, at the request of the Supreme Court, withdrew parliamentary immunity from President Carlos Andres Pérez of Venezuela, and he became former President Pérez. The charge against him was embezzlement, one of his methods a currency scheme originally described by the journalist, José Vicente Rangel.

On 2 March 1989 the government exchange house (RECADI) was used to purchase dollars at the preferential rate of B 14.5/US$1, these immediately sold at a street value which Rangel set at B 43/US$1 and which resulted in a gain of B 600 million. Seven days after this currency manipulation Pérez "closed the doors of RECADI forever" as he had promised to do in his election campaign. Funds from such embezzlements were apparently used, for example, to fund Violeta de Chamorro's Nicaraguan presidential campaign, an activity in which former President Pérez now contends (EFE, 1 June 1996) he engaged in order "to support democracy" in Nicaragua.

On 18 May 1994 the Supreme Court "jailed" him—house arrest since he is over seventy. Legal maneuvering postponed his sentencing for "generic and aggravated embezzlement" of $17.2 million until last month when he was given a sentence of two years and four months that will be completed in September 1996. Pérez's own Democratic Action Party (AD) expelled him in 1993, petitioning the Socialist International (SI) to revoke his vice presidency in that organization this spring. Still under study are charges of his having opened various foreign bank accounts with his *amante*, Cecilia Matos, now residing in New York with their two children.

Pérez was born on the family coffee plantation in the Andean State of Tachira in 1922. His political training began early; by age eighteen he was attending his first AD convention, and he became Romulo Betancourt's secretary in 1945.

Betancourt (b. 1908) was expelled from Venezuela in 1928 for organizing strikes against President Gómez. Drifting to Costa Rica he was the Communist party head there from 1930 to 1935 (*La Hora* [San José], 25 September 1934) when he bequeathed the party to his brother-in-law, Mora Valverde. Returning to Venezuela he formed the Venezuelan Revolutionary Party (ORVE) which evolved into the AD. In 1945 Betancourt was civilian head of a military junta which seized power, only to lose it again in 1948, leaving the country with his protégé, Pérez.

For a time Pérez was a "journalist" with *La República* (San José), then returned to Venezuela with Betancourt when the Jiménez government was driven out by a new coup. Betancourt received acclaim as a "democrat," although Olin Johnston, senator from South Carolina (D) called him the "communist leader of Latin America." Carlos Andres won a senate seat in Venezuela, only to resign it to take the Interior Ministry (police agency) in the Betancourt government.

This led to his first presidential election in 1973, the fruit of a campaign urging "democracy with energy." His term as president then lasted until 1979, a crucial period in the FSLN campaign in Nicaragua and one during which Carlos Andres Pérez supplied arms to them in Costa Rica through Caracas, the FAL[41] rifle shipment perhaps being the most notable. In the AD primary election of October 1987, Pérez received 65.27 percent of the vote. In the elections of December 1988 Pérez, the avowed candidate of Fidel Castro (AFP, 31 May 1988), received 54.87 percent to defeat his nearest rival, COPEI candidate Eduardo Fernández, with 33.91 percent. His second presidential term ended with his expulsion from the Presidential Palace in 1993.

For many years Carlos Andres Pérez has been a power in the SI, the lineal descendant of that First International established by Heinrich Karl Marx, serving that body as its president and as one of its directors or vice presidents.[42] It was through this organization that he cooperated with Noriega to whom he would offer asylum in the spring of 1989.

This socialist is a wealthy man who has spent his life in politics, not in any sort of endeavor which might legitimately generate wealth. Perhaps the tedious legal action against him explains the source of that wealth, certainly the bank accounts with Cecilia, reported by apparently reliable authorities in New York and Switzerland, could have the same source.

No sooner had Carlos Andres assumed the Venezuelan presidency in 1989 than he hosted what Pedro J. Chamorro[43] described (6 February 1989) "as a secret meeting" in Caracas. At this meeting were, inter alia, Nicaraguan president Daniel Ortega, Cuban caudillo Fidel Castro, Peruvian president Alan Garcia,[44] LibTheo cleric and Nicaraguan foreign minister Miguel d'Escoto, and (alleged) Esquipulas Accords author Oscar Arias[45] who described him as "leader of Latin America." Reestablishing diplomatic relations with Cuba shortly thereafter, Carlos Andres continued his agitation in favor of hemispheric "normalization" of relations with Castro's island.

One author accuses Pérez of "sticking his *narices* (nostrils) where they don't belong," one way of describing his fine Italian hand in the back offices of so many Latin American governments. The Salvadoran elections of the mid-1980s found his minions in the Duarte camp, one of his protégés from the late 1970s that same Edén Pastora whose lieutenants convinced the LANS editor in the 1980s that he was "the Counterfeit Contra" (see chapter 3, "Nicaragua"). Pérez financed what was allegedly a Contra organization, Southern Opposition Bloc (BOS), from which would arise Nicaraguan assembly president Alfredo César. But his "nariz" activity, which perhaps had the most recent effects, began with Doña Violeta de Chamorro's visit to him in 1989 (AFP, 7 January 1989), a visit repeated after her nomination as UNO presidential candidate.

Petroleum shipments to Nicaragua from the U.S.S.R. were to end with Doña Violeta's inauguration in 1990. At a private meeting, described to the LANS editor by one of the participants, Pérez offered to replace the Soviet oil with Venezuelan oil if Madame President would retain Humberto Ortega as Sandinista People's Army (EPS) chief. Humberto remained, the petrol continued to flow, and Vice President Godoy Reyes was excluded from presidential society for his protest.

WILL VENEZUELA EMERGE FROM "SOCIALIST PREHISTORY"?
(WKLY 1.11, 18 JULY 1996)

IMF director Michel Camdessus answered "yes" to this question (AFP, 4 June 1996), but no attempt will be made to answer here. However, an idea as to how Venezuela reverted to "socialist prehistory"[46] may be obtained.

As has been discussed above, the International Socialist and Betancourt protégé, Carlos Andres Pérez, was removed from the presidency of Venezuela in May 1993 for vast embezzlement.[47] On 2 February 1994 Rafael Caldera was inaugurated Venezuelan president ending the interregnum which had begun with Pérez's ouster.

There was a seventeen-candidate field in the elections of 5 December 1993 which Caldera won with 30.95 percent of the vote. The wire services, with what may be called poetic license, described the four principal candidates as "center left." As a youth, Caldera had formed COPEI, first assuming the presidential sash under its banner in 1969–1974. In 1993 he was the candidate of the candidate of the CN coalition of COPEI "dissidents," MAS, PCV, and a dozen *chiripero* parties. The other candidates have been mentioned in chapter 1. The election was enlivened with charges of fraud.

When Caldera assumed the presidency, Venezuela was in deep economic trouble. This was partly due to a vast corruption such as that which brought down Pérez, a corruption which Uslar Pietri[48] attributes to the immense shower of "petrogold" which had made it possible for a series of governments to indulge their subjects and themselves in a welfare bacchanal.

The Venezuelan government had long owned and controlled the petroleum industry. The boom in this commodity began in 1973, following Uslar Pietri's account, as its price passed $2 per barrel on its way to an eventual $34. In about fifteen years that little nation had $200 billion showered on its government, a sum which transformed its entire economy into what he calls "a dependency of the monstrous state," a huge and heterogeneous collection of state enterprises which have offered immense opportunities for corruption and vast inefficiency. As Chelminski noted, "...the government devoted itself to planning the economy, to transferring to the State the profitable industries and distributing its risks."

"What is Caldera going to do?" asked *Semana* (Bogotá), then dodged its own question, apparently unwilling to consider what the basic socialism of the new president inferred. In his inaugural address Caldera pledged "to exchange the pilferage of the past for austerity in the budget" while vowing not to reduce government payrolls. His "strategy to reduce the deficit"—$5 billion or one-third of the GDP in 1993—included improving tax collection with "equity," combating inflation, and "encouraging production." Some were asking how any of these objectives were to be attained by a president who had pledged himself not to privatize a "huge and heterogeneous collection of state enterprises," reduce the size of government or otherwise move away from state interference in the economy.

What he did was seek his solution in the gamut of "government" solutions to economic problems: taxes, price and exchange controls, bank intervention, arrest of bankers, suspension of constitutional guarantees (for example, the right of private property), a tourist dollar, issuance of bonds, and so on. In November 1995 he announced that "I feel like shooting…those who go abroad and say you can't invest in Venezuela, they are enemies of the country." He did not carry this out, but it is the ultimate government economic "solution." His 1996 New Year's message called for "sudor" (sweat).

In late 1995 inflation for 1993 was being reported as 45.9 percent; for 1994, Caldera's first year, 70.8 percent. His government was projecting an inflation rate of 50 percent for 1995, but it had projected 60 percent for 1994. Inflation is, of course, a function of the value of the currency. President Caldera's inflation reduction method was: In June 1994 it was reported that the Bolívar had fallen from B 117/US$1 to B 200/US$1. So the Caldera government introduced exchange controls as the solution, attributing the inflation to "speculative pressures" and "rumors which have bewildered" the national life. First, a presidential decree suspended articles of the constitution-guaranteeing private property, the free choice of professional activity, the inviolability of a person and his home, and so on. Although the numbers vary somewhat depending on the source, in June 1994 the "controlled" exchange rate was established at B 170/US$1. It was "adjusted" in December 1995 to B 290/US$1. Of course Brady bonds denominated in dollars had been sold on the Caracas exchange since mid-1995. These were only symptoms of the malaise.

After President Caldera had been in office for two years, he perforce changed his program, perhaps most remarkably as concerned the IMF and, later, other international lending agencies. During his election campaign Caldera had "satanized" (EFE, 3 March 1996) the IMF. By early January 1996 he declared that he was going to reopen dealings with that organization, by May these reopened relations were to include the WB and the IDB.

Which will, for example, call for "strong measures" such as reducing the government subsidy on gasoline, a commodity which, on 17 April, was raised in price from B 5.20 per liter to B 50 per liter, that is, from $.03 per liter to about $.288 per liter ($.114 per gallon to $1.09 per gallon). Various privatizations of government enterprises have been announced, these ranging from iron, steel, and aluminum production to telecommunications and airlines. If all these measures are carried out, perhaps Michel Camdessus's roseate vision of the Venezuelan economy will become a reality.

In the meantime, however, Chelminski is apparently correct in stating that, while Caldera took the first steps toward a solution on 15 April, "in comparison with the rest of the modern world, we continue in socialist prehistory."

Notes

1. Argentina had left the IMF in the fall of 1994, allegedly to avoid IMF criticisms of high state expenses and falling state income.
2. Joseph A. Page, *Perón*, Random House, 1983.
3. Torquato Luca de Tena, *Yo, Juan Domingo Perón*, Editorial Planeta, 1976.
4. Anticipating Soviet behavior against Japan, Argentina declared war on the Axis in the spring of 1945, long enough before German surrender to allow confiscation of a number of German firms.
5. See note 2, this chapter 2.
6. David Rock, *Argentina, 1516–1987: From Spanish Colonization to Alfonsín*, University of California, 1987.
7. Carlos Aloe, *Gobierno, Proceso, Conducta*, Editorial Sudestada, 1969.
8. William S. Stokes, *Latin American Politics*, Crowell, 1959.
9. See note 6.
10. Sebastian Edwards, *Wall Street Journal*, 30 September 1996.
11. Garcilaso de la Vega, *Comentarios Reales*, Plus Ultra, [1609] 1967.
12. A. Ostria G., *Un Pueblo en la Cruz*, Editorial de Pacifico, 1956.
13. Jule Dubois, *Operation America: The Communist Conspiracy in Latin America*, Walker, 1963.
14. "Bolivia has literally millions of acres of undeveloped land.... Instead of providing for use of these lands, the Agrarian Law concentrated on the expropriation of lands which were already in use.... Why Bolivia should...go beyond...the systems of [the] Guatemala [of Arevalo and Arbenz] and [the People's Republic of] China, needs to be examined." (p. 183 of Stokes, *Latin American*).

15. These parties' names are spelled out in chapter 1, "The Political Situation in the MERCOSUR Nations."
16. The coca leaf is harvested from various South American shrubs, in particular, the species *Erythrollylon Coca*, cocaine then produced from these leaves into the crystalline alkaloid $C_{17}H_{21}NO_4$.
17. Briefly discussed in Wkly 1.13 below.
18. "Good things" and "bad things" are discussed by Walter Carruthers Sellar and Robert Julian Yeatman, *1066 and All That: And Now All This*, Dutton, 1931–1932.
19. Portugal was still a far-flung empire with possessions in Africa and Asia.
20. *Grito* is "cry" in both Spanish and Portuguese.
21. Professor Dulles is University Professor of Latin American Studies at the University of Texas. He has published many books on Brazil, these being remarkable for his interviews with immense numbers of Brazilians, all of whom were important to the subject under treatment. In his *Castello Branco: The Making of a Brazilian President* (Texas A&M, 1978) he details the circumstances leading up to the Goulart ouster. His most recent book on Brazil is *Carlos Lacerda, Brazilian Crusader: The Years 1960–1977* (vol.2), (University of Texas Press, 1996).
22. Such political aloofness, in the case of the German military, contributed to the rise of Hitler.
23. Eudocio Ravines, *The Yenan Way*, Scribners, 1951.
24. Perhaps for political purposes, the Brazilian government has designated this welfare program as the "centerpiece." From the economic point of view, the "centerpiece" was the balancing of the budget.
25. Vargas's suicide has been discussed above. For further information on Vargas, cf. J.W.F. Dulles, *Vargas of Brazil: A Political Biography*, University of Texas Press, 1967; for Lacerda, cf. Dulles, *Carlos Lacerda, Brazilian Crusader*, University of Texas Press, 1991, and note 20 above.
26. Stated another way in a recent Prospectus on Brazilian 8-7/8 Notes of 2001, the "real reached its highest quotation versus the U.S. dollar on 14 October 1994 at R$0.829 per U.S. dollar. The cumulative devaluation of the real in the period from 14 October 1994 through 30 September 1996 was 23.2 percent."
27. The immense featherbedding in the Argentine nationalized railway system has been discussed, for example, in chapter 2, "Argentina."
28. The U.S. Social Security system, when introduced, was allegedly to establish a "trust fund" with the workers' and employers' contributions. Had this fund actually been established and kept sacrosanct, a recent calculation indicates that the worker would have enjoyed the income from something like $1 million on retirement. But, as rapidly as contributions flowed into the "trust," the politicians absconded with them for pet projects of their own. The result is a Ponzi scheme whereby today's workers pay minimal benefits to the retired workers. The solution to this is, of course, privatization, whether in Brazil or the United States.
29. The Rossi is a competitor of the Taurus so that this argument is apparently unaffected by the change from the latter to the former.
30. Oscar Reyes, *Breve Historia del Ecuador*, Editorial Voluntad, 1965.
31. The ABC powers are Argentina, Brazil, and Chile.
32. The *audiencia* was a form of high court and its jurisdiction.
33. In DOT order 96-7-5, p. 4, appendix note 21 states, inter alia, "200 tons of explosive." LANS learned from DOT that a "note" from Peru had modified this to "20 tons."
34. AAN is the Andina News Agency.

35. President Fujimori of Peru posed the rhetorical question, "Why are some U.S. circles deploring our purchase of MiG-29s when they did not deplore the Ecuadoran purchase of the Israeli K-fir?" He went on to say that Foreign Minister Francisco Tudela had informed the "highest levels" in Washington of the sale by Byelorussia.
36. This is a simplification in that loans and a letter of credit would be negotiated. Of course the latter is transformed, gradually or otherwise, into the former at which point the interest question arises.
37. A festive air would be added to the proceedings by Latin American Episcopal Council (CELAM) president Monseñor Oscar Rodríguez who accused the international lending agencies of being "usurers"—at 1 percent and 2 percent interest rates—for not simply forgiving the debts of the "poor countries." Perhaps with Rodríguez's remarks in mind, WB president James Wolfensohn told a Washington, DC, press conference on 28 September 1996 that "The increasing economy in Latin America is good, but its principal problem is the distribution of wealth..." He went on to say that the WB's principal objectives are the reduction of poverty and resolution of the "poorest countries'" indebtedness [Pierrot: "We are like Robin Hood..."].
38. P. H. Lewis, *Paraguay under Stroessner*, University of North Carolina Press, 1980.
39. That there is a HL (Hemispheric Left) with such objectives will be discussed in chapter 3. This was demonstrated, for example, at the 12 October 1993 Summit of Latin American Presidential Candidates at Cartagena de Indias, Colombia, at which those present could hardly be described as other than "far leftists." That anti-neoliberalism is the battle cry of the HL is made clear in the Manifiesto de Indias which the LANS editor obtained from M-19 director Abraham Rubio during an interview the following year.
40. Confidential Costa Rican sources have informed LANS that U.S. pressure forced the appointment of Gaviria as OAS secretary general. These sources should have been well informed since the Costa Rican foreign minister had certainly appeared for some time to be in line for the position.
41. The FAL (Fusil Automatique Léger) rifle takes a 7.62mm NATO round. First manufactured by Fabrique National d'Armes de Guerre, Belgium, in 1950, it has since been widely distributed and adopted.
42. The AD is a social democrat party and hence a member of the SI. In May 1996 the AD asked the SI to expel Pérez as no longer a social democrat.
43. Pedro J. Chamorro is the son of assassinated *La Prensa* (Managua) publisher Pedro Joaquin Chamorro and President Violeta de Chamorro.
44. Alan Garcia is the avowed marxist who was (a) the college roommate of MRTA (Tupamaro) terrorist boss Polay Campos and (b) the president of Peru until 1990.
45. Oscar Arias received a Nobel Prize as the author of the Esquipulas Accords which allegedly brought "peace" to Nicaragua. From sources very close to Arias the LANS editor learned that Arias's alter ego, John Biehl, was almost certainly the instigator of Esquipulas. Biehl was the roommate of Arias in college, later apparently in the Allende government which he fled with the latter's ouster. Biehl would become Chilean ambassador to the United States in 1996.
46. The phrase, "socialist prehistory," was used by Caracas Chamber of Commerce director Vladimir Chelminski in an insightful article of July 1996.
47. Perhaps the original whistle-blower on the Pérez embezzlements was the journalist, José Vicente Rangel. Rangel's son-in-law, Carlos A. Totessaut Salicetti, was murdered with three rounds to the head on 20 June 1996.

48. Arturo Uslar Pietri is a literary figure and a successful businessman. He was minister of education in the government of President López Contreras (1936–1941), serving in the administration of President Medina Agarita on the presidential staff, in the Treasury, and in the Interior Ministry. Medina was overthrown by the Betancourt coup of 1945. Uslar was a presidential candidate in 1963 and is still active in literary and political affairs.

3

The Hemispheric Left (HL)

Introduction

The Hemispheric Left (HL) is a loose association of Marxist and Marxist-Leninist (ML)—amorphous and militant—left organizations. For ease of presentation, the amorphous Marxist portion of the HL will be taken as roughly exemplified by that gaggle of Social Democrat parties known as the Socialist International (SI).

The SI is the lineal descendant of the "International Working Man's Association" or First International which was formed by Heinrich Karl Marx on 28 September 1864 with the intention of uniting the various forms of socialism—that of Mazzini, Proudhon, Bakunin and Lasalle's German Socialist Movement—which had emerged to that time.[1] The First (Socialist) International soon foundered, to be replaced by the Second (Socialist) International with the opening of the International Socialist Bureau in 1896. Ulianov (a.k.a. Lenin) was unable to obtain dictatorial control over the Second International or SI—Mensheviks for convenience—and formed his own Third International or COMINTERN (Communist International)[2] which opened its First World Congress in Moscow on 2 March 1919.

From this date the SI was generally, and allegedly, on its own. However, did such stalwarts as Venezuelan Carlos Andres Pérez the Sandinista supporter, Peruvian Alan Garcia the "believer in Sendero 'principles,'" Costa Rican Pepe Figueres the Sandinista supporter, and other prominent SI figures wittingly or unwittingly give their aid and comfort to HL operations? Whatever the answer, the benefit to these HL objectives was the same, and it is reasonable to take the amorphous portion of the HL as exemplified by the SI. This is not to say that other portions of this amorphous HL are to be neglected, nor is it to indicate that no portions of organizations such as the SI are connected with:

The Marxist-Leninist Left

This portion of the HL was, until the implosion of the Soviet Union,[3] an extension of the Kremlin's international apparat. Between 1919 and 1943 this was, of course, the COMINTERN which in a fruitful disinformation operation,[4] the Kremlin allegedly dissolved in 1943. In reality, as Schapiro has shown,[5] it simply moved the COMINTERN personnel from its Gorky Street headquarters into a newly created "International Department" (ID) in the Central Committee (CC), Communist Party of the Soviet Union (CPSU). From 1943 to 1947 then, the primary apparat for the militant HL was the ID. In 1947 the Supreme Junta for the Liberation of Latin America (JSLA), created that year in Prague, assumed an intermediate position in the chain of command. The JSLA was moved to Mexico in the early 1950s and then to Cuba shortly after Castro's takeover.

Since the time of JSLA peregrination to Havana, the headquarters of the HL has been in that Cuban capital, although three organizations would replace and/or supplement it. The first of these was Latin American Solidarity Organization (OLAS) which emerged from the Tricontinental Conference (see "Umbrella Organizations and Activities" below), the second the Americas Department (AD) of the CC, Cuban CP. The AD is the bailiwick of Manuel (Redbeard) Piñiero Losada whose "red" beard has turned white and who has had his AD buried in another CC department. The third of these HL arms is perhaps the most important at present, this the São Paulo Forum (FSP).

Before discussing the HL and its components, it is appropriate to discuss its chief, Fidel Ruz Castro.

Fidel Ruz Castro

THE BACKGROUND OF FIDEL RUZ CASTRO
(SPCL 2.15, 30 NOVEMBER 1996)

The titular deity of the Nicaraguan Sandinista National Liberation Front (FSLN), Augusto Calderón Sandino, the patron saint of the FSLN, Carlos Fonseca Amador[6] and the longtime head of the HL, Fidel Ruz Castro,[7] share two common characteristics: their bastardy and their "aggressively antisocial" hatred of the society into which they were born, a hatred which stems from their bastardy. Sandino was born in 1895, Castro in 1926, and Fonseca in 1936. Such personalities are often susceptible to the death-and-destruction theme in ML philosophy.

On 2 December 1961, safely installed as Cuban caudillo, Fidel Castro publicly declared, "I am a Marxist-Leninist and have been all my life." If "all my life" is taken as "after seventeen years of age," the available evidence appears to support this statement. Before his 1956 departure on his Cuban adventure, Castro's Marxism-Leninism may be conveniently divided into four phases: (1) his recruitment as a Kremlin agent; (2) his service in the Caribbean Legion; (3) his participation in the Bogotazo; and (4) his activities prior to the *Granma* sailing.

Soviet supervision of Latin American operations during the 1943–1956 period include two major command phases: (1) the International Department[8] Phase, 1943–1947; and (2) the JSLA Phase, 1947–1966. General Jan Sejna of Czechloslovakia, the highest level defector from the Soviet Bloc since World War II, was in a position to be familiar with the JSLA and its operations. He confirmed to LANS that the JSLA was run by the Communist Information Bureau (COMINFORM) out of Prague. Since the COMINFORM did not come into existence before 1947, the JSLA was apparently not formed until that date. In referring to the COMINFORM, this source used the familiar term, "'Peace and Socialism' Organization," a name adapted from its periodical. The source stated further, "The P&S organization in Prague was run by the KGB and the International Department." In the secret documents of the Soviet Bloc the name was later changed to "Freedom and Justice."[9]

Castro's Recruitment

The U.S.S.R. having been recognized by Cuba, its first ambassador, Maxim Litvinoff, arrived in Havana on 7 April 1943, to be replaced a few months later by Andrei A. Gromyko whose entourage consisted of 150 Russian functionaries among whom was the spymaster, Gumer W. Bashirov. Bashirov, a Soviet officer fluent in Spanish, had recruited young Spaniards during the Spanish Civil War. In keeping with his new recruiting mission he was installed away from the Soviet Embassy in House No. 6, Second Street between First and Third Avenues, in the El Reparto Miramar section of Mariano, a Havana suburb. His recruiting began immediately as did clandestine photography of his recruits during their monthly visits to collect their expense money. Among the various agents who were observed and photographed visiting Bashirov's house was Fidel Castro.[10] File A943, containing 268 pages of Castro documents and photographs was kept on the second floor, No. 558 G Street, Vedado. Through "loose lips" Guevara discovered the location of the file and destroyed it on 23 January 1959.

To the testimony of Diaz Verson may be added that of Rafael Lincoln Diaz Balart,[11] Castro's brother-in-law and the Cuban KGB (DGI) officer[12] who added the information that the Soviet spymaster, Grobart, sent by Dzugashvili (a.k.a. Stalin) to Cuba in 1928, recruited Castro into (Agencia) Caribe.

Castro in the Caribbean Legion

As time ran out for the Soviets in Spain (9 March 1939) a meeting took place in Madrid at which was formed the National Committee of the People's Front (CNFP) from which emerged Emigration Service for Spanish Republicans (SERE). SERE was charged with shipping handpicked "Kremlin line" personnel to Latin America. Another such organization, Spanish Republican Aid Junta (JARE), was formed in July. From the "refugees" shipped out of Spain by such organizations came many of those who would agitate the hemisphere for many years. For example, the father of the "red-diaper baby" and Nicaraguan KGB (DGSE) chief, Lenín Cerna, was one such. Another was "General," actually colonel, Alberto Bayo Giraud (a.k.a. Bayo Gosgayo) who would train Castro in 1955 but who first played a role in the Caribbean Legion (CL).

The Army of Liberation of the Caribbean was renamed the CL by Jerry Hannifin of *Time* in 1948. In 1946 the CL was organized by Romulo Betancourt (1908–1981) and Guatemala's Arevalo. The latter will be encountered below. The CL was trained by Spanish "Republicans" at Cayo Confites off Cuba and bankrolled by the "Frederick Vanderbilt Field of the Caribbean,"[13] José Manuel Alemán, with $2 million from his Cuban Education Ministry. It was intended to bring the blessings of "liberation" to the nations of the Caribbean.

Among the CL trainees on Cayo Confite was Fidel Castro.

The Bogotazo

This, although important to Fidel Castro, is of sufficient importance to "Colombian Terrorism" per se to be treated with relation to that subject area below.

Castro's Activities to **Granma** Sailing

After their "triumph" in the Bogotazo Fidel Castro and Alfredo Guevara Valdes asked to be sent to Czechoslovakia.[14] Guevara was allowed to go, but Castro's request was refused, the reasons alleged by Castro for the refusal contained in his letter to Abelardo Adan Garcia, another Bashirov recruit then in Prague. In the letter, which was intercepted by Diaz Verson, Castro claimed he was being kept "in reserve for greater tasks."

In 1952 Cuba broke relations with the U.S.S.R., Bashirov moving to Mexico City. On 11 July 1952 Castro, using a forged passport in the name of Federico Castillo Ramírez, followed him there on Mexicana Airlines. The following month he returned with "full subversive plans" and a promise of Kremlin support. He was to become active in the Orthodox Party, as he did, receiving his instructions from Basily Bogarev at the Orthodox Club (109 Prado Street, Havana). Jailed for the murderous fiasco which was his "attack" on the Moncada Barracks (26 July 1953) and whence the name of his terrorist movement, his contact there was Caridad Moncado (San Vicente Heights, Santiago de Cuba). In May 1955 Batista "amnestied" Castro.

Castro again slipped out of Cuba, this time proceeding to Quintana Roo, Mexico, where Alberto Bayo, who has already been encountered, had a ranch. Here Fidel and others to include Ernesto Guevara, were trained in guerrilla terrorism. Returning to Mexico City after his training, Castro and his brother Raul found "the weapons and the ship with which he was to undertake his bold adventure" waiting.

WHO ARE YOU, MR. CASTRO? (WKLY 2.20, 26 DECEMBER 1996)

ALPHONSE EMANUILOFF-MAX,[15]ASSOCIATE EDITOR, LANS

January 1 will mark the thirty-eighth anniversary of his triumphal entry into Havana, saluted by the whole world, and especially Latin America, as the "great democrat who came to liberate Cuba from the bloody tyranny of Batista and proclaim the message of continental liberation." This ritualistic proclamation could be heard from every corner of the world for many years and still today continues to be heard spasmodically. I always suspect that when many people assert the same thing, it could be false…Those who, as with he who is writing this, tried—discretely—to disagree, were anathematized and declared "incapable of recognizing the direction in which history is marching"…We are not going to continue with this and create a mournful chronicle of the eight lustra of his duration of power, and of the methods utilized to effect this authentic achievement (one must recognize it!) which con-

sists in having established institutionalized crime as a form of government before the eyes of the world, and, in spite of this (or would it be as
a result?) surviving. Because tyranny tends to rule until checked,,,

Fidel Castro is, and I write it without ire, a chromosomatic traitor. In
the course of his long, too long, life, he has betrayed everyone: family,
children, people, social class, religion, wives, comrades, allies, friends,
his own past...All the problems with which Castro has been confronted,
Castro has resolved with blood and violence.

Nevertheless, Fidel Castro has one great involuntary merit of benefit to the West: Cuba was one of the principal causes of the Soviet
Union's collapse! Let us explain ourselves.

The maintenance of Fidel Castro's regime during more than six lustra
cost the Kremlin an average of $4 billion per year. The return from this
absurd investment was nil, if not to say negative. The Russians used
the Cubans (preferably those of color for purposes of mimicry) as pe-
ons of war and cannon fodder in Africa and various Latin American
countries. Castro charged by the head and his billing drained, to the last
penny, everything possible from the needy Soviet economy which had
commitments in other scarcely more profitable parts of the world: subversion, espionage and, finally, Afghanistan. Naturally, this enormous
investment had no political return and even less economic, to the point
that Gorbachev, accompanied by Raisa, had to go personally to tropical
Havana, imploring the understanding Castro, in order to warn him that
this El Dorado could not continue. But the most interesting aspect of
all this is that, while the bountiful Gorbachev fell from power at the
end of 1991, the consignee of the bountiful one continues in Havana as
if nothing had happened. This also has an explanation.

Fidel Castro, the Soviets' most costly useless one, was transformed,
in spite of himself, in the course of his long term in power, into a su-
premely beneficial factor to North Americans. And without costing
Washington a penny. Nothing is sadder than rendering service to an
enemy, and this gratuitously. We will see how.

With the withdrawal of Soviet nuclear missiles from Cuban soil in
1962–1963,[16] the danger which Cuba would have represented to the
United States disappeared. From this moment on, everything that Castro
did by orders of Moscow, directly or indirectly, favored the United States.
The distinct continental organizations, which Havana set in motion
during the 1963–1964 period and which had to coordinate the various
Latin American terrorist movements, produced the concrete result of
cohesion of all sorts of then existent regimes on the continent around

the United States, these ranging from the traditional dictatorships to parliamentary democracies. These organizations were also responsible for the establishment of strictly military government from Tierra del Fuego to Mexico. All this thanks to Castro, the obstetrician in spite of himself, of Latin American neo-militarism.

On the other hand, the continuing and predictable impoverishment of Cuba was a warning even for that Latin American left which in the beginning approved "in principle" the Castro regime. But such enthusiasm is cooled by the enumeration of those excesses which the maintenance of that regressive Utopia demands and which, even under these conditions, are accepted as "historically justified." Some leftists were sufficiently lucid (e.g., Vargas Llosa[17]) to comprehend that Castroism per se was the very problem for which the same Castro was recommended as the unique solution...

Thus, for example, the Cuban military presence in Havana was favorably received by some State Department functionaries who considered the Castroite troops disembarked in Africa a contribution to regional stability. In an area plagued by fratricidal wars among the various tribes on the one hand, and by the Chinese, Soviet, and South African guerrillas on the other, fighting among themselves, the planting of Cuban mercenaries was evaluated in terms of its final effect, with formidable moral indifference, as objectively positive for Western interests. Moreover, the bills for services rendered and the accounts of expenses which Castro periodically presented to the Soviets for this presence of his myrmidons (not only in Angola) in the bottomless pit which was Africa, was one of the elements contributing to the financial and political fall of the Soviet Union. Moscow had to prove that Castro was the dearest of all those whom it was maintaining, and, in its global arrangements with the West, cut the provisions without more ado. It was Castro, in the final analysis, who exploited the Russians, and not the other way round. And when the Kremlin finally understood that its accounts were not closed in any rubric and that the exploiter had been transformed into the exploited, it knew that the raison d'être of the system had been exhausted. Will it not be the "indigenous vivacity" of the grotesque Caribbean buffoon, selling "stamps" like a gypsy to the Russians, which contributed to the ultimate overthrow of the U.S.S.R.?

* * *

Therefore, it cannot be a surprise, although it could sound cynical to some anorectic intellectuals, that the United States has no interest in the immediate disappearance of a senile Castro, because a Cuba freed of him would be transformed for Washington into an inevitable regional economic, migratory and, in the end also, social problem. The Government of the United States is not interested at this moment in the abrupt fall of Fidel Castro. His disappearance from power would mean a mega-exodus of Cubans satiated with having lived so many years in the island misery toward the south of the United States. In contrast to the exiled Haitians, who were sent back, hundreds of thousands of Cubans, Cuba once de-Castroed, would arrive in the United States, with or without permission to enter and reside, and would be settled very easily thanks to their family connections. The problems for the authorities of the Office of Immigration are predictable. Moreover, that fall of Fidel Castro would also signal the massive withdrawal of funds by many Cuban Americans from the banks and the economy of the United States with the resulting partial decapitalization of the State of Florida for investment in a liberated Cuba. Precipitate investors from France, Germany, and Italy will present themselves promptly once the inevitable occurs.

But still there is no scheduled fall of Castro and his regime, (His place of refuge in Galicia is arranged. Ask Fraga Ibararne about it…) Knowing the manifest and natural susceptibility of Washington to all that surrounds it, especially Cuba, it appears doubtful that Paris, Bonn, and Madrid, its allies in NATO, would have risked investing in the island if this would have caused serious concern to the U.S. government. Moreover, the White House would consider the investments of its allies as arguments for stimulating its own opposition to its Republican opponents.

* * *

Those who think that Castro, on the altars of his own survival, will be tempted to change and liberalize his regime, are deluding themselves. He knows very well, having observed and survived the disappearance of the U.S.S.R. and its satellites, that a tyrannical system such as his, runs the most serious danger at the moment it begins to change. The Castro regime is more secure if it remains in a position of social and political immobility and solidification, than if it begins a risky reformist seachange. Moreover, viewing the inextricably entangled situation on the island, it appears obvious that Fidel Castro is now too weak to yield. Only total inanition could oblige him to take the aircraft with the last load of fuel remaining on the island, with destination Galicia and liberate the shackled Cuban people from his

presence. But, as we have inferred above, there is not too much hurry in hastening such a disentanglement...
                    —Translated from the Spanish by the LANS editor

CASTRO AT THE WORLD FOOD SUMMIT (SPCL 2.15, 30 NOVEMBER 1996)

Cuban ML caudillo Fidel Castro is one of the four vice presidents of the Food and Agricultural Organization (FAO) which held its World Summit on Nutrition at its headquarters in Rome from 13 to 17 November 1996. On 16 November 1996 Vice President Castro spoke before that august body, his harangue entitled "What We Must Do to Prevent One Million People from Dying of Hunger Every Year" and heavily larded with the propaganda of the HL. The speech was of course published in his house organ, *Granma* (Havana, 18 November 1996),[18] which referred to the caudillo as "Commander in Chief...First Secretary of the Central Committee of the Cuban Communist Party and President of the Council of State and Ministers." The flavor of his oration may be captured by a reproduction of its seventh paragraph which allegedly answers the rhetorical question in its title:

> Capitalism, neoliberalism, savage market laws, foreign debt, under development, unequal exchange are what kill so many people in the world.

Which is one way of saying that the free-market economy is responsible for these deaths from hunger, a state of affairs which could be corrected by Castro's Marxist-Leninist economic models. This does not appear to have been the case in the defunct Soviet Union or, indeed, in Castro's economically disastrous fiefdom. But in order to more precisely delineate the fatuousness of the vice president's remarks, LANS consulted the ultimate expert on Cuban economic affairs, Dr. Antonio Jorge. Dr. Jorge is professor of economics and international relations at Florida International University.

"First of all," Professor Jorge told LANS, "since the end of World War II the economies of all the Third World countries have grown twice as fast as those of the Developed Countries such as those in Europe and North America. In fact, the countries in the Developed World have never in their history experienced economic growth as rapid as have the Underdeveloped Countries (UC) in the last fifty years. During the nineteenth and twentieth Centuries, for example, Britain and the United States experienced economic growth of about 2 percent. The UC have enjoyed economic growth fluctuating between 4 percent and 5 percent.

"It is paradoxical," Professor Jorge went on, "to blame Third World poverty on the very system which has brought affluence to so many countries in North America, Europe, and other regions such as Japan. What Castro is doing here is recommending a system which had catastrophic effects on Russia and on his own country.

"His economic problems were certainly not caused by the blockade which is nothing more than a porous commercial embargo through which he can buy as much as he wants to include U.S. goods," Professor Jorge explained. "And furthermore, Castro seldom referred to the 'blockade' before 1990. That was when the immense Russian subsidy stopped.

"For thirty-one years Castro received $5 billion per year from the Soviets for a total of some $150 billion. This was almost ten times the cost of the Marshall Plan—$17 billion—which brought the economic recovery of Western Europe after the Second World War."

LANS: Did not Castro take over one of the most robust of the Latin American economies in 1959 and almost totally destroy it?

"Absolutely," Professor Jorge replied. "In a recent report one of Castro's own 'think tanks,' the Center for the Americas in Havana, reported that the Cuban GDP declined 50 percent from 1990–1991 to 1995."

ZEDILLO, JIANG, AND CASTRO
(SPCL 2.15, 30 NOVEMBER 1996)

On 22 November 1996 President Ernesto Zedillo Ponce de Leon of Mexico and President Jiang Zemin of the People's Republic of China met in Beijing for discussions in which they "decided to promote" the rejection of the Helms-Burton Law, an end to nuclear testing,[19] restructuring the UN Security Council and the reelection of Boutros Boutros-Ghali as UN Secretary General. It probably can be said that all of these measures met with the approval of the ML Cuban caudillo, who had visited his Asian ML brethren such as Jiang some months before; it certainly can be said that the agreement on opposition to Helms-Burton met with his approval.

And one more incident of a Mexican head of state laboring for Castro was played out. Once again, it is probably a question of Castroite blackmail to which Mexico appears at times to be particularly susceptible. Perhaps the most recent example of this has been Zedillo's treatment of the Zapatista National Liberation Front (EZLN).

BROTHERS TO THE RESCUE SHOOTDOWN (WKLY 1.2, 15 MAY 1996)

Two unarmed Cessna aircraft piloted by members of the Cuban refugee group, Brothers to the Rescue, were shot down over international waters at about 1515 eastern standard time on 24 February 1996 by one Cuban Revolutionary Air Forces (FARC) swing-wing MiG-23MF "Flogger" with an R20 or R23 missile and one FARC MiG-29 "Fulcrum" with an R72. The MiGs were piloted by Francisco and Alberto Pérez Pérez, both trained in the U.S.S.R.

In a 7 March 1996 interview General Rafael del Pino, a 1987 defector, told LANS the probable reason for the shootdown: the Castro government needed a foreign enemy to unite the Cubans and distract them from the internal crisis. The crisis during the Mariel Boat Lift yielded a similar remedy.

In May 1980 a Cuban fishing boat operating in Bahamian waters was detained by the Bahamian Coast Guard vessel, *Flamingo*. Castro ordered del Pino to sink the *Flamingo* which he did with two aircraft from Holguin. During the Grenada Operation, Castro did not invoke the contingency plan which he had prepared, destruction of the south Florida nuclear plant, General del Pino said.

LANS' description of the base, which Russia has established and maintains in Cuba,[20] have appeared in various publications. The information which LANS has been gathering may be summarized as follows:

1. General del Pino told LANS that there are "more than 300" Russian aircraft in Cuba, MiG-21s, MiG-23MFs, MiG-23Bs, MiG-29s. A "half-dozen" aircraft are at San Antonio de los Baños (Lourdes) operating out of the base (La Cayuba) established there by the United States during World War II. Another half-dozen operate out of Holguin, Oriente Province. The remainder of the aircraft are stored in hangars at Santa Clara and Holguin or in the multilevel underground hangaring in San Antonio.

2. Also at Lourdes Russia maintains and operates one of the world's greatest electronic espionage bases outside the U.S.S.R./C.I.S. This was admitted by the United States in early 1995 when Under Secretary of State Watson defended before Congress the right of the Russians to operate this base (cf. AFP, 18 March 1995). Russian personnel operate this base as they do the Cienfuegos nuclear submarine base.

3. Russia continues to operate the ballistic missile submarine base at Cienfuegos Bay which was established in 1971. In the summer of 1995 one Polaris-type submarine was reported operating from there; in the fall of last year three such subs were reported operating from there.

4. The evidence that Soviet missiles were not removed from Cuba after the so-called Missile Crisis of 1962 has grown to substantial proportions.[21] At that time no inspections were made in Cuba, no Soviet vessels boarded for inspection of canvas covered deck cargo alleged to be missiles. Surface emplaced missiles were reported removed to the U.S.S.R.-improved cave system, later generation systems since reported brought on line. These are now reportedly siloed with their headquarters northeast of Cienfuegos.

On points 3 and 4: A treaty was signed between the United States and Russia in Switzerland on 28 September 1995. The operative paragraph is: "The parties understand that the treaty does not prohibit them from translating the ICBM [Intercontinental Ballistic Missile] and SLBM [Submarine Launched Ballistic Missile] outside their national territories."

5. The Russian commitment to complete the Comunidad Jurigúa (Cienfuegos Bay) nuclear power plant was reaffirmed this year. Whatever the level of Chernobyl-type accident risk such a power plant may pose, it should provide a source of weapons-grade fissionable material.

Insofar as responsibility for the shootdown of the Brothers to the Rescue aircraft is concerned, it was carried out with Russian aircraft and Russian-trained pilots. Russian vice premier Oleg Soskovets paid a six-day visit to Cuba in October 1995 (cf. AFP wirephoto, 11 November 1995: Raul Castro et al. greeting Soskovets), ostensibly to arrange for continuing exchange of Russian crude for sugar, the harvest of which is reportedly a disaster. Perhaps more relevant to the visit was the *Nezavisimaya Gazeta* article (18 October 1995), "Cuba is Attracting the Russian Military, Submarines May Arrive at the Island following Soskovets."

The shootdown was generally condemned. However, Sandinista secretary general Daniel Ortega defended Cuba while Russian president Boris Yeltsin urged "calm" and mentioned "improving relations" between his country and Castro's.

The HL: Umbrella Organizations and Activities

The objective in the organization of this section is to provide a hemisphere-wide glimpse of HL organizations and activities. That such a treatment should precede that of individual terrorist organizations and regional groupings is necessarily a subjective decision. Those groupings which LANS has treated begin with the TCC (Spcl 2.1), to be followed by the FSP (Wkly 1.6), and the Chiapas Encounter (Wkly 2.1). Among the honored guests at Chiapas was Danielle Mittterand, wife of the former French president, and Debray. Which justifies the inclusion of Debray.

THE TRICONTINENTAL CONFERENCE (SPCL 2.1, 15 AUGUST 1996)

The "Intercontinental Encounter for Humanity and Against Neoliberalism" was held in Chiapas State, Mexico, from 27 July to 3 August 1996 and hosted by ML terrorists of the Zapatista National Liberation Army (EZLN). The EZLN is treated in Wkly 2.1 below. This "Encounter" was held on the thirtieth anniversary of the "First Afro-Asian-Latin American Peoples Solidarity Conference," more commonly known as the Tricontinental Conference (TCC), and would be more appropriately called the Second TCC. Such is the case even though an almost unnoticed Second TCC was called for Cairo in 1968, a call irrelevant to the Latin American situation.

The First TCC was held from 3 January to 16 January 1966 in Havana, Cuba. It is described in detail in the report of the OAS[22] on security. Page 0 of the report will hereinafter be referenced as TCC0. The first point to be made about the TCC is its evolution from a series of previous conferences which had preceded it whereat the "aim of international communism" was "to extend its subversive action to other continents"(TCC9).

The first of these conferences was the Bandung Conference (Indonesia) in April 1955, apparently sponsored by the People's Republic of China (PRC). The "First Afro-Asian Peoples Solidarity Conference" was held at Cairo, Egypt, from 26 December 1957 to 1 January 1958; it emerged from the "Council for Afro-Asian Peoples Solidarity." The Second Conference was held at Conakry, Guinea, in April 1960; the Third took place in Moshi, Tanganyika, from 4 to 10 February 1963; the Fourth convened in Accra, Ghana, from 9 to 16 May 1965. At the Conakry Conference the Afro-Asian Peoples Solidarity Organization (OAAPS) action group was organized; at the Moshi Conference the inclusion of Latin America was suggested; at the Accra Conference it was agreed that the TCC should be held in Havana. "The Accra Conference was attended by some 300 delegates from seventy political organizations of Africa, Asia, and Latin America...all the participants were either militant communists, crypto communists, or fellow travelers closely associated with Peking or Moscow" (TCC13).

In what was clearly the result of careful, long-range planning, a Committee of Preparations for the suggested TCC met in Cairo, Egypt, on 1 and 2 September 1965, preparing an agenda which stressed the "struggle against imperialism,"; "anti-imperialist solidarity among the Afro-Asian and Latin American peoples,"; and "political and organizational unification of the efforts of the African, Asian and Latin American...struggle for 'national liberation'" (TCC13). Moroccan leader Ben Barka clarified the thrust of the coming TCC with his description of it as representing the two currents of world revolution "originating from the socialist October Revolution (in Russia, 1917) and that of the national revolution of liberation" (TCC14). The reason for the selection of Havana as the site of the TCC "was to identify it with 'peoples seeking liberation' following Cuba's example" (TCC15).

A sampling of Conference officers includes the president, Cuban foreign minister Raul Roa Garcia, and the vice presidents, Venezuelan terrorist Pedro Medina Silva and Viet Cong Nguyen Van Tien. The number of delegates was variously reported from 483 to 522, the number of delegations from seventy-nine to eighty-four. The large Soviet delegation to the TCC was led by Sharaf P. Rashidov, a member of the CC, CPSU, a Supreme Soviet deputy and first secretary of the CP, Uzbek SSR.

In his opening remarks, Mr. Rashidov eulogized his "dear Cuban brothers," expressing the support of "the Soviet people" for the Latin American "liberation wars." "We express our fraternal solidarity," said Rashidov, "with the armed struggle being waged by the Venezuelan, Peruvian, Colombian, and Guatemalan patriots...," concluding his long speech with the hope that "this conference increase and strengthen the unit of our ranks, and impart new forces to the liberation struggle throughout the world" (TCC27-29).

The conference did "increase...the unity" of Soviet geostrategic operations, particularly in the Western Hemisphere through the formation of that OLAS which emerged from it. Twenty-four hours after the TCC adjourned, the OLAS formation meeting convened, presided over by Comandante Pedro Medina Silva, the Venezuelan National Liberation Armed Forces (FALN) terrorist who would direct OLAS.[23] One of Castro's periodicals described this gathering by declaring that "representatives of the national liberation and anti-imperialist movements of the hemisphere" unanimously agreed to set up such an organization in Havana.[24] That its mission was to support and coordinate Latin American guerrilla-terrorist operations is made clear throughout the communique with declarations such as "[OLAS]...will use all means within its reach to support the liberation movements..." Which OLAS did, initially through an Organizing Committee comprised of representatives of the "anti-imperialist groups" from various countries whose function was "to orient the work" of the new organization.

Bethel has laid to rest the mythology wherein Castro "upstaged" the Soviets at the TCC, the U.S.S.R. did not really take part, and so on.[25] If the *New York Times* editorial of 10 August 1967 did not instigate the myth, it was typical of it: "The OLAS [Latin American Solidarity Organization]...gave the already fractured Communist movement another gaping wound. This one came in a vote to condemn the Soviet Union's economic policies in the Western Hemisphere." The editorial was apparently based on a Reuters dispatch which the *New York Times* published the next day.

Said the dispatch, "[OLAS] approved a resolution today condemning Soviet economic and technical policy in the Western Hemisphere." As Bethel asks, since Western journalists in Havana were allowed into none of the OLAS sessions, what was the source of this dispatch? A second-hand source must have furnished this information in a typical disinformation maneuver, since, as Bethel points out, "of the twenty resolutions passed at the OLAS conference, not one of them clashes with the Russians," and there is no resolution "condemning" Soviet policy. That OLAS was a creature of the U.S.S.R. was confirmed by Leonard Brezhnev at the Twenty-third CPSU Congress with "special mention must be made of the courageous liberation struggle of the peoples of Latin America..."

Haydee Santamaria, general secretary of the OLAS Organizing Committee, announced that the First OLAS Conference would be held in Havana from 28 July to 5 August, its slogan "the duty of all revolutionaries is to make revolution" (*Granma*, 26 February 1967). At this Conference an organization for "coordinating and supplying" terrorist operations in various Latin American countries was established and manned with representatives from each of these countries. In the Second TCC of Guillen (see below), this head Zapatista doubtless envisions some such hierarchial role for himself in some similar organization of the HL.

THE HEMISPHERIC LEFT (WKLY 1.6, 13 JUNE 1996)

Whether one does (PC) or does not (PIC) "believe" that the U.S.S.R. has transmogrified itself into a free-enterprise democracy, there does remain a Western HL of which the investor-entrepreneur, the tourist, or anyone with an interest in the Latin American-Caribbean region should be aware. Various of the still active ML terrorist groups are considered below; here an important umbrella organization, the São Paulo Forum (FSP), will be discussed. Save for the Hispaniola head of state, the FSP has placed none of its candidates in presidential palaces. However, in the 1993–1994 round of presidential elections, the substantial majority of the victors were strongly influenced by the HL's campaign against neoliberalism and in favor of Agrarian Reform (AgRef).

The Brazilian leftist, Luís Ignacio (Lula) da Silva (b. 1945), came to public notice at about thirty years of age when he was head of the "communist-oriented" Metal Workers' Union. In the 1975–1981 period Lula was active as a union agitator in São Paulo State, jailed briefly in 1981 for such activities. In his Appendix to the book by Pierre Broue,[26] Lula claims his Workers Party (PT) came into being in February 1980, classifying its militants as "Trotskyites, Castroites, activists of the Brazilian Communist party (PCB) ...[with support from] progressive sectors of the Church...liberation theologists..." In case there is still some question as to PT's orientation, he identifies it with his "Nicaraguan Sandinista comrades, the Salvadoran FMLN...the Colombian M-19."

What Lula does not state is that Castro's cleric, Friar Beto,[27] went to live with him and was the driving force behind PT formation. Indeed, the close relation between the Brazilian union leader and Castro developed from Beto's introduction of the two. Da Silva and Castro put together the FSP idea in the Havana of 1989 as described in *Granma* (12 January 1989). With the exception of 1995 when Lula was running for president of Brazil, there was thereafter a yearly "Encounter" of this alliance of ML terrorist, "former" terrorists, left parties, and organizations from throughout Latin America.

The first such encounter appropriately took place in São Paulo, Brazil, on 3–4 July 1990 (*Granma*, 3 July 1990) and drew more than 42 "parties and Latin American left organizations." The rhetoric for the subsequent forums was established there and was concerned with "the neoliberal offensive in the capitalist countries and the transformations which are occurring in Eastern Europe...representatives of Argentina, Cuba, and Mexico[28] analyzing the new forms of capitalism...in the inaugural session" (ibid.). The theme had been established and would be carried through the later sessions.

The Second FSP was held in Mexico City on 12–15 June 1991 (*Granma*, 15 June 1991), this preceded by a meeting between Lula's

PT and the Cuban CP in March (ibid., 25 May 1991), 62 organizations from twenty-two countries allegedly participating. Neoliberalism, the electoral defeat of the Nicaraguan Sandinistas, threats against Cuba, the "invasion" of Panama, and so forth, were condemned while Haiti's Aristide, Salvador's Farabundis, Nicaragua's Sandinistas, Guatemala's URNG, inter alia, were lauded. All this condemnation and praise appeared in the Final Declaration of the Second FSP. Those more or less familiar organizations listed as participating in the Second FSP were the Mexican PRD, Lula's PT, the Salvadoran Farabundis, the Nicaraguan Sandinistas, the Venezuelan Movement Toward Socialism (MAS),[29] the Panamanian PRD,[30] the Colombian Unión Patriótica, and CNG. The CNG is the Colombian terrorist umbrella organization to be discussed below.

The Third FSP took place in Managua, Nicaragua, at the Mercedes Motel immediately across from the airport terminal, on 15–19 July 1992, allegedly drawing "60 representatives of organizations, parties and fronts" (*Granma*, 14 July 1992). The themes were the same. The first three FSPs appear to have built toward the fourth.

The Fourth FSP was held in Havana, Cuba, on 21–24 July 1993 with (allegedly) 112 member organizations and 25 observers (*Granma*, 24 July 1993), its themes anti-neoliberalism, anti-Yankee imperialism, pro socialism and the creation of "supra national countries" in Latin America as a "sort of re-edition of a soviet-type union in Latin America."

Cuban CP Politburo member José Balaguer opened the Fourth FSP with a speech (ibid.) wherein two remarks are worthy of note: (1) The FSP "transcended the symbolic figure of more than 100 member parties and organizations and expanded its field of action with new organizations and movements from the English-speaking Caribbean"; and (2) it was meant "to achieve these objectives and advance to the eventual institutionalization of other [FSP] structures…" At a meeting on the second day, "attended by our commander-in-chief Fidel," Friar Beto, editor of *América Libre*, presented his review as an instrument for continental integration (*Granma*, 23 July 1993) while Cuauhtémoc Cárdenas said "neoliberalism implies the unemployment of much of the population…," and so forth. He condemned "humanitarian operations such as Somalia is suffering today." Sandinista secretary general Daniel Ortega then, inter alia, "transmitted a message to the Forum from the Libyan leader, Colonel Mu'ammar Qaddafi."

Thirty new members of the FSP are listed in addition to those attending the Second FSP, most of them obscure, a more or less complete catalog appearing in *Correio Brasilense* for 14 August 1994. Perhaps most important to the *Granma* listing are the two Dominican parties. More to the point, "At the Fourth FSP," LANS associate editor and São Paulo, Brazil, expert on the FSP, Dr. Graça Wagner, pointed out, "eighteen left-wing Dominican parties were coalesced. From this arose the candidacy of Peña Gómez."

The Fifth FSP was held in Montevideo, Uruguay, in May 1995, there having been no FSP in 1994. Attendees and rhetoric remained more or less constant. Perhaps the most relevant aspect of this Encounter was enunciated by Dr. Graça Wagner: "It was decided, then, at the Fifth Encounter that Chiapas would become the model for the new stage of Latin American battles." There would appear to be a certain amount of wishful thinking in such a decision since success in Chiapas by the EZLN was the direct result, as will be seen below, of the Mexican president calling on a Sandinista and a Farabundi for guidance.

The Sixth FSP is to be held in San Salvador, El Salvador, next month.

INTERCONTINENTAL ENCOUNTER FOR HUMANITY AND AGAINST
NEOLIBERALISM (WKLY 2.1, 15 AUGUST 1996)

Thirty years after the TCC[31] was held in Havana; what amounted to a the Second TCC, the International Encounter for Humanity and Against Neoliberalism, was hosted by the ML terrorists of the EZLN in Chiapas, Mexico, from 27 July to 3 August 1996.

Although the Mexican government had been aware of EZLN existence for some time prior to 1 January 1994, it did not admit as much until the "uprising" of that date. The reaction was initially routine, but, in a few days, Mexican president Salinas de Gortari declared "peace," leaving the Zapatistas in effective possession of Chiapas State. Why?

In a 14 August 1996 interview with the prominent Nicaraguan banker and syndicated columnist, Roberto J. Arguello, the LANS editor found out "why." Arguello's sources within the Mexican government told him that, within hours of the 1 January 1994 Zapatista "uprising," Mexican president Salinas called Sandinista general Humberto Ortega to ask him what to do. In a short time Ortega and former Farabundi terrorist Joaquín Villalobos had flown to Mexico City and *told* Salinas what to do. Before releasing this information, Arguello recently interviewed Ortega in Managua and obtained direct confirmation of this vital information. The Mexican president followed this ML advice and declared "peace."

This Second TCC was reported (*Excelsior* [Mexico], 28 July 1996) as drawing 3000 people, "representatives of forty-two countries." The names of the enemies had been changed from the "colonialism" and "neocolonialism" of the First TCC to the "neoliberalism" of the Second TCC, but it occasionally bubbled up that it was the same "great capitalism" excoriated by the Bolshevik, Ulianov (a.k.a. Lenin). And the rhetoric and posturing remained the same, perhaps even amplified with the appearance of the terrorist chief Guillen (a.k.a. Marcos) *a caballo* (on horseback), the affected ski masks, the ubiquitous Indian headdress.

The leftist affair was romanticized in various publications, extensively so in *La Jornada* (Mexico) beginning with a clutch of four articles on the day after the start of the Second TCC (28 July 1996) and floating through article after article, perhaps to peak but not to end with Bellinghausen's account of the press conference by Guillen on 3 August 1996. The questions for Guillen could well have been prepared by Guillen. The *New York Times'* Julia Preston asked how the transformation of the EZLN into a civil force was proceeding and what was the future of "Marcos," receiving a lengthy reply. Gianni Mina, the Italian journalist described herein as "viejo lobo de mar" (old sea wolf), asked what were the minimum conditions which would render the dialog a success. This of course evoked a lengthy reply, winding up the "conference."

Adolfo Gilly reports a press conference held by "Cmdte. David" (*La Jornada*, 30 July 1996), allegedly held to explain "the debates in the tables of Oventic." We do not learn much about the debates, but we do learn what a fine fellow David is, of his direct and not evasive responses. Most remarkable is Gilly's opinion that "I have before my eyes [personified by David] a living confirmation that those who say that the EZLN is the product of a leftist conspiracy do not know what they are talking about." Which is interesting because the "correspondents" tell us the next day that Guillen says the EZLN "is formed in the mountains by a group which comes with the tradition of the Latin American guerrilla of the 1970s, [a] vanguard group, [of] Marxist-Leninist ideology, which seeks the transformation of the world, trying to arrive in power in a dictatorship of the proletariat." Of course he says later that "armed 'zapatismo' began to change itself into something new," but this bears not at all on his first statement.

ML gatherings are frequently typified by gibberish which was here characterized by the delightful Guillen statement in the same article, "We lack the time and distance to be able to reflect on what we are doing, since above all it is a kind of self-concentration which may or may not coincide with what occurs in reality." As to the "tables of debate."

On the first day (27 July) of the "Encounter," the activities were to begin at 1900 but were delayed until 2140. They were to take place at the Ejido[32] Oventic in San Andres Larrainzar some forty kilometers from San Cristobal de las Casas. They were to be held in five "tables," the physical location of which were at various points in the jungle and on the Heights of Chiapas. The five "tables" allegedly comprehended (1) politics, (2) economy, (3) culture, (4) society, and (5) diversity. While the Zapas assured the throng that this was a simple give-and-take among the attendees, it appears to be clear that the "discussions" were transparently pre-orchestrated.

This may be illustrated with the remarks of "Major Moisés" who inaugurated the "political table" (Bellinghausen, *La Jornada*, 30 July 1996). After Moisés, described as "military commander in this part of the jungle," Guillen and a score of Indigenous Clandestine Revolutionary Committee (CCRI) members staged their entrance on horseback, "Moses" more or less began with "What is urgent for us human beings is to think what we are going to do." Later, he would add, "Nobody is going to think for us. We are the exploited, the ravished, the crushed, those who must think." The "thinking theme" was pursued through a discourse—even "the rain tells us that we must think"—which demonstrated that the thinking had already been done. Moisés: "We must be organized, prepared, united" was a remark almost indistinguishable from "Workers of the world unite. You have nothing to lose but your chains."

A stereotypical performance closed this opening. First, the "youth group," "9 de Febrero" sang "El horizonte," another danced "El Colas." Then a mob of boys with cardboard hats and wooden rifles, and masked girls in colored dress, recited, then sang, the verses of "Carabina 30-30": "With my thirty-thirty I am going to march/In the ranks of the rebellion..."

The Zapas had convened this encounter "to construct a tomorrow of inclusion and tolerance," something that apparently exists now in Castroite Cuba. In actuality, they convened it because they had agreed to do so at the Fifth FSP in Uruguay in 1995 as LANS associate editor Graça Wagner has demonstrated. "Major" Ana María told the arriving delegates that "in the mountains of southeast Mexico, on the five continents, we are fighting for life against death." "Death" is "neoliberalism," as it was "colonialism" at the time of the First TCC, as it is and has been the "chains of capitalism." This was the theme which was

repeated throughout. If there was any dissent, it must have been difficult to find.

In sum, the Second TCC was one more bombastic stage-managed
ML performance, and the question naturally arises: Is it not simply a
joke? Perhaps but, again, perhaps not. Castro and his Twenty-sixth of
July Movement was essentially a joke, but, after he attained what U.S.
Ambassador Spruille Braden called "Robin Hood status" from Herbert
Matthews, his bandits in the Sierra Maestre were, not able to "win a
war"—Batista never fought one—, but able to occupy the power vacuum
after Batista fled and cause an as yet unassessed amount of misery and
hardship in the Hemisphere.

That Castro is the power behind the Zapas appears beyond any doubt.
Although he has come close to winning other wars since 1 January
1959, even in the single Nicaraguan success, he did not "win" militar-
ily, he won through the isolation of Caudillo Somoza—who also fled—
ultimately effected by the turning back of the Israeli supply ship. Can
he win anything here? With the help of Humberto Ortega, he has already won the first stage with the Mexican Government's allowing a
Cuban-backed armed force to occupy virtually all of one Mexican state.
For this reason it may not be wise to concentrate on the bombastic
posturing of these terrorists to the exclusion of the possible mischief
which they may yet accomplish.

WHO IS RÉGIS DEBRAY? (WKLY 2.19, 19 DECEMBER 1996)

He is the "sociologist" and militant of the International Left (IL)
who has written another book.[33] Until the Socialist François Mitterand
recently exited the presidency of France, Régis Debray was his "advisor" on Latin American affairs. That he was an ML, at least until his
"break" with Fidel Castro, his life and the career of his wife attest. To
ask if Debray is or was a "communist" is a non sequitur. Entirely too
much attention has been paid to the word "communist" which, although
perhaps enjoying the virtue of brevity, generally means only a formal
member of a CP. Since the "useful idiots" (*tontos utiles*) of Ulianov
were routinely more valuable than the "communists," ML, as descrip-
tive of Debray, is considerably more informative. But he was a
showpieced treasure at last summer's Zapatista gala in Chiapas.

It appears straightforward to link Debray's rise to prominence in the
IL with the appearance of his tract[34] which was an apologia for his
friend, Fidel Castro. No sooner had this piece appeared in France—and

of course in Cuba—than it was dissected by the Angels on Pinheads (AIP) "philosophers" of the IL. At that time, for example, Paul M. Sweezy and Harry Magdoff were editing *Monthly Review: An Independent Socialist Magazine.* They rushed into print a book on the Frenchman[35] which featured a gaggle of seventeen authors led off by Juan Bosch.[36] But even before his rise, Debray had been active with the bizarre Ernesto (Che) Guevara.

Debray and Guevara

That Guevara was a "legend in his own mind," as he has been described, is easy to understand, given his personality. Perhaps it is also easy to understand why someone like Debray would adopt the same attitude. In any event, doubtless to preserve his "heroic" Bolivian campaign for a waiting posterity, the "legend" kept a diary which is really rather pitiful, and should be of more interest to a psychiatrist than a strategist. In any case, it has been published in an excellent and well annotated English translation by Daniel James.[37] Guevara apparently lost head and hands in his "adventure," but his friend, Debray, survived the experience.

On 7 November 1966 the "legend" began his "Bolivian Campaign," hoping to create "another Vietnam" and a Latin American reaction against "Yankee Imperialism." He traveled to that country from Cuba via Prague, Czechoslovakia; Frankfurt, Germany; and São Paulo, Brazil, finally landing in La Paz with an Uruguayan passport identifying him as "Adolfo Mena González." Perhaps the most interesting member of Guevara's small terrorist group was the spy, Haydee Tamara Bunke Bider (a.k.a. Tania la Guerrilla), who had been recruited by the East German Ministry of State Security when she turned twenty-one, then coopted by the KGB to keep an eye on the "legend" during his wanderings around Bolivia.

The basic decisions about Guevara's campaign were made in Havana in January 1966 at the Tricontinental Conference which was attended by, among others, Mario Monje Molina, first secretary of the Bolivian CP (PCB), Mario Miranda Pacheco, executive secretary of the PCB-inspired National Left Liberation Front (FLIN) and Gabriel Porcel Salazar representing Nationalist Left Revolutionary Party (PRIN). Guevara was under wraps to these people during the TCC so that Monje and Castro dealt directly on the upcoming Bolivian operation as may be learned from the diary of Pombo, one of Guevara's underlings. As James remarks, "the Cuban government was the sponsor and sole directing force behind the...movement Che led." What would happen after Guevara's arrival in Bolivia was the establishment of a "base"—at Nancahuazu—to which Guevara expected his volunteers to flock. As with the Guatemalan Guerrilla Army of the Poor (EGP) six years later, which in four years grew from twenty-five to fifty, nobody flocked, and the "legend" ended by being quite dead.

If, in this adventure, Tania la Guerrilla was the most interesting character, Régis Debray was certainly the second most interesting. Before Nancahuazu was finally chosen as the "base," Debray arrived using what was doubtless to him the romantic alias of Danton.[38] The diarist Pombo (James, ibid.) was told by another of Guevara's band "about the visit of Danton whose mission is to make a geopolitical study of the selected 'zone' in the Beni."[39] He also acquired the "military maps of the country" which Guevara had requested. This is important, however incomplete, because Debray would later claim at his trial that he was a "newsman." These activities, whether he squeezed a trigger or not, are considerably more those of a terrorist than of a "newsman."

On 3 March 1967 Guevara's terrorists fought their first "battle," ambushing a thirty-two-man Bolivian Army patrol at Nacahuanzu, Santa Cruz Department, killing seven, wounding six, and capturing eleven for which he received publicity out of all proportion to his "accomplishments." He would enjoy no later "victory" as impressive as his first. Guevara's little band, mostly Cubans, moved north through the department, its furthest point of "advance" being Samaipata, the civilian population of which he briefly "captured."

In the meantime, the Bolivian Army had been largely occupied with a violent strike in the mines from which it could now extricate itself and start after the Cuban terrorist. The Army caught him at Quebrado del Yuro (9 October 1967) and executed him, apparently removing head and hands. The U.S. CIA officer, Félix I. Rodríguez, who was almost certainly slandered by Terry Reed,[40] was present at the capture and has some interesting points to make about it.

Early in this brief "campaign" (20 April 1967) Debray (a.k.a. Danton), Carlos Bustos and a British "newsman," Roth, were dropped off at Muyampa in Chiquisaca Department, northwest of Camari, Santa Cruz, in order to make their escape from the country. Captured the same day, "Danton" was brought to "swift and speedy" trial in Camiri on 21 April 1967 and given twenty years imprisonment for terrorism. Debray considers his sentence cruel and unusual punishment. The evidence would appear to indicate otherwise. While available evidence indicates that Mr. Roth was a newsman, it indicates that Mr. Debray was working for Guevara and hence a terrorist.

It has been asserted that Régis Debray "broke" with Castro. This is the sort of assertion made, inter alia, by Debray himself, that perhaps cannot be definitively disproved. But here a mention of Debray's spouse, Elizabeth Burgos, is all that can be added.

Burgos is the author of the "autobiography" of Rigoberta Menchú.[41] The inside of the cover is graced with a photograph of Elizabeth and Rigoberta allegedly taken in 1982 during the production of the book. Perhaps Régis has been as ignorant of the Castro situation as his never-questioned statements indicate, but such an ignorance of Rigoberta by Elizabeth would, from the contacts which would have been required in producing this "autobiography," be even more difficult to believe.

The terrorist Guatemalan National Revolutionary Union (URNG) had been put together in Sandinista Managua less than two years before the photo was purportedly taken. Two of Rigoberta's brothers were in the URNG, and the LANS editor has viewed a photograph in Guatemala City of an individual taken at about that time (1982) and alleged to be Rigoberta, complete with terrorist garb and terrorist companions. It certainly looks like a younger and slightly less plump Rigoberta. That Ms. Menchú has been a spokeswoman for the URNG for many years has been continually demonstrated to anyone following her career.

But above all, she is clearly one of Caudillo Castro's "people," a fact perhaps most concisely demonstrated in a wirephoto in the LANS files of about two years ago. Rigoberta, the Nobel Peace Laureate, is rather short and stout. In the photograph she is standing in front of Castro, simpering—the only description—up at him as he bestows the Order of Ana Guadeloupe on her.

"LOW-INTENSITY WARFARE" BY THE HEMISPHERIC LEFT[42]
(WKLY 1.8, 27 JUNE 1996)

In our country (Brazil), Sem Terra (Landless Peasant) Movement (MST), supported by the Workers Party (PT), carries out a series of actions which constitute "low-intensity warfare."

Through 1995 and into 1996 these "actions" have continued a Brazilian escalation with MST occupation of lands in alleged AgRef "low-intensity warfare" which, if not directed out of Havana, is coordinated and encouraged from there. Pope John Paul II (*Jornal do Brasil*, 6 February 1996) declared that, with the fall of the Berlin Wall, "also fell

Liberation Theology (LibTheo)." Nonetheless, Brazilian LibTheo clerics assembled at Itaici in February 1996 aligned themselves solidly with Sem Terra.

In a gaffe so extreme as to appear deliberate, *Gazeta de Alagoas* (Brazil, 17 March 1996) "reported" that Tiberius (Gracchus) tried to introduce AgRef "three thousand years before Christ."[43] Since Tiberius lived in the second century B.C. (c. 163-133), and his biographer, Plutarch,[44] no more than two centuries later the three-millennia claim is bizarre. The Tribune Tiberius G. did, late in the second century B.C., try to introduce AgRef. It is next appropriate to consider Heinrich Karl Marx.

The concept of private property was anathema to Marx who advocated "1. Abolition of property in land..."[45] The Bolshevik Revolution (1917) introduced the notion; in the Western Hemisphere leftist Mexican president Lazaro Cárdenas[46] was one of the first to implement it. Shortly after seizing power in Cuba Castro introduced (May 1959) an AgRef law written by Marxists to include Antonio Nuñez Jiménez, the geographer-speliologist who had sent his Cuban cave mappings to the U.S.S.R. in the early 1950s and who would head Cuban AgRef (INRA). The defector, Manuel Artime, was briefly in INRA and has recounted Nuñez' "INRA is the real Cuban state..."[47]INRA's promulgators would be involved in Brazilian AgRef, first in the "Peasant Leagues."[48]

On 21 July 1961 Clodomir dos Santos Morais and eleven other Brazilian members of the Tiradentes Revolutionary Movement (MRT) deplaned in Havana to begin terrorist training, the first in a series of such arrivals. The MRT was a part of the Leagues, the "honorary president" of which was Francisco Julião. The League headquarters were at 216 Respiola Street, Recife, its avowed objective the "peaceful promotion of the farmers' interest," an objective which did not square with the flow of arms to the organization's terrorist training camps in six Brazilian states. The Peasant Leagues would subside, to be replaced twenty years later by an MST which would prove as militant and, instead of being opposed by the clerics as were the "peasant unions," supported by those of LibTheo persuasion.

Stripped of its fancy dress, AgRef consists of taking property from its owners and giving it to others for political purposes. In the course of this action the procedure is justified by reports of unequal land distribution, insufficient utilization, and so forth. The statistics used by the Brazilian pro-AgRef people have been shown contradicted at times by their own government numbers, but an exhaustive consideration of this is impossible here. Three general conditions for AgRef activity are: (1) an alleged justification for the procedure; (2) a constitution which does not guarantee private property; and (3) a government which is anti-neoliberal, that is, not free market.

With regard to condition (2): The Brazilian constitution of 1967 reads, inter alia (chap. 4, art. 150, par. 22), "The right to own property shall be guaranteed, except in case of expropriation for public necessity or utility or *social interest...*" (emphasis added).

With regard to condition (3): President Henrique Cardosa is a Social Democrat, by definition a socialist, who appears basically favorable to AgRef, but who has limited his implementation of it.

Brazil is under discussion here, but the same thing is going on in Mexico, Guatemala, Colombia, etc., all with the enthusiastic support of *Granma*, the newspaper of Castro's Central Committee. Replete with communist propaganda, which is to be found repeated in certain Brazilian publications, these articles report tens of thousands of landless campesinos waiting to be settled on land which is rightfully theirs. There are a great many people in the camps which MST has organized, but it is doubtful that anyone has studied what relation they have had to agriculture. And earlier this year (*Jornal do Brasil*, 18 February 1996), Workers Central (CUT) announced that it was joining forces with MST to "recruit" 100,000 jobless from the cities to invade the farms. With this evolution the idea of AgRef as a front for "low-intensity warfare" by the HL became more clearly delineated.

Nor is this notion belied by the "leaders" of the movement. Lionized by a media which appears to have him in the Robin-Hood category, a ranking chief is the thirty-five-year-old José Rainha Junior whose newly acquired house boasts four pictures of Mao Tse-tung and the works of Castro's LibTheo coordinator and Lula da Silva confidant, Friar Beto. In Brazil, Rainha's MST is supported by Lula da Silva's PT. At the 1996 meeting in Chiapas, billed as the "Forum for Humanity and Against Neoliberalism" and hosted by Zapatista terrorist R. S. Guillen (a.k.a. Marcos), the latter declared himself prepared "to coordinate the entire continent in civil resistance to neoliberalism" (*La Jornada* [Mexico], 19 April 1996). Now all that was needed was a "human rights" campaign for the HL Support; this materialized.

On 18 April 1996 the police were disposed near Eldorado de Carajas, Para State, Brazil, to prevent the MST from lawlessly invading a farm. They apparently did so, in the process killing what was first reported as twenty-six, then twenty-three, then nineteen. This was described by the press as a "massacre," a "slaughter," and so on. Whatever the facts of the matter may be, the MST now has a *cause célèbre* and may henceforth do whatever it wishes with no fear of opposition.

President Cardosa was quick to condemn the incident and declare that he would reach his goal of turning over lands to 240,000 families, whatever the costs or difficulties, during his four-year term of office. (Or 380,000 [AFP, 4 June 1996], etc.). Three MST and two guards died in an "armed confrontation" in Marinhao State on 12 June 1996, and a few days later the government was blaming PT for "inciting" MST to the invasion (EFE, 19 June 1996).

A footnote: A headline in the 15 January 1996 issue of *O Estado de São Paulo* asked: WHAT DOES THE U.S. GOVERNMENT WANT TO KNOW ABOUT MST?—the question prompted by the visit of Vice Consul Delwek Mathews of the United States to the MST collective farm at the former Fazenda Pirituba. U.S. farmers have reportedly been asking the same question.

HL Terrorist Organizations: Colombia

THE BEGINNING OF COLOMBIAN TERRORISM: THE BOGOTAZO
(SPCL 1.2, 1 JUNE 1996)

At 1305 on 9 April 1948 Jorge Eleicer Gaitan, the popular Liberal Party leader, was hit by four revolver bullets as he was leaving his office in the Nieto Building (Bogotá, Colombia), the shots fired by Juan Roa Sierra, age twenty-six, who was literally torn to pieces by the mob but not before being gunned down by his "associates." This assassination signalled the beginning of a well-organized revolution, the Bogotazo, preparations for which had been underway for months. That it was well-organized was attested by several eyewitnesses, among them: Inter-American Workers Confederation (IAWC) president Bernardo Ibañez had an appointment at 1700 with Gaitan on the day of his death. Ibañez reported (*Inter-American Labor News*, May 1948) the "crime and provocation [were] peculiar to the Russians," the careful planning reflected in the fact that "fifteen minutes before the attack on Gaitan all the radio broadcasting stations in Bogotá were taken over by the Communists through workers and students...Precise instructions...issued to plunder arms deposits, hardware stores..."[49] This description was generally confirmed by IAWC vice president Juan Laro. U.S. Ambassador to Colombia Beaulac further described the organization of building burning by small groups equipped with naptha and sprayers.

The Bogotazo was a Kremlin operation, its short-range objective the disruption of the Ninth Inter-American Conference (IAC), its long-range objective the takeover of strategic Colombia overlooking the Panama Canal and both the Atlantic and Pacific Oceans.

The Ninth IAC of twenty-one American republics was called for 30 March 1948 in Bogotá, with George C. Marshall, the U.S. secretary of state, to attend. The IAC was to adopt a charter reaffirming the solidarity of the American states in mutual defense and resistance to international communism. Communist reaction was rapid, the Colombian Community Party (PCC) drawing up an ambitious program to disrupt the IAC[50] (dismissed by the Kremlin), Lombardo Toledano's Marxist CTAL Latin American Labor Federation (CTAL) loudly condemning it, a parade of agents beginning to arrive at Soviet spymaster Gumer W. Bashirov's Havana headquarters (House no. 6, Second St. between First and Third Avenues, el Reparto Section, Miramar suburb)[51] on 2 February 1948, the first being World Federation of Democratic Youth (WFDY) treasurer Frances Demot with $50,000 in her suitcase. On 25 February Soviet Youth Society president Basily Bogarev headed the arriving contingent including the Spanish communist Luís Fernández who was immediately sent on to Colombia. Fernández's report torpedoed the PCC plan and resulted in the dispatch of Fidel Castro and Alfredo Guevara Valdes to Colombia. What happened next is best described by Colombian national security chief Alberto Niño H.[52]

Rumblings from the coming storm began reaching Niño early in the year. His agents warned him that the terrorist operation would occur on "4 or 5 April"; it did not. Some in the government of Conservative president Mariano Ospina thought Gaitan behind it; Niño did not. And "packets of various sizes" were reported moving out of a Soviet embassy which was removing its forest of radio antennas. Red Friday (*viernes rojo*) arrived, and the slaughter and havoc of the Bogotazo began. *The Daily Worker* (New York, 12 April 1948) was delighted: "Interruption of the foreign minister parley is a sock in the jaw to the big business men of the State Department."

Bogotá suffered heavily, but the revolution was squelched in a matter of days by the coalition government president Ospina quickly formed with the Liberals. Using information such as that published by *El Colombiano* (Medellin, 13 June 1948) on four Soviet agents brought in just before the attempted coup, the Colombian government announced on 13 April that two "Soviet agents" and thirteen other foreign agents had been "caught in the act" of fomenting trouble, then broke relations with the U.S.S.R.[53] The investigation of the attempted revolution continued, detectives from the Federal Bureau of Investigation (FBI), Scotland Yard, and Military Intelligence (MI5) arriving in June.[54] A footnote on Castro's contribution:

El País (Caracas, 27 March 1948) carried a photograph[55] of a beardless Castro and Rafael del Pino (not to be confused with the Brothers-to-the-Rescue Del Pino of p. 93) on the way to Colombia which they entered that day through Medellin, proceeding to Bogotá. According to Niño's detectives, the pair was seen with the assassin, Roa, "a few days" before the ninth. On 3 April they were picked up in the Colón Theater for throwing leaflets from the balcony, these printed in Cuba and attacking the United States and Britain. The Cubans were taken to their room in the Hotel Claridge where enough material was found to warrant taking them to National Security Headquarters. Reporting back on 7 April because of passport irregularities, they were printed and mugged, all these records destroyed on 9 April with the building. On 13 April Guillermo Hoenigsberg, a Claridge guest, told detectives he had heard the Cubans boasting of their part in the coup.

During the riots U.S. Ambassadors Pawley and Donnelly heard the following on their car radio in Bogotá:

> This is Fidel Castro from Cuba. This is a communist revolution. The president has been killed, all of the military establishment are now in our hands. The Navy has capitulated to us, and the revolution has been a success.[56]

The statements were nonsense, and Castro escaped Colombia through a mistake which Cuban Ambassador Belt long regretted, to be accepted in the United States ten years later as a "noncommunist."

From the Bogotazo arose La Violencia (LV), a seventeen-year bloodletting in which perhaps 100,000 to 200,000 died. Most of the treatments of LV ignore the information presented above. Henderson,[57] for example, ignores the Bogotazo, describing it and LV as the fruit of a 100-year struggle between conservatives and liberals, pleading ignorance of the "dynamics" of it. Future president Lleros Restrepo,[58] Guzman Campos et al.[59], and the like, partly with obvious political motivation, likewise ignore the Bogotazo, treating LV as a simple extrapolation of the long liberal-conservative struggle. Others, such as Nieto Rojas,[60] admit what they know of what has been reported above.

In ignoring Soviet involvement in the Bogotazo these authors seriously distort the historical reality. Even Gaitan's daughter, Gloria, who was long understandably seduced by Castro, admitted (July 1993) the latter's involvement, albeit, she had an agent from the then nonexistent CIA helping him. But the details of LV are indeed murky, partly because many of the participants have political reasons that they remain so.

It glimmers through the murk that, in the midst of LV (1957), Manuel Marulanda Velez (a.k.a. Pedro A. Marín Marín; Tirofijo) founded the Colombian Revolutionary Armed Forces (FARC), the first Colombian terrorist organization. Whether or not it was ML when he founded it, it became so within a few years, and remains the backbone of narcoterrorism.

COLOMBIAN TERRORISM, 1957–1996 (SPCL 1.3, 5 JUNE 1996)

In 1997 FARC will celebrate its fortieth anniversary. How this group could function for forty years under both liberal and conservative governments is illustrated by the following events:

After 1982 terrorism in Colombia steadily accelerated as governments from each party called for peace and talked dialogue. The terrorist war mushroomed to the point that, by 1 November 1988, the important banana area of Uraba had to be supplied by sea and air. So on 4 November 1988 Defense Minister General Rafael Samudio ordered negotiations with the terrorists to cease, the war for their destruction to begin. By 5 November President Virgilio Barco had dismissed Samudio, telling the National Police that "the politics of public order must be treated...[by] reconciliation." Terrorist violence continued to increase. In late May 1996 FARC "is [still] willing to negotiate."

In mid-March 1995 the alleged FARC director, Ivan Marquez, told Radio Super that Manuel Marulanda Velez (a.k.a. Pedro Antonio Marín Marín; Tirofijo [Deadeye]) died in bed on 13 March 1995 at the age of eighty-one.[61] Marín had formed FARC in 1957 and run this narcoterrorist organization until his death. FARC has long been designated as "Moscow Line," as other terrorist groups have been designated "Maoist," "Trotskyite," and so forth.[62]

FARC is and has been the largest of the Colombian terrorist[63] groups. In October 1986 Radio Caracol reported the group to have between twenty-three and thirty-five "Fronts" (sub-units). In December 1987 Samudio reported its strength at 4500 men in thirty-nine fronts (FARC was claiming twice this number). By mid-1993 *Semana* (Bogotá) was reporting 6000 in forty-five. Observation of this situation has indicated obvious useful truths about front size.

The details on specific operations over the years have indicated a clear pattern of front size: these vary between 100 and 200 men, usually closer to 100. This is to be anticipated since a company-strength unit (about

100) is the maximum which can be effectively controlled by a unit commander in much of Colombian terrain. Thus, the 6000/45 of 1992 is internally consistent (130/front, company size). [In mid-February 1996 the Army seized a FARC plan for AgRef of its coca-leaf production—Ed.]

National Liberation Army (ELN)

The next Colombian terrorist group, the ELN, arose in 1963, originally led by Fabio Vásquez Castaño (a.k.a. Cmdte. Alexander) and his brother, Manuel. This "Castroite" group was reported fielding 950 men in fifteen fronts in December 1987, 2000 in 1992. One of ELN's most famous members was the cleric, Camilo Torres Restrepo, this terrorist group having been reported (AFP, 24 October 1989) with twenty-nine clerics in its command structure. Its present commander, the Spanish cleric Manuel Pérez (a.k.a. Poliarco), began his narcoterrorist career as a founder of EPL (see below) in 1968, his connection with ELN not surfacing until the mid-1980s when, described as a "friend of Torres" (UPI, 19 February 1988), he was first reported as ELN leader. By late 1989 Pérez was claiming twenty years with the ELN (AFP, 24 October 1989).[64] (ELN third-in-command Antonio Garcia told Cambio 16 Colombia in February 1996 that his group had no intention of negotiating with a government "on the verge of falling.")

People's Liberation Army (EPL)

This terrorist group was put together in 1968 by Olonso Ojeda and Manuel Pérez, the latter probably moving to the ELN in the 1980s. This view is supported by the routine appearance of Ernesto Rojas as terrorist chief by then (NYT, 25 July 1984). The group is described as "Maoist," allegedly aligned with the Colombian CP/Maoist line. In December 1987 Samudio told the Colombian legislature that the group mustered 750 men in fifteen fronts. (The portions of these terrorist groups which have allegedly become peaceful are discussed below, see Wkly 2.15.)

Nineteenth of April Movement (M-19)

General Gustavo Rojas Pinilla lost the presidential elections of 19 April 1970, this allegedly sufficient to warrant Jaime Bateman Cayon, a former FARC chief, forming M-19. Bateman was killed in an aircraft "accident" in 1983, to be succeeded by Ivan Marino Ospina (killed

1985), who would be important to a national terrorist army. (In February 1996 the government was "negotiating peace" with "dissident" M-19 group Jaime Bateman Cayon.)

Marino was succeeded by Carlos Pizarro Léon-Gomez who negotiated "peace" and was running for president when shot. It was reported that ELN chief Pérez had ordered the killing, a report angrily denied to the LANS editor by M-19 coordinator general Abraham Rubio. Pizarro was succeeded by Navaro Wolff, a distant third in the 1994 presidential elections.

Quintin Lame Front (FQL)

Carlos Lehder Rivas now resides in a Florida jail,[65] there for narcotrafficking, his terrorist activities seldom mentioned. He was the (or a) boss of FQL, apparently first reported active in Cauca Department in September 1985. This "indigenous" group was named for Manuel Quintin Lame who led the Indians of Valle del Cauca in a rebellion during the 1920s.

In October 1986 Radio Caracol reported FQL fielding two fronts in Cauca. In December 1987 Samudio did not mention FQL although it was reported fighting alongside M-19 the following year. This group may have been a shadow organization manned by terrorists from other groups to attain indigenous support. It was certainly the youngest and smallest when it made "peace."

COLOMBIAN TERRORIST ACTIVITY (WKLY 2.7, 26 SEPTEMBER 1996)

On 25 September 1996 AFP reported from Bogotá that the "armed conflict," which had been concentrated in the south of Colombia, had worsened in the previous forty-eight hours in the north with the blocking of highways, kidnappings, and murders. The "paramilitary" groups announced their intention of opposing the terrorists.

On 23 September the Colombian minister of defense, Juan Carlos Esguerra, announced that, as a consequence of this increased subversive activity, several thousand reservists would be called to active duty beginning in October.

UPDATE ON COLOMBIAN TERRORISM (WKLY 2.15, 21 NOVEMBER 1996)

"Alto, moreno, bien parecido" (tall, dark, and handsome) as what was probably a lady interviewer called him, twenty-nine-year-old

"Cmdte. Sarley" and his 118-man Bernardo Franco "dissident" Front of the now allegedly "peaceful" EPL last month laid down their arms. He is worthy of remark as a typical example of (1) recruiting age—he claims to have been sixteen when recruited—and (2) recruiting propaganda. Since he was a terrorist boss, Sarley's testimony is highly suspect,[66] but some probably valuable points may be sifted.

"Many young people, including my friends, entered the guerrillas... for political reasons," he said. At sixteen a youth's political maturity is hardly such as to make this a meaningful statement, and it is immediately belied by the ML propaganda which he quotes from his EPL recruiter. Then too, he neglects to mention the "drafted" (kidnapped) youth which have made important contributions to terrorist recruiting everywhere. The interview (*Semana* [Bogotá], 12 November 1996) with "Cmdte. Sarley" and "Cmdte. James," who defected with twenty-six men from FARC Front Fifty-eight, leaves no doubt about the ML nature of either EPL or FARC, but it does carefully avoid any references to the sources of these two terrorist groups' very substantial incomes: kidnappings, extortion, and narcotrafficking.[67] A bizarre twist on the first of these is the reason LANS felt it appropriate to revisit Colombian terrorism at this time.

On 30 August 1996 FARC terrorists carried out an attack on a village in southeast Colombia, the details of which have varied considerably in allegedly serious reports. LANS has correlated various reports and believes the details to be about as follows:

Originally, it was reported that the target was a village "on the border" between Caquetá and Putumayo Departments. (The Putumayo River defines the southern boundary of Colombia with Ecuador to the west and Peru to the east.) It appears, however, that the target was Las Delicias in Caquetá which is some miles downstream from the confluence of the Orteguaza and Caquetá Rivers, the latter defining the Putumayo-Caquetá border and hence probably explaining the earlier discrepancy. All of this is in Amazonia to the southeast of the Eastern Range (Cordillero Oriental) of the Andes, a sparsely populated region. The aeronautical chart (ONC L-26) says of the Las Delicias region "maximum elevation figures are *believed* not to exceed 3000 feet." They probably do not.

On 30 August (31 August is apparently incorrect) a large unit of terrorists "attacked" Las Delicias. The number has been given as "500." In early October a dispatch stated that twenty-seven military were killed, twenty wounded, and sixty-seven taken prisoner. Because of the circumstances the casualty figures should probably not be taken as precise, this based on the proviso that the winning side had access to body counts and related numbers, the side deserting the battlefield not so blessed. The new Colombian Army commander, General Manuel José Bonnet Lacarno, is claiming sixty, not sixty-seven, and this could be more accurate.

Since 30 August the terrorists have copied the tactics of other Latin American subversive groups, dangling the promise of imminent hostage—these sixty are more appropriately "hostages" and not "prisoners"—release before the Colombian government while escalating its terrorist demands and activities in that country. The chronology of the two-and-a-half months to mid-November will be detailed, but an update of Colombian terrorism as presented in Spcl 1.3 is first appropriate.

FARC. Based on reports obtained in 1995, LANS reported in Spcl 1.3 that Tirofijo was dead of natural causes. In the summer of 1996, however, additional information indicated that he was still alive. This largest and oldest of the Colombian terrorist groups remains active.

ELN. A dissident faction of ELN allegedly desiring peace, the Socialist Renewal Movement (CRS), arose in 1993. The present ELN commander, the Spanish cleric Manuel Pérez (a.k.a. Poliarco), began his narcoterrorist career as a founder of:

EPL. This group allegedly made peace in 1990 becoming the Hope, Peace, and Liberty Party (PEPL), although a "dissident" faction remained active. The "Cmdte. Sarley" mentioned above in this report brought in 118, this number bringing the total for 1996 to 224 and largely dispensing with the EPL. The 118 "will receive money, land, work and education," said an official of the Presidential Office of Reinsertion.

M-19. Under Carlos Pizarro Leon-Gómez M-19 allegedly made peace in 1990, entering the political arena as M-19 Democratic Alliance (ADM-19). Pizarro was assassinated, to be succeeded by Navarro Wolff. A "dissident" faction, Jaime Bateman Cayon, was operating in Cauca Department earlier this year.

FQL. This smallest and youngest of the terrorist groups has been "reintegrated" into Colombian society.

Peace at Any Price

The government of Colombia, under either the Liberal or Conservative Party has demonstrated an unwillingness to deal with its terrorists which is particularly curious when the importance of these terrorists to narcotrafficking is considered. Or perhaps it is not. Again during this fall of 1996 this "peace at any price" mentality has done little more than fret and fume while FARC and ELN continually increase their terrorist activities, the former having carried out a direct campaign of contempt with the sixty hostages for almost three months.

There are various theories as to why this malaise has affected Colombia for so many years, but one or two facts may be mentioned. First, although President Samper has thus far escaped any actions against himself for alleged support by narcotraffickers, enough members of the government have not escaped so that the possibility of terrorist collusion with parts of the government exists. Second, the collusion of lower echelon government officials with these terrorists is an open secret, for example:

In early November 1996 Mayor Antonio Sánchez of Milan was arrested by police as the intellectual author of the murder of Caquetá Department governor Jesus Angel González. The governor was killed by FARC terrorists when on a trip involved with release of FARC kidnappees. This highlighted government officials' claim that the mayors of Colombia's 1,050 municipalities collaborate with the terrorists who appear to have a presence in 560 of them. So political reasons for "peace at any price" exist.

Finally, one specifically identifiable reason for refusal to deal with terrorism and hence also narcotrafficking has to do with Colombian terrain. The three ranges of the Andes, which flow through Colombia to more or less coalesce on the Ecuadoran border, cover much of the land area to the west of what can be called Amazonia. Nearly all of these ranges tower above 12,000 feet, many of their peaks exceeding 15,000 and a substantial number exceeding 20,000. Such terrain is obviously difficult for the sort of search and destroy missions which would be routine against these terrorists. It is not impossible, but it is expensive.

Whatever the "reasons" for the mentality, it has existed for decades as has been discussed in Spcl 1.3 above and may be illustrated with a brief sketch of this decade and the last.

President Betancur came to power in 1982, in August of that year offering the "white flag" of truce to Colombian terrorists. As Colombian journalist Guillermo Zalamea remarked in latter 1985, "the famous peace of Betancur...has converted [the nation] into an urban and rural armed camp." President Barco's 1988 dismissal of General Samudio for attempting to deal with the terrorists has been mentioned. Terrorist violence has continued to increase since that time.

By this fall the relatively unimportant M-19, EPL, and FQL have been apparently eliminated, the oldest and most powerful groups, FARC and ELN, have "negotiated" their way to ever increasingly powerful positions. These two are still allied under the National Guerrilla Coordinating Group (CNG). By early November 1996 a congressional committee, which is "studying" a war tax to fight the terrorists, reported that FARC and ELN have an annual income of $720 million from their narcotrafficking and other activities. [This, of course, does not include the immense losses the country has suffered from, inter alia, wanton destruction of oil pipelines— Ed.] Fifteen years into the "peace" of Betancur, it might be supposed that sufficient "study" had been carried out, but this is apparently not the case. General John Thompson of the United States, who presides over the Inter-American Defense Council, headed a delegation which arrived in Bogotá in October, presumably for more "study."

A "war tax" has been proposed and calling up army reservists is apparently still under discussion, both measures indicating an intention, at least in some quarters, of dealing more realistically with Colombian terrorism. In the meantime, however, Colombian terrorism is dealing routinely with the Colombian government.

The FARC Hostage Campaign

On 30 August 1996 FARC seized sixty military hostages at Las Delicias in Caquetá Department. This act of war was almost immediately followed by cries for peace and the formation of a commission which, Colombian Episcopal Conference (CEC) president Alberto Giraldo declared, "had the complete endorsement" of the Samper government. Appropriately enough, this commission included Augusto Ramírez, former President Betancur's foreign minister.

The next step in what would be a FARC campaign of contempt for the Colombian government was a "warning" against any decision by the military high command to rescue the hostages "a sangre y fuego" (with fire and the sword), insisting instead that the "mothers" of the hostages be utilized. The terrorists have toyed with the Colombian government for almost three months, matters now apparently standing as follows.

FARC has demanded that the Colombian Army "demilitarize" a vast area of Caquetá Department meaning that the garrisons be removed, inter alia, from La Montañita (or Montañitas) and Cartagena del Caguán (or Cartagena del Chaira). La Montañita is nineteen miles southeast of Florencia in the foothills of the East Range. Cartagena del Caguan is forty-three miles almost due east of La Montañita and lies near the Chaira Lagoon which is why it is referred to as either Chaira or Caguán.[68]

If these are all the towns which the terrorists are demanding be "de-militarized," this will still constitute a vast amount of territory for release. To this point the military—or their civilian superiors—have agreed to Chaira and refused Montañita.

COLOMBIAN SURRENDER TO FARC TERRORISTS
(WKLY 2.18, 12 DECEMBER 1996)

In the 1920s the American gangster, Al Capone, routinely sent his thugs through a U.S. Army weapons course. Whether or not FARC sends its terrorists through Colombian Army training, its bosses routinely demonstrate a proclivity for "playing soldier" which they share with terrorists in other Latin American countries. And the press, bemused by romantic illusions about these terrorists and woefully ignorant of military matters, describes run-of-the-mill terrorists such as the Farabundi, Joaquín Villalobos, as "military strategists." Perhaps against such a background the events of the last 100 days in Colombia do not appear as bizarre as they really are.

In Wkly 2.15 (above) the FARC attack on the military base (camp) at Las Delicias, Caquetá Department, Colombia, was preliminarily described. The appearance of a report on this attack by the Colombian Army and the initiation of preparations for the return of the military hostages warrant this further coverage of the situation.

On 30 August 1996 FARC overran the military camp at Las Felicias in Caquetá Department some miles downstream from the confluence of the Orteguaza and Caqueta Rivers to the southeast of the Eastern Range of the Andes, a sparsely populated region. This facility was built in the early 1990s and had not been previously attacked. Following the attack and the lack of response from the Colombian government, the Army dispatched what has been described as a "handful" of intelligence officers to the region.

A voluminous intelligence report was compiled from the testimony of various recently captured terrorists and from various documents seized in recent counter terrorist operations. What follows appeared in this report.

The details of whatever terrorist "plan" there may have been remain obscure, but it appears unlikely that any meaningful military "tactics" were employed. It appears to have been merely the concentration of a superior force about the camp, a force which began firing its weaponry—to be listed below—then overran a camp which may have been largely asleep. Whatever the plan, it was developed last April by a terrorist named Milton de Jesus Toncel Redondo (a.k.a. Joaquín Gómez, a.k.a. Usurriaga).

Toncel, thirty-eight years of age, allegedly joined FARC in 1983 and, according to the account, rose rapidly within its command structure. In June 1992 he was appointed commander of the FARC Southern Bloc which is made up of ten terrorist fronts totaling 1000 personnel and operating in the departments of Putumayo, Caquetá, south Huila and northwest Amazonas. Amazonas is the southeast department of Colombia which borders on Brazil to the east and Peru to the south. Putumayo is west and slightly north of Amazonas and borders on Peru to the east, Ecuador to the west. Caqueta borders Putumayo to its southwest, Amazonas to its southeast. Finally Huila is to the northwest of Caquetá in the Eastern Range. (The formerly somewhat different organization of FARC activities in this coca-producing region will be discussed under "Narcoterrorism.")

Toncel drew 415 men from Fronts Three, Fourteen, Fifteen, Thirty-two, and the Teofilo Forero Company of Front Fifty-five. He also used the so-called Bloc Special Forces and Company Timanco and called in one physician and ten nurses. The operation is supposed to have cost 56 million pesos and utilized the following weaponry: 312 rifles, 770 pounds of explosive brought in from Ecuador, six machine guns (MGs), three rockets and two mortars, a heavy MG installed as anti-aircraft on a nearby hill. And some sort of "attack" was carried out. But on what?

The military base, but with what troops was it garrisoned? The initial reports which LANS published said that 27 military were killed, 20 wounded, and 60—67 by some reports—were taken hostage. Since the base was overrun and left in "ashes," this would indicate that the total garrison was 107 men. But more recent reports claim 28 dead, 60 hostages, and no wounded, numbers which appear rational when, presumably, the hostages would have included any wounded. This would amount to a total of 88 men. The garrison of, say, 88, did get off a few effective rounds, the terrorist boss of Front Forty-eight, "Pedro Martínez" (alias), and nine other terrorists killed, "about 25" wounded. In the "attack," Bloc boss Toncel was well out of the line of fire, his assistant, Ezequiel Huelguia Cruz (a.k.a. Rolando Romero), in command of the operation.

Rudyard Kipling's questions have been answered save for his "Why". His "Who" in slightly more depth largely provides the basis for whatever conclusions are drawn for the necessarily speculative

"Why." There is a specific reason for the action which will be given, but more generally:

These FARC personnel are anything but the military servants of their country whom Dumas Père delighted in describing with his "arms ennoble a man." These are ML terrorists who seek whatever power and perquisites of power they can gain through terrorism, drug dealing, kidnapping, and extortion. And in the eyes of the citizens they apparently have it.

In latter June 1996 a poll was carried out by the executive board of the National Liberal Party, that of President Samper, in which 1200 people over the age of eighteen and resident in fourteen of the largest Colombian cities were questioned. Twenty-five percent felt the terrorists to be the most powerful grouping in the country, only 19 percent considering the government to be so. The 16 percent, which considered "narcotrafficking" the most powerful force, might well be added to the 25 percent already in awe of the terrorists. The reasons for the citizenry making this not unenlightened choice have been reviewed in Wkly 2.15, this subsection.

100 Days of Surrender

In the face of the military "hostage" situation the Samper government has refused to allow the Army to go after its own, instead calling on the world to "save" the troops. During a period of almost 100 days FARC toyed with the Colombian government, then laid down the conditions—which were accepted—for the return of the sixty military personnel.

At midnight on 5–6 December 1996 a terrorist "truce" was initiated, this allegedly to last for ten days. The military forces were to be restricted to their barracks at the bases in Remolinos del Caguán, Tres Esquinas, Cartagena del Chaira, Leguizamos and La Tagua, this restriction to include military overflights and military vessels on the waterways. The area which is thus being delivered to the terrorists is 14,000 km^2 or 5400 mi^2 or 3,450,000 acres.

The area lies almost entirely in Caquetá Department, although, for example, La Tagua is on the right bank of the Caquetá River and hence in Putumayo Department. Cartagena del Cagua (or Cartagena del Chaira) is about 55 miles east-southeast of Florencia which is in the foothills of the East Range, Tres Esquinas at the confluence of the Arteguaza and Caquetá Rivers some 55 miles south-southwest of

Cartagena. La Tregua is 55 miles south-southwest of Tres Esquinas. The area in the triangle with these three cities as its vertices is about 2090 mi^2 and more or less delineates the "truce" region. This area is in the Caguán (Cartagena del Caguán, Remolinos del Caguán) with reference to which the intelligence report stated, inter alia: "We have destroyed various cocaine processing laboratories in the Caguán, precisely in the zone which they have asked be demilitarized in order to turn over our soldiers. But in reality what they wish is to return to a zone occupied by us because we believe that the soldiers are in Putumayo." (Putumayo Department is, save for La Tagua, south of the zone.)

AN INTERNATIONAL TENTACLE OF THE HL
(WKLY 2.18, 12 DECEMBER 1996)

On the night of 15 August 1995 eight masked, armed men, "some" wearing ELN armbands, broke into the Schoene condominium in the Medellín suburb of Llanogrande. They kidnapped Frau Brigitte Schoene, her five-year-old son and the maid; her husband, Ulrich Schoene, was absent in Valencia, Venezuela, on business at the time. On returning to Colombia the following day Herr Schoene contacted the Metropolitan Police and the English firm, Control Risk, experts on kidnapping, which had been under contract with the firm of which Schoene had been president for some years, BASF Quimica.

At dawn on 17 November 1996 Werner Mauss, who has some twenty aliases of which this may be one, was arrested at the Río Negro National Airport (Antioquia Department) some forty kilometers east of Medellín when he was in the process of spiriting Brigitte Schoene, under the name Barbara Baum, out of Colombia. After the arrest Antioquia governor Alvaro Uribe and Medellín police chief, General Alfredo Salgado, accused "Mauss" of belonging to an "international arm" of the ELN.

This is of considerable importance because of the crucial role played by the international support received by many HL terror groups, LANS having encountered such support for terrorist groups in Mexico, Guatemala, El Salvador, Nicaragua, and Peru. In the past much of the support for Colombian terrorism has been funneled through the headquarters for the HL, Cuba.

Mauss was traveling under the alias Norbert Schroeder and accompanied by an individual called Sylvia Schroeder whom Mauss claimed to be his wife. Although the accounts given by the Schoenes support the charge of kidnapping brought by Governor Uribe, General Salgaso, and various completely independent witnesses, the honorary German Consul in Medellín, Helmut Luecker, maintained that the Schroeders were innocent of all charges and had simply been carrying out a "humanitarian" action.

The Schoenes gave a detailed account of their ordeal to *Semana* (Bogotá, 10 December 1996), Frau Schoene's clearly the more harrowing. The key to the whole affair was Mauss, who was introduced on 14 September to Herr Schoene by the then head of the German embassy in Bogotá as an individual with a great deal of experience with kidnappings. Either way this was probably true. Mauss was now Jürgen Seidel who told Schoene that "by order of high functionaries of the German government I have carried out a series of investigations of the case of his wife Brigitte."

From this point it was a matter of Mauss first maneuvering Schoene into taking the Metropolitan Police and Control Risk out of the picture and putting everything in his hands. Frau Schoene was told on 14 November by a young terrorist dressed like Che Guevara that she would be freed on 16 November, and at 2000 that day a jeep arrived with a driver, a priest—the ELN is the "clerics' terror group"—and two Germans, Werner and Michaela Mauss. The group proceeded to Río Negro International where Mauss told Brigitte that they were boarding a charter flight for Cartagena, Colombia, whence they would fly to Caracas, Venezuela, then to Germany where they would meet her husband and the son who had been released.

But Colonel Mauricio Santoyo and his men, who had been on Mauss' trail, arrived at the airport, arrested a now flustered Mauss and released Brigitte Schoene. There are apparently some who, innocently or otherwise, continue to support "Mauss." Nevertheless, this multiple agent had in his possession various passports, a document from the German embassy in Bogotá asking collaboration with "Schroeder," satellite communication equipment, mobil cellular telephones, and a list of eighty-three world terrorist organizations to include those in Colombia.

When Santoyo's men arrested him, "Mauss" played his last card. Grabbing his cellular phone, he punched a number, then began hollering "¡Aquí está el embajador!...¡Aquí está el embajador!" Colonel Santoyo seized the cellular, looked "Mauss" straight in the eye, and turned it off.

HL Terrorist Organization: Mexico

MEXICAN TERRORISM (WKLY 1.9, 4 JULY 1996)

There has been an ambivalence in Mexican relations with Cuba's Fidel Castro which reflects that within the ruling Institutional Revolutionary Party (PRI).[69]

Thus, the Cuban- and Sandinista-trained terrorist, Rafael Sebastian Guillen (a.k.a. Marcos; El Mejicano)[70] could officially institute a copybook terrorist "uprising" in Chiapas (1) on the thirty-fifth anniversary of Castro's Cuban takeover, 1 January 1994, and (2) after U.S. ratification of NAFTA, although the Mexican government had been aware of the Zapatista National Liberation Front for some time (EZLN).[71]

In June 1996, the People's Revolutionary Army (EPR), an allegedly "new" terrorist organization, surfaced in Guerrero State. In reality, this may be one of the five Mexican terror groups which, in addition to the EZLN, emerged in 1994. Three of these were in Chiapas, two in Guerrero. Various of these may be bogus, that is, the creation of an individual with a typewriter. The two Guerrero groups were the ELS Southern Liberation Army (ELS) (EFE, 27 July 1994) and the Mexican Revolutionary Armed Forces (FARN) (AFP, 11 September 1994). The HL has followed a routine wherein multiple terrorist organizations allegedly "arise independently" in a given nation and are then consolidated as in Guatemala, Colombia, and elsewhere. Such a progression could be underway in Mexico.

THE ZAPATISTA CHIEF RAFAEL SEBASTIAN GUILLEN
(SPCL 1.7, 17 JULY 1996)

Rafael Sebastian Guillen Vicente (a.k.a. Jorge Narvaez; El Mejicano; Subcommandante Marcos) is anything but the romantic figure from a Romberg operetta which a part of the press has attempted to portray. He is an ML terrorist who, as Ruíz Pavon has phrased it, was nurtured in that "vast net of subversion which Castroites and Sandinistas wove in the Latin America of the 1980s."

Guillen officially emerged on 1 January 1994 when the copybook ML "uprising" was announced in commemoration of the thirty-fifth anniversary of Castro's seizure of power. As has been pointed out, the Mexican government had been aware of this group for at least two years, but it behooved it to be officially unaware until after NAFTA had been ratified by the U.S. Senate. Young Guillen (b. 19 June 1957, Tampico) had been groomed for this almost from birth.

La Jornada (Mexico), in early 1995, secured a copy of a Mexican government report which, in establishing Rafael's father, Alfonso, as an ML, effectively established the boy as a "red-diaper baby," appropriate since he would train under the classic "red-diaper baby" and Nicaraguan KGB (DGSE) chief, Lenín Cerna. This fourth of eight children studied, or was indoctrinated, at the Jesuit-run Tampico Cultural Institute, in 1980 obtaining a degree in philosophy from Mexican National Autonomous University (UNAM). The government profile says that "the majority of elective courses taken by Rafael Sebastian, among them 'Political and Ideological Philosophy of the Society,' are connected with the study of Marxism-Leninism." According to a widely circulated puff piece, he taught a "design" course at the University of Mexico in Xochimilco from 1979 to 1984. In reality, after receiving his degree from UNAM his internship began in the Sandinista Managua of 1980.

According to *La Tribuna* (Managua, February 1995), Guillen arrived in Nicaragua in 1979 as a member of the "promotion of culture brigades," a Sandinista program which brought thousands of young terrorists from all over the world to the country. Here, with the Mexican, Gloria Valdes, he matriculated in the first "militia" training course, appropriately enough under LibTheo cleric, Sandinista and minister of "culture," Ernesto Cardenal. Cardenal's assistant, Señora Luz Marian Acosta, has recently attested to this being the same man in Chiapas save he is "thinner" now.

Guillen's time in Nicaragua is appropriately divided into two periods, the year 1984 marking the division. During the first phase he was engaged in intense political activity with frequent trips abroad, particularly to Cuba and El Salvador. As former Sandinista militiaman and *Barricada* (Managua)[72] reporter, Oliver Bodán, has written, Guillen's immediate superior was Secret Police chief Lenín Cerna; he was trained in Brigade 3-68. This organization had responsibility for the defense of Jinotega, a northern Nicaragua department fronting Honduras and having considerable Contra activity at the time, notably in the San José de Bocay region. In the Sandinista ranks Guillen was known as "Jorge Narvaez," in the mountains as "El Mejicano."

Roberto Orozco of *La Prensa* (Managua) reported that, "about" 1985 Guillen moved into the Linda Vista section of Jinotega City with the Salvadoran terrorist, Silvia, and various Mexican "comrades." A young German terrorist, Heidrum Neith, disappeared about then—"Buried in the basement?" asked the neighbors—his Salvadoran amante killing herself amongst the AIDS rumors. Guillen then began more frequent travel to El Salvador, his "comrades" giving him up for lost until he reappeared at a Sandinista celebration in Managua.

Another of his companions was the Basque Homeland and Liberty (ETA) terrorist, Ana Uriz, also active in Nicaragua and El Salvador. The extensive involvement of this Basque terrorist group in Central America—wherein Chiapas may practically be placed—has been prominent to the present.

The "spontaneous uprising" of 1 January 1994 had been carefully planned for several years to take place as and where it did. As Pedro Cifuentes reported from Cuba in the fall of 1994, the commanders of this operation were all trained in Cuba, logistics would originally be arranged by Cuban ambassador to Mexico José Fernández Cosiio, and the final touches were put on the operation in the 1993 Foro São Paulo Encounter in Havana. The FSP was clearly replacing OLAS as hemispheric terrorist command and coordination center.

But Guillen's training and indoctrination neither started nor stopped when he was given nominal command.[73]

More direct testimony has been given on his frequent visits to Cuba for such training. The trips date from the fall of 1981, not long after his establishment in Managua. In October 1981 he took the first of these trips, as journalist Gustavo de Anda discovered and Santiago Aroca verified through the testimony of his roommate, Eradio Morena, the Sandinista mayor of San Juan de Río Coco. The mayor lived with him and "shared many of his ideas as to how to bring the revolution to Mexico." The courses which he was taking at the time were, of course, given by "Redbeard" Piñiera's Americas Department, CC, Cuban CP, Castro's personal command post for hemispheric terrorism.

Ruíz Pavon's observation is worthy of repetition: Guillen was nurtured in that "vast net of subversion which Castroites and Sandinistas wove in the Latin America of the 1980s."

THE MEXICAN PEOPLE'S REVOLUTIONARY ARMY (EPR)
(WKLY 2.5, 12 SEPTEMBER 1996)

There have been two complete successes by the ML terrorists in the Western Hemisphere, that of the Twenty-sixth of July Movement in Cuba (January 1959) and that of the Sandinistas (FSLN) in Nicaragua (August 1979). In neither case did the terrorists attain their success by "force of arms." The "victories" were obtained by the occupation of the power vacuums created by the "well-meaning" (*tontos utiles*) in the Hemisphere who drove out the reigning caudillos, Batista and Somoza, the MLs moving in and taking their place. The *tontos utiles* did this because they had fallen victim to the propaganda of the HL and HL Support. The machine continues to function smoothly, even enjoying success with the time-worn "babies-and-bayonets" tale.

What may or may not be another HL disinformation operation began in the Mexican State of Guerrera on the morning of 27 June 1995, mentioned here only because of its relation to the emergence of the EPR. A confrontation between police and members of what Guerrera governor Ruben Figueroa called "the tiny radical group," Campesino Organization of the Southern Mountains (OCSS), left seventeen dead and twenty wounded, four of the wounded police according to AFP dispatches. It was also reported that the OCSS people *said* that the police were waiting "to ambush them," the ten policemen accused of "guilt" in the affair maintaining that the OCSS people attacked them. *La Jornada* (19 June 1995) published a lengthy article recounting the claims by the campesinos, but from which, nonetheless, certain holes in their story may be gleaned.[74]

Before long the governor of Guerrera would be driven out of office by the affair, the press having labeled it a "matanza" and a "masacre." The importance here is the use to which the confrontation was put.

On 28 June 1996 FSP member and PRD[75] head Cuauhtémoc Cárdenas, his PRD National Executive Committee, and various "human rights" organizations were gathered at Aguas Blancas ford to commemorate the first anniversary of the "massacre." The meeting was officially a function of the Broad Front for the Construction of the National Liberation Movement (FAC-MLN). They would all deny any connection with what happened next.

Some[76] men and women appeared, taking over the stage and its environs. *La Jornada* (16 June 1996) reported that the FAC-MLN "cordon of security" (with yellow caps) about the gathering "protected the entry of the armed group." The members were uniformed in olive drab with shoulder patch, combat boots, and masks and carried AK-47s or AR-15s. A "short youth" took over the microphones: "Comrades," he told the crowd, "we are combatants of the People's Revolutionary Army and we are here to render homage to our comrades fallen on 28 June..." After an offering "made of field plants" and the firing of seventeen volleys by other performers, the youth read the "Manifiesto de Aguas

Blancas" which the EPR "General Staff" directed to a FAC-MLN "facing institutionalized violence, [who realize that] the armed battle is a legitimate and necessary recourse of the people to reinstitute its sovereign will and the state of law."

The manifesto listed five points for which the EPR "is fighting." The first is to overturn the "anti-people, anti-democratic, demagogic government" in the service of "national and foreign big money." The second would reestablish the people's sovereignty by the "establishment of a people's democratic republic." The third promises to "solve the people's problems," the fourth "to establish just relations with the international community," and the fifth vows to "punish the guilty." Throughout the manifesto there was considerable use of various ML expressions calling for "revolutionary, armed, peoples...organizations to battle exploitation and repression," promises to form "a single political force" "to battle for liberty, democracy..."

If the FAC-MLN directors are to be believed, they had no idea such an eruption of armed men would occur at their protest meeting. If the reports of the affair are to be believed, however, their members cheered lustily during and after the reading of the manifesto. Such was the official announcement of what purports to be a "new" ML terrorist organization. LANS has reported the alleged existence of five other terrorist groups in Mexico during 1994 when the EZLN was attracting most of the attention. Such proliferation has been important during the last two decades because of the routine amalgamation of such collections into umbrella groupings such as the URNG (Guatemala), the FMLN (El Salvador), the trisected FSLN (Nicaragua), the CNG (Colombia), and so forth. Such a development may be irrelevant in Mexico, but it is early in such a process to ignore the possibility.

Alleged EPR Background: The Last Link

Leaving the documents in a park and notifying the press, the EPR issued two "communiqués" dated 7 August 1996. The first was of eight pages and was entitled "Manifesto of the Western Sierra Madre," the second of fourteen pages, "Historical, Economic, Social and Political Foundation." In the first of these the EPR described itself as "the last link in the symbiosis of diverse clandestine organizations, heirs of the 1960s–1970s guerrillas with a single objective: Taking power in order to transform the country to socialism." (*La Jornada*, 23 August 1996). In the same document the EPR announced the alleged[77] formation of the People's Revolutionary Democratic Party (PDPR) on 18 May 1996.

The appearance of the Mexican terrorist is taken as coincident with the 23 September 1965 emergence of Arturo Gamiz and Pablo Gómez who led a group which attacked the Madera Barracks in Chihuahua, justifying their action with references to "the despoiling of lands and the chastisement of cattlemen." From this action allegedly arose the Clandestine Revolutionary Workers Party (PROCUP—see below), founded by H. E. Hernández Castillo (d. 1978) and others. The Liga de Septiembre[78] appeared next, its last director, D. Jiménez Sarmiento (d. 1976), dead in an attempted kidnapping of Margarita López Portillo. At about this time the Zapatista Urban Front (FUZ) also arose with its "spectacular" kidnapping of the director general of airports, J. Hirschfeld Almada, on 29 September 1971. Revolutionary Action Movement (MAR) was created in 1968 and eliminated with the capture of thirty-one terrorists in 1971. Peoples Armed Commandos (CAP) was dissolved by the government on 17 September 1971. People's Revolutionary Armed Forces (FRAP) materialized and kidnapped U.S. Consul General T. G. Leonhardy. American United Proletarian Party (PPUA) surfaced at about the same time and operated until the end of the decade.

It is claimed that the rural terrorists developed principally in Guerrero under Gonaro Vázquez and Lucio Cabañas, the former heading the José María Morelos Front of the National Revolutionary Civic Association (ANCR), the latter the director of the Party of the Poor (PDLP), both notorious for kidnapping. Meanwhile, in Oaxaca PROCUP was consolidated, PDLP "establishing contact" with it in 1976 and entering into a closer alliance three years later. The People's Liberation Army José María Morelos (EPLM) made itself known on 11 August 1992 as allied with PROCUP-PDLP, the MRP in 1985, various others such as the Mexican Revolutionary Movement (FARM) emerging in the next decade. How many of these are bogus—"one man with one mimeograph machine"—is probably not known, but more can be found in *Proceso* (Mexico 23 August 1996). The point of this "history" is that the EPR claims to be the "last link" in the chain of such organizations.

EPR "Actions" Since 27 June

There have been a few EPR terrorist activities during the summer of 1996, perhaps the most notable occurring on 29 August when small groups of armed personnel appeared in various locations, *La Jornada* reporting the maximum number of twenty in Tlaxisco (Oaxaca State) and fifteen in Huatulco. (Such reports are routinely high.) A number of mostly untargeted rounds were fired in a number of locations, a road was blocked in Chiapas. The Mexican government reported the casualty tally from these activities at sixteen dead and twenty-eight wounded among Army, Navy, police, and civilian personnel. This is the largest "operation" which the EPR has mounted, and it appears to support the contention of the Mexican government that this is no true guerrilla-terrorist force but a small group intent on political destabilization. Although the EPR claimed 500 members at Aguas Blancas, that it is probably much smaller—no more than 100 the government maintains— was scarcely belied by this noisy but hardly massive operation. The majority of the EPR activities support such a conclusion.

For in their majority EPR overt activities have consisted of issuing "manifestos" and conducting pc's (press conferences) with costumed commandants. The "manifestos" have been discussed; the 28 June affair at Aguas Blancas amounted to the first pc (not to be confused with PC or Political Correctness—or is it?). Another was held in early August at a "secret camp" in the Eastern Sierra Madre, "around thirty [?]" armed personnel present, "Cmdte. José Arturo" spouting standard ML rhetoric. The performance was repeated by "Cmdtes. Vivente and Oscar" at a "safe house...less than three hours from the center of Mexico City." The rhetoric was the same, that of this performance spiced by a manual, *Curso basico de guerra*, with which the "officers" of the EPR allegedly "instruct their new militia in guerrilla war" (*La Jornada*, 25 August 1996). The covert activities of the EPR can hardly be laid out with the same precision, but the group is clearly active in directing its supporters in such as the OCSS in their reactions to government activities. The press has published a great deal of what is at least exaggeration in the comments of these supporters.

The Origins of the EPR

In 11 September 1996 interviews, sources as different as Dr. Fernando López, Mexican Interior Ministry director of press relations, and Mr. Rafael Pérez-Gay, head of Cal y Arena Publishers and editor of *Nexos* magazine assured the LANS editor that there was no question that PROCUP-PDLP and OCSS are involved with the EPR. As Vice Minister of Interior Arturo Nuñez of Mexico told a press conference[79] on 29 August 1996, "documents on the formation of the EPR have been found which make public [the fact] that it constitutes the armed branch of the…[PROCUP-PDLP]." These documents also establish the goals of the EPR as "fight[ing] and destroy[ing] the power of the bourgeoisie…to seize political power, to establish the rule of the proletariat and to build socialism." Nuñez went on to say that "the documents identify those [groups] operating as fronts in its political activity, especially…[OCSS],…Emilio Zapata Eastern Mexico Democratic Front [FDMEZ]…and…People's National Democratic Front [FDNP]." Organizations such as the OCSS have denied these suggestions, but there are independent pieces of evidence which tend to support them.

The EPR and the EZLN

As LANS has reported (Wkly 2.1 above), Mexican president Salinas de Gortari declared almost immediate "peace" with the EZLN because Sandinista People's Army head Humberto Ortega flew to Mexico City and advised him to do so. The Zedillo government was then faced with a *fait accompli* in its dealings with the EZLN which is to say nothing of the "wisdom" of its dealings with that organization. When the EPR emerged, however, the reaction of the Mexican government was quite different.

Some sources attribute the difference in treatment to the influence of Fidel Castro on the Mexican government, the Cuban dictator demonstrably involved with Guillen and allegedly opposed to the EPR. Whatever the merit of such an argument, the Mexican government has maintained from the beginning that the EPR situation differs from that of the EZLN in that the former does not have the "popular base" enjoyed by the latter nor has it shown the same willingness to "negotiate."

THE MEXICAN PROCUP-PDLP (SPCL 2.5, 13 SEPTEMBER 1996)

As has been remarked in the last article, there appears to be no question that "documents have been found demonstrating that it [the EPR] constitutes the armed branch of the PROCUP-PDLP [Clandestine Revolutionary Workers Party-Party of the Poor]." Which demonstrates the importance of understanding the PROCUP-PDLP. The following history of this organization was developed from documents graciously supplied to LANS by Dr. Fernando López L., Mexican Interior Ministry foreign press director, and from other sources. The account begins some thirty-two years ago.

The first militant nucleus of the People's Union (UP) was developed in 1964 by students from the University of Guadalajara and from Oaxaca Autonomous University Benito Juárez (UABJO). These "scholars" began carrying out terrorist acts four years later (October 1968) in small groups of six to ten as members of the Antonio Briones Montoto Brigade. From within this terrorist milieu arose Clandestine Revolutionary Organization-Union of the People (ORCUP) which went public with terrorist activity in 1972, the brothers Tiburcio and Gabriel Cruz Sánchez prominent members. At that time the principal members of ORCUP were Hector Samudio Fuentes and Jaime Bali West, both professors at Chapingo Autonomous University where, with the Guatemalan, José María Ortiz Videa, they were training members of the organization in guerrilla-terrorist tactics.

ORCUP continued its activities into 1976, that year approaching PDLP with the idea of combining efforts and developing joint ventures. The following year (1977), working through groups called "Coyotes,"[80] ORCUP linked up with the movement headed by the rector of UABJO, Felipe Martínez Soriano, whose ideas of academic activity differed considerably from the traditional. Both Martínez and the Coyotes nursed an "ideological antagonism" against the secretary general of UABJO, Carlos Hernández Chavarria, which was apparently strong enough to result in the murder of the latter on 23 February 1978. The ORCUP murderers of the secretary general declared in their statements to authorities that they had been following the orders of Maribel Martínez Martínez, the daughter of Martínez Soriano and head of the Coyotes. A month after the murder ORCUP claimed responsibility for it and described it as an "execution" as Sendero Luminoso (Peru) would do with its mock trials and throat slashings. This sequence of events appears to coincide with the time at which ORCUP began to be known as PROCUP and merged with the PDLP.

The "new" terrorist organization was faced with the necessity of establishing a process for the defense of its members who had been detained and, at that time, of functioning as an open political front. On 3 October 1978, Felipe Martínez and his wife, Josefina Martínez Rojas, founded the Independent National Committee for the Defense of Prisoner, Persecuted, Detained-Disappeared and Exiled Politicians (CNI) in order to deal with this two-pronged problem. The use of the term "politician" to describe these terrorists is extremely important and essentially adumbrates our later discussion of the Hemispheric Left Support (HLS).

His wife remaining as director of CNI, Martínez Soriano founded the Peoples National Democratic Front (FDNP), another HLS organization which would be laboring with the CNI. With this network of supporting organizations then, PROCUP-PDLP began to show itself as a subversive group the objectives of which were the taking of political power through the installation of a "dictatorship of the proletariat" and the "construction of socialism."

Investigation no. 7A/1427/990-04 was initiated against members of the organization for the crimes of homicide, kidnapping, aggravated robbery, criminal association, and concealment, and these charges were brought before the Fourth Criminal Court in the Federal District. Two males and three females acknowledged their participation in various criminal acts[81] among which were robbery at the Iberoamerican University, the kidnapping of J. K. Siguchi Hoshino and the murder of two guards at *La Jornada* newspaper. In this investigation various documents, found in a "safe house" in Los Reyes La Paz (Mexico State), were entered into the record as were the declarations of those mentioned above.

From these documents and statements the organizational structure of PROCUP-PDLP could be detailed. It was a typical ML organization having the standard "commands" and "committees" and of course including a Central Committee and a Politburo. This organizational structure, which was apparently in force until about 1990, maintained some "subversive presence" in the states of Oaxaca, Jalisco, Puebla, Michoacan, Guerrero, Hidalgo, and the Federal District with a "secondary" presence in Morelos and Veracruz. The organization allegedly directed its "recruiting activities" at the usual societal segments: workers, campesinos, students, independent unions, and "dissident" managers.

Immediately after the 2 April 1990 murder of the *La Jornada* guards, it was allegedly confirmed that this clandestine organization had carried out assaults on banks, kidnappings, and "actions collecting arms" similar to those which, in the 1970s, ORCUP had carried out in Jalisco and Oaxaca and PDLP had perpetrated in Guerrero.[82]

A few days after Serafin Gervasio (a.k.a. David Cabañas Barrientos), half-brother of the defunct director Lucio Cabañas Ruíz, was detained (12–13 June 1990) as guilty of the murder of the *La Jornada* guards, the group began violent terrorist activities demanding the release of its members, these outrages to include bombings in Oaxaca, Guerrero, and the Federal District.

On 7 June 1991 four PROCUP-PDLP militants were picked up for possession of illegal firearms, and they subsequently identified them-selves as members of the Recuperators of Arms Command, their im-mediate objective the Metropolitan Auxiliary Police Armory. On 19 June 1991 eight members of such a "command" hit the Sixty-third Auxiliary Police group and stole firearms, two alleged members of this command picked up on 7 August 1991. A number of bombings were perpetrated that summer—banks, a Nissan Agency, the IBM building, McDonald's of Villa Copa, and so forth—and the number of impris-oned PROCUP-PDLP members grew, these joined in April by various Liga Comunista 23 Septiembre militants.

Inside the prison the Political Prisoners' Collective (CPP) had arisen and contained members of various ML groups. The CPP branch in Reclusorio Norte has produced a "history" of the subversive organiza-tion and a number of "communiqués" to the general population con-taining routine ML rhetoric have been issued. The CPP has taken its place with the FDNP and the CNI as another member of the HLS.

PROCUP-PDLP greeted the overt appearance of the EZLN in 1994 with a wave of bombings, these having graduated from the simple deto-nation of explosive charges to the more sophisticated vehicle bomb. The Mexican government claims to feel this to have been a campaign "to take advantage of the EZLN" eruption, the official position being that there is no connection between the two terrorist groups or, now, between the EZLN and the EPR. It would appear wise to reserve any conclusions as to the lack of connection or enmity among these terror-ist organizations.

HL Terrorist Organizations: Central America

Guatemala

THE REALITY OF GUATEMALAN TERRORISM (WKLY 1.7, 20 JUNE 1996)

Dame una ametralladora y una ideología y aplaudireis mis crímenes[83]
—Francisco-Felix Montiel

At the Twenty-sixth General Assembly (Panama, 3–7 June 1996) of the Organization of American States (OAS) the thirty-four nations represented aligned themselves solidly against the United States in the matter of the Helms-Burton Law on the Cuban Embargo, this under the leadership of U.S.-backed secretary general César Gaviria Trujillo. Less remarked but of more interest here was the OAS announcement that the organization will develop "a special program of support for Guatemala…to consolidate democracy, peace, reconstruction and reconciliation." More specifically, the OAS will secure World Bank, IMF, IDB, etc., money for the Guatemalan National Revolutionary Union (URNG) use in order to "integrate themselves into Guatemalan society." Few, if any, of the delegates had (1) that in-depth understanding of terrorism in Guatemala or (2) that knowledge of similar past "peace" processes which would allow a "consolidation" program to be rationally created or implemented. In the meantime, 14 June 1996 saw the Mexico City beginning of the "ultimate stage of peace negotiations between the Guatemalan government and the URNG."

The complexity which has fed this confusion may be somewhat alleviated by dividing the 1945–1996 Guatemalan terrorist period into (a) the Arevalo-Arbenz Era, 1945–1954; (b) the First Interregnum, 1954–1960; (c) Castroite Terrorism phase 1, 1960–1970; (d) the Second Interregnum, 1970–1972; and (e) Castroite Terrorism phase 2, 1972–1996.

The Arevalo-Arbenz Era, 1945–1954

In this much truncated treatment, Ubico's political demise (1944) is passed over and the period summarized with James's description of Guatemalan communization: "By the time Arevalo [inaugurated president 15 March 1945] turned over the reins to Arbenz in March 1951, the nationalist revolution had been submerged in a rising tide of Communism…Whereas Arevalo had flirted with the Communists, Arbenz became one with them."[84]

And so, on 29 June 1954, Arbenz was ousted by Colonel Carlos Castillo Armas. Schlesinger and Kinzer[85] have set forth the position of the HL which Ravel[86] has described as "pure Marxism…private capital summoning the imperial state to its rescue." U.S. Ambassador Spruille Braden[87] long ago detailed the fact that Castillo led a spontaneous revolution which was not assisted by the United States until it was almost too late to matter, many pertinent details being available in the House Select Committee Report.[88]

The First Interregnum, 1954–1960

At 2100 on 26 July 1957 President Carlos Castillo Armas was struck and killed by two bullets fired by one of his guards, Romeo Vásquez Sánchez. Was this Kremlin "wetwork"? LANS has encountered evidence moving this answer from "possibly" to "probably." Possible: Vásquez's correspondence with Radio Moscow's Ludmila Riausova was innocuous (NYT, 30 August 1957), but his diary could link him (UPI, 28 July 1957). Probable: An interview by the LANS editor with Nicaraguan president Luís Somoza's security chief (30 May 1985) showed that Dominican caudillo Trujillo had called President Somoza in the middle of the night to warn him that his friend (Castillo) had "a scorpion in his shirt." Somoza sent off his intelligence chief immediately, but Castillo just laughed—and died. The Caribbean knew before the fact.

After Castillo's death Kremlin operatives began flowing back into Guatemala (Paul Kennedy, NYT, 10 November 1957); with Castro's takeover his embassy in Guatemala began to play a key role in the planned and coming rebellion while arms shipments escalated.

Castroite Terrorism, Phase 1: 1960–1970

And then came the anything but spontaneous "uprising" of November 1960.[89] The principal myth of this "uprising" was that it was led by "younger officers." The rebel leader in the Ruffino Barracks (Guatemala City) was Colonel Sesan Pereira and in Puerto Barrios, Colonel Llerena Miller, while Colonel Paz Tejada and Villamar Contreras were in overall command. The "uprising," directed by Arevalo and Arbenz from Cuba, was put down in a few days, the ranking officers fled and two lieutenants took to the hills with a handful of men and fed the Sigmund Rombergs of the press the "younger officers" myth. Lieutenants Yon Sosa and Turcios Lima[90] fled to the Lake Izabal region, there forming the first ML terrorist group in Guatemala, the Thirteenth of November Movement (MR-13), the Revolutionary Armed Forces (FAR) subsequently evolving. By 1966 Yon was heading MR-13, Turcios FAR. On returning from Castro's TCC in 1966 Turcios rejected President Méndez Montenegro's offer of a truce. FAR had no more than 300 members although press reports indicated "weekend volunteers," "students" who joined on weekends to "kill a cop." Turcios was dead in 1966, Yon killed by Mexican troops in 1970 at the Río Lacantun.

The Second Interregnum, 1970–1972

Thus, by 1970 Guatemalan terrorism had ceased to exist with the disappearance of MR-13 and FAR. That terrorism was dead was effectively admitted by the abandonment of these terrorist groups. A *new* FAR would arise in the 1970s, but it was admitted even by the apologists for these terrorists that this was *not* the FAR of the 1960s. It has only been the lack of knowledge of those recently covering Guatemalan terrorism, combined with the terrorists wish to establish a false longevity for their operations, which has many believing that there is an unbroken history of Guatemalan terrorism tracing back to 1960. In reality the terrorism of the 1970s, 1980s, and 1990s began with an *invasion* from Mexico in 1972.

Castroite Terrorism, Phase 2: 1972–1996

Today's Guatemalan terrorism began with an invasion from Mexico on 19 January 1972, the details of which have been provided by one of the terrorists.[91] He says "the Edgar Ibarra guerrilla detachment [of twenty-five men and boys] penetrated Guatemalan territory." This would be the Guerrilla Army of the Poor (EGP). By 1976 EGP had only grown to fifty and done little save murder an occasional "hated landlord." Three additional terrorist groups would then arise. One of these was a *new* FAR, but even the apologists for these terrorists such as George Black (below) have admitted that this was *not* the FAR of the 1960s.

In addition to EGP and the new FAR, Organization of the People in Arms (ORPA) and Guatemalan Workers Party (PGT) came into active existence. A notable apologist for these terrorists is George Black, author of the Introduction to the Payeras book. His breathless description of these terrorist groups includes an account of a peace-loving PGT which, in the early 1970s, was "sticking to semi-legal [*sic*]...work." Their departure from "semi-legal work" apparently occurred in the spring of 1979 when they claimed "credit" for the murder of a rancher and his three bodyguards.

A meeting among Guatemalan terrorist leaders, Cuban and Nicaraguan personnel was held in Managua in September 1980. Secretary General Manuel Mora of the Costa Rican CP, Secretary General Efraín Cardona of the Honduran CP, and Humberto Ortega and Bayardo Arce of the Sandinistas took part. Presiding over the meeting was the head of Castro's Americas Department, Manuel (Redbeard) Piñiero Losada.

Out of this meeting arose the URNG. Three of the important meeting documents have been published by the U.S. Senate Subcommittee on Security and Terrorism (Y4.J89/2:J-97-97, 1982). These documents are valuable to any analysis of these organizations.

THE POSSIBILITY OF A URNG "VICTORY THROUGH PEACE" (SPCL 1.6, 26 JUNE 1996)

In Wkly 1.7 immediately above, the apparently emerging "peace" agreement between the Guatemalan government and the URNG terrorists were discussed, it being pointed out that the same powers are supporting this as supported the Chapultepec Accords which allegedly brought "peace" to El Salvador. If such is the case, these Chapultepec Accords comprise necessary background to serious consideration of the apparently emerging accords with the URNG.

[Although of considerable consequence to the URNG accords, this Report deals primarily with Salvadoran matters and is hence reproduced below, see "El Salvador"—Ed.]

GUATEMALAN "PEACE" (WKLY 1.9, 4 JULY 1996)

The Guatemalan government and the URNG "concluded a new round of dialog" (AFP, 25 June 1996) on 23 June, "peace talks" during the next three weeks to be between the government and UN mediator Jean Arnault. The subjects which have been discussed were apparently quite similar to those delineated in Spcl 1.6 (above). An interesting double standard has evolved, on the one hand, the URNG terrorist chiefs telling the press (EFE, 17 June 1996) that an amnesty for them "is not negotiable," on the other, prosecution of the Armed Forces for "human rights" violations is demanded (EFE, 19 June 1996).

GUATEMALAN "PEACE" ACCORDS (WKLY 2.14, 14 NOVEMBER 1996)

Precision in language is essential to understanding. Therefore, to call ML[92] groups such as the URNG "guerrillas," that is, members of "an irregular military unit," being incorrect *a priori*, leads to misunderstanding. Those who make war on the civilian population as does the URNG are appropriately called "terrorists" whether murdering a "hated landlord" in Guatemala or blowing up the Murrah Building in Oklahoma City. In Guatemala further misunderstanding has been engendered by deliberate misrepresentation, or ignorance, of the five phases of the 1945–1996 terrorist period: (a) the Arevalo-Arbenz era; (b) the First Interregnum; (c) Castroite Terrorism, phase 1; (d) the Second Interregnum; and (e) Castroite Terrorism, phase 2. In the more civilized nineteenth century guerrillas were executed out of hand, as the great Marshal Davout threatened to do during the Jena-Auerstädt Campaign.[93]

In the late twentieth century such terrorists, supported and coordinated from outside their own country, are not dealt with summarily. Instead they are rewarded with "peace" accords as was done by the Chapultepec Accords which awarded Salvadoran Farabundo Martí National Liberation Front (FMLN) terrorists a level of political power and government funding which they would never have attained with their "military" impotence or their unpopularity with the civilian population.

Why then do the governments of these nations surrender these victories? There are three principal reasons: (1) pressure from their "allies"; (2) international acclaim for their chiefs of state; and (3) the disinformation operations of the HL Support. The United States has been the principal "ally" of the beleaguered Latin American nations. The LANS editor, over a period of time, has encountered various examples of U.S. pressure against these "allies" to fight no-win wars. As he was told by an intelligence chief, had the United States fought World War II like this, "there would have been a Nazi Storm Trooper in the White House." Such pressure goes along with the "stop-sign" mentality wherein the electioneering promise of a "stop sign" can be fulfilled— the stop sign erected—when "peace" replaces the terrorist threat.

Former President Oscar Arias of Costa Rica received the Nobel Peace Prize and the international acclaim that accompanies it for having brought about the Esquipulas Accords which allegedly brought "democracy" to Nicaragua. President Arzú of Guatemala expected a "pat on the back" at the Fifth Iberian-American Summit; perhaps he expects the Nobel Peace Prize after the accords. But the disinformation operations of the HL Support, which have often led to U.S. pressure, are probably the most important instrument for obtaining these accords.[94] Motivations are to some extent speculative, but the realities of the accord process and the accords themselves are not.

Alvaro Enrique Arzú Irigoyen was elected Guatemalan president in a runoff election of 7 January 1996. The month before, while still a candidate, he had a secret meeting with the URNG terrorists in El Salvador, allegedly to promote the "peace process." Taking office on 14 January 1996, President Arzú was in Mexico City a month later (20

February) in a "historical contact" as the first Guatemalan president to meet with the Guatemalan terrorists. From this point President Arzú has shrugged off every provocation by these terrorists and continued to assure all and sundry that he will make peace. Various sources have told LANS that peace through surrender is always possible. A few days later (27 February) the terrorists showed their contempt for President Arzú by ambushing a military patrol, killing one and wounding nine, in Playa Grande (Quiche Department).

In March the "General Staff" of the terrorists announced from its seat in Mexico that it was ordering a cease-fire. President Arzú then ordered the Army to cease all counterinsurgency operations and hurried to the military base at Playa Grande (21 March) "to personally order the cease-fire." The terrorists promptly carried out an "attack" on a barracks in the northwest of the country, an attack which Arzú "denounced." A few days later President Arzú "warned" the terrorists that their "propaganda armada" put the treaty with the Army "at risk." With regard to this sequence of events, a Guatemalan source paraphrased the Khrushchev remark, "You spit in his eye, and he calls it dew." In the meantime, the Arzú government turned over "concrete" proposals on the "socioeconomic and agrarian" conditions which the terrorists had been demanding.

The eruptions of the terrorists continued, the Army, under orders from its commander-in-chief, Arzú, doing nothing when, toward the end of March, the terrorists brazenly entered Siquinala, ninety miles from the capital, disarmed the police, then left. In early April the terrorists announced that they would "reduce" but not suspend the so-called "war tax," a simple extortion practiced on anyone from whom money can be obtained. Since 20 March then, the Arzú government has suspended all military actions to be sneered at and taunted in return by continuing terrorist operations.

The terrorists have applied a "carrot and stick" control method to the Arzú government, dangling the carrot of "peace" before the president, then whacking him with the stick of contempt, only to be showered with fresh concessions. In June Peace Commission (COPAZ) president Gustavo Porras told reporters of his optimism about "a solid and definitive advance of the negotiations," and almost immediately the terrorists occupied La Democracia (Escuintla), one of them posing prettily with an M-60[95] for the AFP photographer. The performance may well be rewarded with a Nobel Peace Prize for the Guatemalan president; indeed, he told the Fourth Iberian-American Summit on 10

November that Guatemala is on the point of "successfully closing the pacification process in Central America." But this will call for considerable funding, most to be given to the terrorists.

On 28 May 1996 Planning Secretary Mariano Rayo told the AFP that some $2.3 billion will be required for "the reinsertion" of the terrorists into "productive life," the "reduction" of the Army and the "reeducation of the Armed Forces." Elsewhere, restriction of internal security tasks to a national police has been mentioned and can probably be expected. In short, the same sort of victories by the terrorist which were won in the Chapultepec Accords for El Salvador have apparently been written into these Guatemalan "peace" accords.

Group of Friends of the Peace Process

The Group of Friends (GF) is an interestingly mixed bag of nations made up of the United States, Spain, Venezuela, Colombia, Norway, and Mexico. Perhaps most interesting in the group is Norway because of what LANS has learned of the relation of a Norwegian entity to the URNG terrorists. According to Guatemalan sources, most of the money for the URNG is laundered through the State Church of Norway, an organization which has likewise been reported supporting other terrorist groups in Latin America. The sources which have furnished this information feel that most, if not all, those directly involved with the State Church of Norway are unaware of what they are doing (*tontos utiles* again). It is interesting that Colombia, so unsuccessful in dealing with its own terrorists, is a member of this group, but Venezuela's involvement is probably a hangover from Carlos Andres Pérez (see chapter 2, "Venezuela").

But more interesting than the GF is the Foro Regional convoked for 22–23 February 1996 by the Central American Parliament (PARLACEN).

Foro Centroamérica por la Paz y la Reconciliación
(Central American Forum for Peace and Reconciliation)

In the Havana of 1989, Brazilian Lula da Silva and his mentor, Fidel Castro, put together the idea of the FSP (chapter 3, "The HL"). This HL grouping contains still active terrorist groups such as FARC and URNG and now allegedly "peaceful" groups such as the Salvadoran FMLN and the Nicaraguan FSLN. When PARLACEN and COPAZ president

Manuel Conde convoked a Foro Regional meeting he effectively called together the FSP members from El Salvador and Nicaragua, albeit, these are all now allegedly peaceful. The coincidence is fascinating.

The Central American Forum for Peace and Reconciliation (FCPR) was actually convoked in order "to seek actions which smooth the road toward effective pacification and generation of development in the region." For this alleged purpose the following were invited:

From the Nicaraguan FSLN (orthodox) Tomás Borge, from the FSLN ("reformed") Domingo Salazar and Ricardo Zambrana, from the Salvadoran FMLN Eugenio Chicas and Sigfrido Reyes, from the FMLN ("reformed") Ana Guadelupe and Jorge Meléndez and from the Nicaraguan Democratic Action Party (PADN) "the Counterfeit Contra" (see "Nicaragua" below) Edén Pastora. This is the corollary of a money-laundering operation wherein the Narco Syndicate (Foro São Paulo) launders its dirty money through a dummy corporation (the FCPR). Although it is partially speculative, the details of the Guatemalan "peace" accords which have surfaced to this time could well have been formulated by this group of former terrorists.

One More Blow of the Stick

The URNG "peace process" was to have been reinitiated in Mexico City on 9–11 November 1996 under UN moderator Jean Arnault, but the terrorists delivered one more blow: the kidnapping of eighty-six-year-old Olga de Novella and her exchange (19 October 1996) for the captive terrorist chief Rafael Augusto Baldizon Nuñez (a.k.a. Commandante Isaias). That "tensions and doubts" were "provoked by the kidnapping and exchange" (*Prensa Libre* [Guatemala], 9 November 1996) appears to be true enough, but the Guatemalan government again demonstrated its "carrot-and-stick" subservience with its docile return to the "negotiation table."

THE REALITY OF GUATEMALAN TERRORISM, 1995
(SPCL 2.13, 15 NOVEMBER 196)

AMBASSADOR CURTIN WINSOR[96]

In 1994 and 1995 a public-affairs blitz by the self-proclaimed "wife" of a Guatemalan terrorist attracted the sympathetic attention of the Clinton National Security Council (NSC) Staff and the U.S. media (to be discussed in chapter 4, "Target Guatemala"). It could have derailed Guatemala's return to law and order. [It did not, but it may have been to some extent responsible for President Arzú's surrender to URNG demands—Ed.] Ms. Jennifer Harbury claims that her alleged lover, the Guatemalan terrorist Efraín Bámaca Velásquez, was captured and killed in 1992 by Guatemalan military forces.

Any deliberate killing of prisoners, if it occurs, is lamentable. However, it must be noted that Guatemala is a country which has come a long way toward democracy, in spite of a civil war which has claimed the lives of 100,000 Guatemalans. It is no longer the institutionally violent land ruled by the military in the 1970s and 1980s; it is a land which, in less than ten years, has progressed from almost no democracy to a series of successful presidential and congressional elections and the accompanying transfer of power among political parties.

The process has been less than perfect, Guatemala still having deep societal problems which will take years to eliminate completely. But what is most important is the continuation of Guatemalan progress toward true democracy and its most important concomitant, the rule of law. For this conflict has its roots in ancient enmities and a violent history of injustice and vigilanteeism which arose from conflicts between the Spanish landowning class and the country's huge unassimilated Indian majority the diversity of which is capsuled in twenty-two language groups. In recent years Guatemala has sought to do some justice to the Indians of the country's mountainous region while *the Marxist terrorists of the URNG and its allies have continuously used their terrorism to provoke and reignite these conflicts based on ancient wrongs.*

The Army of Guatemala has engaged in a brutal conflict with these guerrillas and terrorists since 1966, a conflict in which it has used systematic violence against groups of people associated, or believed to be associated, with the guerrillas, whose principal organization is now the URNG. These are communist guerrillas trained in or by Cuba and, later, by the Sandinistas in Nicaragua; they have never numbered more than 2000. These terrorists were responsible for the cold-blooded murder of U.S. Ambassador Gordon Mein on the streets of Guatemala City in 1968. They have killed numerous other Americans, to say nothing of Guatemalans and others, since that time.

The URNG has successfully used terrorism to provoke government responses and counterbrutality to an extent out of all proportion to its numbers. Its depredations are a "re-igniter" for the dwindling forest fires of violence in a Guatemalan society which is moving away from institutionalized violence, as it practices political democracy with increasing success.

The struggle between the violence-prone Guatemalan military and the small and public-affairs savvy terrorist/guerrilla URNG has entered a peace process with the signing of the Comprehensive Human Rights Accord of 1994. The Guatemalan people are tired of violence from whatever source and desperately want peace. However, the URNG, numbering fewer than 500 but with a disproportionate share of the publicity, seems willing to delay the peace process, hoping to obtain power sharing and major concessions from the next Government of Guatemala. [When this was written the "next Government of Guatemala" would be the Arzú government—Ed.] Which brings us back to Jennifer Harbury.

She has created sympathy for the URNG outside Guatemala and has given that terrorist group increased leverage at the bargaining table while her supporters have increased pressures to settle on the terrorists' terms with threats of retaliation against the beleaguered Guatemalan government. The resident leftists of the Clinton-administration NSC have cut off all assistance to Guatemala, even the International Military Education Training (IMET) funds being used to create a non-military police force! As a result, peace negotiations have been halted, the URNG has reinitiated violence, ambushing isolated military outposts. The Army may again be forced to become actively engaged, and the terrorist sympathizers are ready with human rights monitors who excuse any activity by the left-wing commandants while seeking the worst from the non-leftists in uniform.

The guerrillas and their foreign sympathizers have adopted Ms. Jennifer Harbury's allegations as a plausible excuse for excoriating Guatemala. Harbury is a Harvard lawyer, longtime supporter of the URNG and, more recently, the self-proclaimed "commonlaw" wife of an allegedly deceased URNG commandant. (Bámaca's parents deny this relationship.) She has used tears and widow's weeds to arouse sympathy in the U.S. Congress among those who have never liked anyone in the military and never disliked a leftist commandant.

She has become a major U.S. news item and she is calling for U.S. aid and trade cut-offs to "punish" Guatemala. Her guerrilla comrades (managers?) hope that the outcry she seeks to evoke will kindle enough chaos to force a military intervention which can only benefit her Marxist guerrilla friends. Any response by the Guatemalan Army entailing repression and brutality would assist the guerrillas, among other things, in reopening their precarious Scandinavian money sources. Such a scenario could transform Guatemala from a struggling neo-democracy to the pariah state which the guerrillas, Jennifer Harbury, and some of her friends on the Clinton NSC staff would apparently welcome. An unambiguous, right-wing pariah state would help Mort Halperin, Bob Fineberg et al. take the heat off Cuba, and it would enable them again to support "reformers from the left."

For Guatemala to achieve the rule of law necessary to continued democracy, the peace process must continue. Both sides must renounce violence, the guerrillas must cease their provocative attacks. [Almost one-and-a-half years after this was written, these terrorists have not yet ceased these attacks—Ed.] The government must guarantee civilian control over the military and an end to impunity for human rights violations of which both sides have been guilty. However, Guatemalan democratic development lacks adequate enforcement agencies.

The United States has an easily identified and constructive role to play in Guatemala, if the leftists of Clinton's NSC would give it a chance. Far from terminating AID to Guatemala, we should be supplying it through the IMET program which is creating civilian-controlled police forces to replace a Guatemalan Army which is trained and equipped to kill terrorists. There exists in Guatemala no middle ground whence law and order can be provided and the vigilanteeism of the right-wing Mano Blanco,[97] for example, rendered indefensible. The U.S. objective for Guatemala, as with El Salvador, must be democracy in practice, not occasional democratic acts called elections. The key to Guatemalan democracy is the protection of citizens against terror from either left or right so they may build an economy, create employment, and generate savings. This can only be achieved by a trained law enforcement organization which can act without that level of force necessary to military operations.

The United States must help Guatemala by supporting the peace process, not by pressuring that country to give the URNG terrorists any concessions beyond a safe stand down and possible economic adjustment assistance. We must not allow ourselves to fall into traps opened by the tears of a very dubious "widow" and leading to ultimate chaos in Guatemala. A properly trained police force will go a long way toward enabling a much needed peace, a peace in the attainment of which the United States can play a modest, but very useful, role.

URNG REIGN OF TERROR (WKLY 2.16, 28 NOVEMBER 1996)

Until quite recently the Arzú government of Guatemala has continued to subject its citizens to terrorist depredations with its "Peace at

Any Price" policy. One of the most recent examples of this occurred at Finca María de Lourdes (Quetzaltenango Department) on 23 November 1996.

Fifteen armed terrorists, dressed in olive drab and identifying themselves as URNG, broke into the home of Ismael Fernández Gonzales, age seventy-six, murdered him and one of his men and robbed the place before leaving.

The next day, Agricultural Chamber president Humberto Preti reported that the agricultural community is seriously concerned over this "reign of terror" through which, previous to the signing of the "peace," the fincas in the interior of the country are living.

Preti went on to say that twelve fincas have recently been assaulted by such groups which are operating with complete impunity since neither the Army nor the National Police—clearly at the order of President Arzú—are doing anything to oppose them.

Whether or not these terrorists in olive drab and identifying themselves as URNG are actually in that terrorist organization, their identification as such gives them a "safe conduct" for whatever terrorist activity they wish to carry out.

President Preti's remarks apparently awoke President Arzú from his dream of peace and peace prizes, for, on 25 November 1996, the Guatemalan president gave the order to the Armed Forces to begin operations against these terrorists whether or not they are part of the URNG.

El Salvador

THE POSSIBILITY OF A URNG "VICTORY THROUGH PEACE"
(SPCL 1.6, 26 JUNE 1996)

[While this article was developed with relation to the previous section, "Guatemala," it basically relates to El Salvador—Ed.]

In Wkly 1.7 (above) the apparently emerging "peace" agreement between the Guatemalan government and the URNG terrorists was discussed, it being pointed out that the same powers are supporting this as supported the Chapultepec Accords (CA)[98] which allegedly brought "peace" to El Salvador. If such is the case, these CA comprise necessary background to serious consideration of the apparently emerging accords with the URNG. A word of background on the Farabundo Martí National Liberation Front (FMLN) is first demanded.

In the Sandinista Managua of 1980, under the aegis of Cuban AD chairman Redbeard Piñiero, five Salvadoran terrorist groups were united into the FMLN. The five groups were the People's Liberation Forces (FPL), the Revolutionary Army of the People (ERP), the National Revolutionary Armed Forces (FARN), the Central American Workers Party (PRTC), and the Liberation Armed Forces (FAL). *All of these groups had arisen, directly or indirectly, from the CP of El Salvador, PCES*, the first of them during the 1960s when Cayetano Carpio (a.k.a. Marcial), in typical ML "theater," had "broken" with the PCES because it was "too peaceful." Further detail on their evolution is unnecessary here.

There was a confrontation between the Salvadoran Armed Forces (FAES) and the FMLN terrorists at the latitude of the Río Frío, San Vicente Department, El Salvador, on 29 June 1991 in which the Farabundi chief, Camilo Turcios, was killed. The LANS editor was asked to translate the cache of documents found on the cadaver. These documents, when compared with the CA, demonstrate the success of the terrorist plan for "victory through negotiation" in a "war" which continued only because international pressure prevented the FAES from cleaning out the privileged sanctuaries from which the Farabundis operated.

These sanctuaries were of two varieties, the first consisting of a string of "refugee" camps, actually villages, which stretched in a band across the northern tier of Salvadoran states and which FAES was not permitted to enter. Routinely, a "refugee" camp would be empty of able-bodied personnel when a terrorist operation was in progress nearby, only to fill again after the operation concluded. The second group of sanctuaries consisted of the so-called *bolsones teritoriales* (territorial pockets) along the border between Honduras and El Salvador, territory which was in dispute between the two nations as a result of the 1968 "Soccor War" between Honduras and El Salvador.

The largest of the *bolsones* was above Morazan Department wherein by 1989 the self-styled "general staff"—Comandancia General[99]—of the Farabundi terrorists maintained a presence. This staff varied somewhat, but a typical lineup included overall boss and head of both PCES and FAL Shafik Handal (b. 1931, Palestine), Joaquín Villalobos of ERP, Eduardo Castañeda of PRTC, Leonel González of FPL, and Ernesto Jovel (a.k.a. Roberto Roca) of FARN. The LANS editor, from the command post at Corinto, has observed a terrorist detachment evading a military trap in a thunderstorm, then slipping across the Honduran border to sanctuary in this bolson. Campesinos from both sides of the border have attested to him of frequently observing these terrorists moving through Honduran territory to their bolson haven.

Protected by their sanctuaries and supported largely by the propaganda of the HL Support, the FMLN terrorists were able to maintain themselves while the interminable negotiations continued, strongly supported by the United States and the U.S.S.R., until the terrorists obtained what they had been seeking in the CA. That the FMLN did attain most of what it had been seeking may be demonstrated by comparing their desires, as taken from the Turcios documents, to the Accords.

In what follows the paraphrase statement in the CA appears as numbers 1 through 4 referring to CA chapter. CA chapter 1 (pp. 1–10) deals with the FAES, chapter 2 (pp. 11ff.) with the National Police, and so forth. The portion of the Turcios documents referring to 1 appears as 1a, 1b,...and are followed by tp. 131,...referring to the editor-ordered set of page numbers. Thus, "1. A process..." is the CA "agreement" on FAES, 1a. "...it is...", 1b. "(5)..." from the captured documents.

CHAPTER 1

1. A process of purification[100] of the Armed Forces is to take place, to be carried out by an Ad Hoc Commission.

1a. "...it is basic that FAES [be] reformed, reduced and [given] a change in its military doctrine...this we will manage strictly in private with whom[ever] the CG considers [appropriate] and the opportune moment will be decided to put it on the table as [a] negotiating proposal. The idea is to create a new PC [Communist Party] in union with GOES [Salvadoran Government], FMLN integrated into all the territory..." [tp. 131]

1b. "(5) Purification of the FAES will be implemented through an evaluation and within a plan of re-education, in accordance with a list pacted by both parties." [tp. 138]

CHAPTER 2

2. It was agreed that the Armed Forces be reduced based on criteria agreed upon by the government and the FMLN. These criteria include the size of the reduced force, the form, the schooling and other factors.

2a. "Also [the] body of officers and chiefs of the END [National Army of Democracy (FMLN)] is to be integrated in [the] FAES in order to bring about the process of reform, reduction and change of the military doctrine..."

2b. "At stake is a solid integration of our permanent forces…our local bases in the participation of our military chiefs in the General Staff and in the destacamento[101] and brigade command of FAES. Changing of the military doctrine to [include] different political tendencies: (a) drastic reduction of FAES[102]; (b) Reforms based on dissolution…[of] nibs of the Armed Forces; (c) New military doctrine…"[103] (tp. 134–5)

2c. (Demands secrecy on the preparation of the draft which there was.) (tp. 135)

2d. "The military school and its curriculum…will be reorganized and…restrictions…for entry will be abolished. [The] direction of the school will be…FAE[S], FMLN,…" (tp. 138)

2e. "(6) FAES will initiate a gradual plan of reduction to 10,000 effectives…" (tp. 138)

CHAPTER 3

The doctrine of FAES will be redefined…It is fundamentally accepted that the mission of the Armed Forces is to defend the national sovereignty of the state.[104]

3a.(2d). 3b (2b). 3C "(2) Change of [the] preambular thesis of accord on FAES and integration of the National Police (PNC). This is a solution to the problem of the future of armies. This is a substantive basis for the change in the secondary phase."[105] (tp. 135)

4. "Ex-combatants of the FMLN will be able to join the National Police…if the aspirants have abandoned…the armed battle. (p. 24 of CA)

4a. "Most important…for the organization of the new PNC a commission with the FMLN-GOES was formed under UNOSAL (UN El Salvador)." (tp. 132) [Such a commission was formed—Ed.]

4b. "[FMLN] personnel to command in the PNC…" (tp. 131)

4c. "Negotiation of a new police law…" (tp. 137)

With the CA the Farabundis entered the political arena with a power which neither their military nor their political impotence would have gained for them, and their chiefs, most notably Shafik Handal, simply transformed themselves from clandestine members of the HL to open members of the FSP. Now a Salvadoran legislator, CP chief Handal visits Havana as regularly as before but not as secretly, appearing as the principal Salvadoran representative at FSP meetings as recently as the Encounter concluded in Havana on 16 June 1996 where he presided over the organizing committee. The URNG, also important to the FSP, will apparently follow the same path, gaining political power and shedding clandestinity following adoption of the Guatemalan Peace Accords.

Nicaragua

[The Nicaraguan situation during 1996 was largely concerned with the second of the general elections since the Esquipulas Accords allegedly brought "democracy" to that nation to replace the rule of the terrorist, now allegedly former terrorist, Sandinista National Liberation Front (FSLN). These elections have been treated in chapter 1. The FSLN remains an active part of the HL, however, Daniel Ortega and Tomás Borge frequent visitors to Castro's Havana. The following Nicaraguan material arose in connection with other matters—Ed.]

ORTEGA AND QADDAFI (WKLY 1.6, 13 JUNE 1996)

In late May *Barricada* (Managua) announced that the FSLN will award its highest decoration, the Order of Sandino, to Mu'ammar Qaddafi, apparently because of his financing of the Ortega election campaign.

EDÉN PASTORA GÓMEZ, "THE COUNTERFEIT CONTRA"
(SPCL 2.3, 29 AUGUST 1996)

Edén is a communist. He breathes through the nose of Fidel Castro; he sees through the eyes of Fidel Castro; he hears through the ears of Fidel Castro.
> —Félix Pastora, Edén's brother, in an interview
> with the LANS editor, 29 November 1987

"I am a Sandinista, a revolutionary and an anti-imperialist," declared Edén Pastora Gómez in Costa Rica (25 July 1987), adding later that "I see myself as president of Nicaragua" (EFE, 12 April 1993). This terrorist prototype, not fated to be president in 1997, left his Sandinista comrades in 1981, either out of pique because he was the tenth man in a government allegedly run by nine, or with the deliberate objective of destroying the anti-Sandinista resistance in the south.

Pastora was born (b. 1937, Ciudad Darío) into a family of staunch Conservatives engaged in farming and ranching. He attended a Jesuit high school in Granada, a Conservative stronghold where he met a man who would be his top commander on the Contra Southern Front, Luís "Wicho" Rivas Leal.[106] Rivas describes "Indian" as short, stocky and a "tough guy," but a dull student. Graduating in 1956, Indian spent a token period at a college in Mexico which introduced him to communism.

Carlos Fonseca Amador formed the New Nicaragua Movement (MNN) in 1958–1959, then the Nicaraguan Patriotic Youth (JPN) in 1960.[107] Pastora was among the handful in this MNN, thus making him a charter member of the FSLN founded July 1961. In his first year as Cuban dictator Castro staged the *opéra bouffe* fifty-man "invasion" of Nicaragua wherein Fonseca was wounded and in which Pastora allegedly took part. For a number of years "the Counterfeit Contra" was an underground member of the FSLN as was the co-founder of that terrorist group, Silvio Mayorga. At that time Pastora was known as a bodyguard for Conservative Party president Fernando Aguero, later a member of the ruling triumvirate. It was during his bodyguard phase that Pastora figured prominently in the armed "demonstration" of 22 January 1967. Picked up with a jeep-load of guns he was bringing into Managua, he was jailed until the amnesty Somoza Debayle declared on his reelection.

During the ensuing years and after the death of Fonseca, the FSLN split into three factions, one claiming the "Yenan Way," one the "Leningrad Way," and, available "ways" having been utilized, the last the Third "Way" (Terceristas). This was all of course camouflage for a power struggle. Since Pastora's deadly enemy, Borge, was in one group, Edén migrated to another, that of the Ortegas (Terceristas). And then came the Borge hunt for Edén with lethal intention, a drama involving his protection by Wicho Rivas, Carlos Coronel, and "Negro" Chamorro, the upshot of it being that he was in Costa Rica in 1976 when the Sandinista Southern Front, a Tercerista operation, began to take shape. But Borge calls for an aside.

Just two years ago this former terrorist showed the power he still wields although having had no official position in Nicaragua since 1989. John Hull, a particular enemy of the Sandinistas who will be discussed in chapter 4 (see "Target NACR") found this out during his escape from Nicaragua in the course of which he was, at 0830 on 7 February 1995, swimming the Río Guasable to safety in Honduras. About half way across he was spotted, and a number of military/police personnel came boiling out of the customs building, shouting that he must be stopped, "¡Borge tiene recompensa!...¡Borge tiene recompensa!" John arrived unscathed on the Honduran left bank to be told by the Honduran police that Borge had a price of $10,000 on his head, dead or alive, the sergeant remarking ruefully that this was twice his yearly salary.

In an amusing episode, Pastora was shipped to Qaddafi's no-booze Libya for guerrilla-terrorist training, hard duty for a man who enjoyed his tipple. A cry to Pepe Figueras for help, and the Costa Rican dispatched Kiki Carreras, the illegitimate son of his longtime chaplain, to save Edén. Kiki got no farther than the bar of the Havana Hilton before finding that "the Counterfeit Contra" had already saved himself.

In early 1978 Rivas was living in Choluteca, Honduras, working under German Pomares on the Sandinista Northern Front. In May Pastora arrived, demanding guns of the "type carried by the Nicaraguan National Guard." Wicho obliged, even providing the old G-3[108] rifle, obtained from a prominent Honduran politician, which would appear on the poster. He arranged Pastora's route to Managua. The terrorist attack on the National Palace (22 August 1978), admired by individuals who should have known better, followed and Pastora became "Commandante Cero." It was here that his second-in-command, Dora María Tellez, was hard pressed to prevent her near-berserk boss from wrecking the operation.

Pastora percolated to Costa Rica, becoming a sort of Sandinista ambassador *extraordinaire* with many doors opening to him after the Palace, particularly in Panama and Venezuela where he became one more protégé of Carlos Andres Pérez. He became one of the key men, if not the key man, in arranging the shipment of arms to the FSLN from these two countries. Possessed of the guns, the Sandinistas filled the vacuum created by the ouster of Somoza Debayle, and Pastora moved to Managua where he became, first, vice minister of the Interior Department under his deadly enemy, Borge, then deputy minister of the Defense Department. On 7 July 1981 Pastora made his exit by automobile from Managua but not before having demonstrated his typical ML brutality as described, for example, by the U.S. ambassador to Costa Rica, Curtin Winsor,[109] who tells us of his involvement "in the initial bloody revenge against members of Somoza's Guardia."[110]

After leaving Nicaragua (7 July 1981) Pastora proceeded to Castro's Cuba and Qaddafi's Libya whence he did not emerge for a year. He reappeared in Costa Rica in the spring of 1982, performing in a press conference there on 15 April. Fresh from Castro's Cuba, he declared

his opposition to the Nicaraguan Nine Sandinista Commanders model-
ing their government after that of Fidel. The U.S. government apparently took these declarations seriously, for this typically embittered, if
histrionically and charismatically gifted, Bolshevik assumed the mantle
of leadership in the Nicaraguan Anti-Communist Resistance as Democratic Revolutionary Alliance (ARDE) military chief. As Ambassador
Winsor put it:

> Pastora has never accomplished a positive military accomplishment as guerrilla
> leader, even when he had significant amounts of supplies and trained men at his
> disposal from 1983–1984...[he] effectively 'sterilized' Nicaragua's southern
> frontier as a source of credible threat to the communist Sandinistas from 1982
> to 1985, by occupying it and making it difficult to use the frontier for effective
> guerrillas...[111]

This viewpoint has been substantiated to the LANS editor in interviews with his brother, with his chief of staff, Rivas, and with other of
his subordinate commanders. For example, Félix, who spent ten months
in the jungle with his brother during the 1984–1985 period, has testified to hearing him talking on the radio to Managua with the Ortegas,
with Nicaraguan KGB (DGSE) chief Lenín Cerna and with other
"former" comrades and in this or in some other way maintaining a liaison with them. But Pastora was apparently involved in something more
than simple "contact," as two examples should demonstrate.

"Luna Roja" was the code name for the narrow strip of Nicaraguan
territory fronting Costa Rica from about El Castillo to about San Carlos
where the San Juan River emerges from Lake Nicaragua. On 7 June
1983 Wicho Rivas began his attack on Luna Roja with a mortar barrage
which sent the green Sandinista troops flying and allowed him to mop
up the strip within three days. He was preparing to take the powerful El
Castillo from the demoralized Sandinistas and secure the strip when
Pastora stepped in. First, he recalled Rivas to San José, replacing him
with Julio Bigotes (a.k.a. Miguel Urroz) whom the men believed to be
a Sandinista plant and under whom they refused to serve. Of the 300
campesinos Wicho had in Luna Roja, all but 27 simply disappeared
when Bigotes assumed command.

Pastora withdrew his troops from around San Carlos and in Luna
Roja and concentrated them at Tango Base, north of the San Juan, in
the face of a known Sandinista buildup at San Carlos. Three days
later, as if on schedule, the FSLN came down river by boat, with
heavy mortars, destroyed Tango and its satellites[112] driving the bloody
remnants across the San Juan. As Rivas, and other commanders not to

be named, told the LANS editor, "You didn't know who the enemy was, really. I thought of his [Pastora's] being an FSLN plant, I thought of it many times."

During that fall of 1983 more and more of Pastora's old sidekicks, now anti-Sandinistas, were removed from positions of authority and replaced by "such as José Davila, Carlos Prado and so on." Commandante Leonel Poveda remarked to Wicho, "We are too anti-Sandinista." Rivas finally gave up in disgust and went to the United States but not before other similar experiences, one of which is worthy of recounting. He had warned Pastora against his projected attack on San Juan del Norte where the river empties into the Atlantic. "You can't hold it," Wicho told him. "The Sandinistas will send down whatever force is necessary to retake it and all you'll get is casualties." After three attempts and heavy casualties Pastora took it, briefly established his "Free Republic of San Juan del Norte," and matters proceeded as Rivas had predicted.

Hugo Spadafora was a Panamanian physician who fought with the FSLN against the Somoza government on the Southern Front. He turned against the Sandinistas after they came to power, and, by 1985, he was leading the Contra Indians out of Costa Rica. On 15 September 1985 his decapitated body was found on Costa Rican soil a few kilometers from the Panamanian border. There are two general sources of information tending to indicate Pastora's involvement in the murder: (1) the testimony of his commanders; and (2) letters and diaries appearing in *Critica* (Panama).[113] Pastora's subordinate commanders believe him to have had ample motive:

They testify that Spadafora was strongly opposed to the narco-trafficking activities of Pastora and Sebastian González; he told Edén to cease and desist or he was going to the press. Testimony on Pastora's involvement in such activities has been given to the LANS editor by these commandants and a source then involved with U.S. intelligence. Comandante A recounted an incident the year before in which Pastora allegedly attempted to kill Spadafora.

In June 1984 various Contra detachments were operating in the mountains of southern Nicaragua, Spadafora leading a detachment of Indians (Miskito, Sumo, Ramo) at the same time. Spadafora was the only "white man" in the detachment. Pastora went on the air and told six of his subordinate commanders to kill the "hombre blanco" (white man) with the Indians as a "traitor" when and if they encountered him.

Six days before his death Hugo visited Comandante B in Iscazu, a San José suburb, and allegedly learned that Noriega was furnishing

Carol Prado, a Pastora confidant, $50,000 per month for Pastora to support the infiltration of Spadafora's group. About 0700 on 12 September, Spadafora called Comandante A and said he was going to Panama the next day, information he had communicated to two friends of Pastora at a meeting in the Hotel Costa Rica the day before.

Critica, which Hugo's brother Winston would not believe, published what it claimed to be (1) a letter from Spadafora to the MISURASATA [114](Indian) leader, Brooklin Rivera, a copy of which he sent to his wife, (2) a letter from Pastora to his "security chief," Julio Bigotes, and (3) entries from Spadafora's diary. All are in holograph. The sentence, "Edén has given orders to assassinate me," forms a cogent part of points (1) and (3) above. Pastora's letter is alleged by the periodical to be an order to kill Spadafora, although it is so allegorical as to mean almost anything. While dismissing *Critica* out of hand as a "Noriega paper," Winston Spadafora did tell the LANS editor that (1) Noriega and Pastora were partners in a business enterprise and (2) while the special prosecutor in his brother's case never brought up Pastora's name, he did bring up the name of Sebastian González whom Comandante A testified had been accused by Spadafora of complicity with Pastora in narcotrafficking.

Far from supporting a characterization of Edén Pastora as a "legendary leader," the evidence strongly supports the characterization of him as "the Counterfeit Contra."

AUGUSTO CALDERÓN SANDINO (SPCL 2.12, 2 NOVEMBER 1996)

Augusto Calderón Sandino is the titular deity of the FSLN. Admirers of Sandino are to be found among admirers of the Sandinistas, among haters of the Somoza Dynasty, and among those who profess the "Big O for Objectivity." Unfortunately, many of those in the last two categories have been victimized by a press which, in the latter part of this century, has been all too kind to Mr. Sandino. With the FSLN at least out of the Nicaraguan Executive on 20 October 1996 it would appear appropriate to put to rest one more of "las leyendas...echadas a rodar el mundo" (the legends...cast forth to wander the world) as Dr. Emanuiloff-Max has phrased it.

Augusto Sandino (b. 18 May 1895) was the "natural child" of Gregorio Sandino, of a well-to-do Niquinohomo family, and Margarita Calderón, an Indian servant. Gregorio had no intention of making an honest woman out of Margarita, and she drifted off, apparently never to be sought for or heard of again. Augusto was taken into the Sandino household as Augusto Calderón Sandino; had he been legitimate he would of course have been Augusto Sandino Calderón. Sandino would later claim the "C" to stand for César, perhaps one of the first of his delusions of grandeur. In 1920 Sandino shot one Dagoberto Rivas in the leg, the latter having made certain remarks about his maternal ancestry, and fled to Honduras. Several years of wandering and fleeing through Mexico and Central America and he was back in Nicaragua on 1 June 1926, the leader of a bandit band four months later.

No attempt can be made here to trace Sandino's subsequent career, but the spirit of the man, so poorly presented in the latter twentieth century accounts which read like Romberg operettas, may be grasped from an example.

A vivid account of one of Sandino's murderous and meaningless raids against U.S. citizens working in Nicaragua appeared in the 27 April 1931 issue of *Time*. The week before the Standard Fruit and Steamship Company's *S. S. Cefalu* had delivered thirty still-horrified survivors of this raid to New Orleans. The survivors had brought with them two of the nine U.S. citizens murdered "by bandit followers of Rebel Augusto Sandino." From their stories *Time* reporters put together an account of the bloodthirsty action which had taken place two weeks before.

Logtown was a small lumber settlement seventy miles inland from Puerto Cabezas which is on the Atlantic Coast about sixty miles south along that coast from the Honduran border. Early one morning a Logtown commissary clerk saw Sandino's bandits emerging from the jungle, screamed "Help" over the telephone to the Wawa Junction operator and fled. With the usual "Viva Sandino" these original "Sandinistas" fell on John Phelps, a Standard Fruit timber inspector, killed him and hacked him to bits. Their blood lust aroused, they threw the Standard Fruit lumberman, Joseph Luther Pennington, into the river, then shot him full of holes. Waking up planter Richard Davis, they murdered him, cut off his head and stuck it on a fence post.

Meanwhile, the Wawa Junction operator had called Puerto Cabezas for help, and U.S. Marine Capt. Harlen Pefley, Standard Fruit Company inspector William Sesler, and a "handful" of Nicaraguan National Guardsmen were making their best speed along the narrow-gauge railway toward Logtown. They were "attacked"—the standard terrorist description of an ambush—near their destination. Pefler was killed, Sesler mortally wounded.

At Moss Farm Standard Fruit's overseers and their assistants had assembled for the run down the narrow gauge to safety when Sandino's thugs fell on them, butchering the overseers, John Humphrey Bryan, Percy Davis, Hubert Ogilivie Wilson, and William Bond, Jr. and hacking off their heads. Cathey Wilson saved herself by jumping into the Wawa River where she hid for two days; James Lloyd took to a ditch and feigned death until the bandits left.

Nine U.S. citizens and eight other foreign nationals were murdered. The Nicaraguans who may be assumed to have also been murdered would hardly have been any happier about the situation than were the foreigners, but *Time* was understandably concerned only with the "gringos."[115]

At the time there were some 300 U.S. citizens resident in Puerto Cabezas who were described by *Time* as "panic stricken" at the news from Logtown, a panic compounded by the report that Sandino's bandits had fired Gracias a Dios sixty miles north along the coast. In the general panic women and children boarded the *Cefalu* and civilians were arming themselves for the defense of Puerto Cabezas when the U.S. gunboat *Asheville* arrived with a detachment of Marines. These were disembarked and the "slim force" of Nicaraguan National Guardsmen hurried off into the jungle after Sandino's Sandinistas.

The U.S. gunboat *Sacramento* arrived down the coast at Bluefields as did the *Rochester*, flagship of the Special Service Squadron from Panama. When the U.S. cruiser arrived at Puerto Cabezas, the *Asheville* moved up the coast to Cracias a Dios. But, other than relieving the National Guardsmen at Puerto Cabezas, U.S. fighting forces did nothing. Which hardly pleased those citizens who had gotten out of the jungle alive. Why, they were asking, did not the United States go after the bandit Sandino as they had other such in the past.

In Washington, D.C., Secretary of State Henry Stimson was composing the answer to this question in accordance with President Herbert Hoover's decision to mute U.S. military strength in Central America. Less than a week after the slaughter of the nine U.S. citizens, Stimson dispatched the following directive to U.S. diplomats in Nicaragua:

> You will advise American citizens that the Government cannot undertake general protection of Americans throughout the country with American forces. To do so would lead to difficulties and commitments which the Government does not propose to undertake. The Department recommends to all Americans who do not feel secure...to withdraw from the country or at least to coast towns whence they can be protected or evacuated. Those who remain do so at their own risk and must not expect American forces to be sent inland to their aid.

This action reversed the Coolidge policy of protecting U.S. citizens and their property wherever they happened to be, but it had been decided upon the previous February by the Hoover Administration. President Hoover stuck to his guns, and, although Secretary Stimson was "pained" by the outcry against his "running up the white flag," his 1927 report to President Coolidge had called for U.S. withdrawal from Nicaragua when that country should be rehabilitated.

"Nicaragua was a 'special case,'" Stimson explained. "The principle of U.S. protection for U.S. interest has not been abandoned, but the Sandino bandits were no better than Mohawk Indians in colonial times; last fortnight's butchers could not be compared to the [Nicaraguan] civil war of 1926 when two regular armies were in the field and the Marines were used to guard neutral zones for the protection of foreigners...The problem before the Government today is not a problem of protection of its citizens from a war but from murder and assassination...We have a situation where small groups of confessed outlaws are making their way through the jungle with the avowed intent of murdering and pillaging."

The basis of this realistic account is the *Time* article of 27 April 1931. Since that time many accounts have transferred the blemishes of the titular deity of Sandinism, Augusto Calderón Sandino, to his opponents.

HL Terrorist Organizations: Montoneros; Coalitions

THE MONTONEROS (SPCL 2.6, 19 SEPTEMBER 1996)

The career of General Juan Domingo Perón has been discussed briefly in chapter 2 (see "Argentina"). Perón was elected president of Argentina in 1946 to have his Corporate State begin to unravel on him in 1954. Fleeing into the Paraguayan Embassy and exile on 20 September 1955, he would return in October 1973 as Argentina's newly elected president, his death the following year seating his vice president and wife, Isabel, on the presidential throne. Her inability to deal with the escalating anarchy resulted in her removal by the military two years later, Perón's legacy having all but assured this.

General Perón—Colonel Kolynos[116] to his detractors—was a power seeker, not an ideologue, a fact which assured the presence within his ranks of the fascist (Corporate State) far left and the communist (Dictatorship of the Proletariat) far left. With Perón's exile began the emergence of that maze of terrorist groups of which only the best known, the Montoneros (Guerrillas), will be considered in any detail here. One of the first of these was the "Peronist Liberation Movement" which

Uturunco began as a camp for twenty guerrilla terrorists in the jungles of Tucumán Province.

The group was supported by John William Cooke[117] who had been a deputy in the First Peronist Congress and whom Perón, in his flight, left behind as his delegate and leader of his Resistencia. In March 1957 Cooke (1920–1968), of Irish extraction, escaped from Argentina's Río Gallegos Prison to Puenta Arenas, Chile, whence he was active in industrial agitation and the instigation of terrorist activity by small bands. His industrial agitation included the 1958 oil-workers strike and, in particular, the 1959 Lisandro de la Torre strike. He sought to turn the latter into a general, revolutionary strike and was jailed by President Frondizi. Taking advantage of the choice the terrorist had of leaving Argentina for good or serving his sentence, Cooke retired to Castroite Cuba in 1960, to return again with President Illia's amnesty.

In September of the year of Cooke's death (1968) the largest guerrilla camp yet discovered, that of the Destacamento Montonero 17 de Octubre (Seventeenth of October Guerrilla Detachment) was wiped out in Tucumán Province. And then in April 1969 occurred a terrorist operation which Emanuiloff-Max has compared to the 1948 Bogotazo, the Cordobazo, a six-hour terrorist takeover of that city (Cordoba) through "cold-blooded, premeditated terror…" In July 1969 a plan for international terrorism was found in Argentina, a plan prepared in Montevideo, annotated by the Paraguayan communist boss Oscar Creydt, approved by Cuban defense minister Raul Castro and later shown to provide the guidelines for the Cordobazo.

Between January and April of the next year, 1970, the Peronist Armed Forces (FAP), in conjunction with other terror groups, carried out a series of attacks on police, military and naval posts in the country, in particular, in remote areas. The stage had, deliberately or fortuitously, been set for the emergence of the Montoneros. With prodding and support from Castro's OLAS (see chapter 3, "The HL") in Havana, and with the influx from other radical left organizations to include that of Camilo Torres in Colombia (see chapter 3, "Colombia"), this terrorist organization apparently felt itself ready for its "revolution" by 1970. This it began that spring (30 May) with the kidnapping of former President Pedro Eugenio Aramburu. A communiqué from the organization "Montoneros," which therein described itself as "Peronist and Christian," declared that Aramburu would be shot on 1 June for his "anti-peronist measures." His body was finally found, shot in the back of the head, on 1 June. On that date a "synchronized mass action never before seen in Argentina" by heavily armed personnel identifying themselves as "Montoneros" took the strategic points in the city of Calera, twenty kilometers from Cordoba, and held them for one-half hour.

Montonero terrorism increased to what appears to have been its apogee on 26 July 1975 when, according to Weathers,[118] the Montoneros "were alleged to have had approximately 6,000 guerrillas engaged in some 250 independent...operations." However exaggerated these numbers may be, there is little question but that this was the apogee of the terrorist group's operations. By this time, Doña Isabel had succeeded to the presidential throne, a Doña Isabel quite incapable of dealing with the escalating lawlessness, particularly in, but not restricted to, Tucumán Province. This led an initially reluctant Argentine military to take a determined stand against the small minority which constituted that terrorist threat. Authors from Ravines[119] to Emanuiloff-Max[120] have stated the reality of Latin American terrorists or "guerrillas": *They are more frequently sociopaths, eager to vent their frustration on society, then ideologues, restless to ennoble it with bombs and guns.* In any event, the military action enjoyed a success which has been detailed by Weathers.

Contributing to this victory was the discovery of considerable infiltration of the Argentine government by the Montoneros and other terrorist groups, perhaps most importantly, the People's Revolutionary Army (ERP). For example, one prominent Montonero chief was identified as the son of former Interior Minister Vaca Narvaj, another as a former police chief. By the fall of 1977 the Argentine military forces reported that they had killed or jailed 80 percent of the terrorists.

While terrorist strength and success claims are often wildly exaggerated, one must also be circumspect in taking such assertions by the military at face value. In the matter of this terrorist elimination, however, events have demonstrated this military claim to be the simple truth. The Montoneros—and the ERP—simply evaporated from the landscape, the credit for kidnapping Under Secretary Miguel Tobias Padilla, claimed in 1978 by the former, being little more than an exception proving the rule.

The reality was to be found in the location of the Montonero "leaders" who were living in Mexico, apparently in comfortable retirement on the "liberated" funds which Castro was holding for them in Cuban banks. As the Montonero R. Galimberti would remark, "The Montoneros must be the only guerrillas...who lost all their troops but kept the money."

Perhaps the Montonero episode might be considered closed with Pres. Menem's pardon of their chief, Mario Eduardo Firmenich. Or can it? A recent AFP dispatch (13 August 1996) reported that Firmenich announced his return to political affairs through a "current of opinion supporting an alternate to neoliberalism." He does not rule out his candidacy in the 1999 elections although he does not yet know whether he will seek the presidency. He was described as having "ideas inspired by Catholicism and Peronism," this the terrorist whose murders included that of industrialist Francisco Soldati for which he was serving a life sentence when amnestied by President Menem.

Many had died and much had been destroyed for this anticlimactic result.

COLOMBIAN AND HIGH ANDES TERRORIST COALITIONS
(SPCL 1.4, 10 JUNE 1996)

[In chapter 3 ("Columbian Terrorism") the principal Colombian terrorist groups (FARC, ELN, EPL, M-19, FQL) have been discussed—Ed.]

Conservative Party president Belisario Betancur came to power in 1982, in August offering the "white flag" of truce to Colombian terrorists. As Colombian journalist Guillermo Zalamea remarked in latter 1985, "the famous peace of Betancur…has converted [the nation] into an urban and rural armed camp." Perhaps this was why preparations for the consolidation of Colombian terrorist groups into a national terrorist army were consummated that year. The first hint of such consolidation appeared on 28 August 1985 when the Army found plans for the logistic support necessary to a national terrorist army in the "safe house" of M-19 boss Ivan Marino Ospina. This army, the National Guerrilla Coordinating Group (CNG), was actually formed in the mountains of Cauca Department in September 1985, there being considerable legerdemain in the makeup of CNG, the FARC charade perhaps most obvious.

FARC was carrying on "peace" negotiations with the Colombian government under Betancur's "white flag" so it could not openly join CNG. However, its "dissident" Frente Ricardo Franco[121] could; therefore, in 1985 the original CNG allegedly contained only Frente Ricardo Franco, M-19, EPL, and FQL. However, when Colombian CP secretary general Vieira announced the emergence of CNG Simón Bolívar from CNG, FARC was specifically included as a member. (ELN's inclusion as a member had begun in 1986.) By mid-1995 CNG was claiming FARC, ELN, the "dissident" Jaime Bateman Cayon Front of M-19, and the "dissident" EPL group, their Comandante Guerrero in Costa Rica conditioning "peace" negotiations on the presence of "foreign observers."

In January 1996 (EFE, 8 January 1996) President Samper "repeated his intention of dialog with the armed groups," this (1) continuing the Betancur approach and (2) lumping the campesino self-defense forces[122] with the terrorists. In discussing the High Andes terrorist army it is necessary to begin with a brief description of Ecuadoran and Chilean terrorists, treating those of Peru later in this chapter (see "Peruvian Terrorism").

The Ecuadoran terrorist group, Alfaro Vive, was formed in 1983 (some claim 1981), allegedly under the "influence of his [Gen. Eloy Alfaro] political thought." Alfaro, dubbed the Old Battler (el Viejo Luchador), took over the Ecuadoran government in 1895, perhaps best known for reducing clerical influence in the state. By 1986 Conservative president Febres Cordero had knocked the Alfaristas out of the war, although his Socialist International (SI) successor, Rodrigo Borja, arranged the "peace," the Alfaristas turning in their arms in 1991. A "dissident" faction under Patricio Baquerizo remained, Pedro Moncada heading the "peaceful" surrender of weapons which was "observed" by an international group including FARC.

The Manuel Rodríguez Patriotic Front (FPMR) has long been recognized as the "military" arm of the Chilean CP. Brock (*Insight,* 15 December 1986) ably reported what was probably its most interesting episode. In a complex operation taking about a year, Soviet and Cuban vessels delivered tons of munitions to the Pacific Coast region near the hamlet of Vallenar. In conjunction with this "largest clandestine arsenal ever found in the Western Hemisphere," "a small military camp," complete with airstrip, hospital, communications and underground facilities, "had been built disguised as a fishing village." The Pinochet government dealt appropriately with the effort.

Also found in Moreno's Colombian safe house were the plans for an international terrorist army, the Bolívar Army. On 23 January 1986 Colombian vice minister of justice Nesly Lozano announced that M-19, Alfaro Vive and Sendero Luminoso (Peru) "have formed a coordinating group." Two days later a bulletin to the press in Popayan (Cauca Department) announced an international organization, Battalón América, not Bolívar Army, had been created, the Senderos confirming their membership the next month, the MRTA (Peru) in August. The close cooperation between M-19 and FARC can be used as a rationale for the practical inclusion of the CNG in the High Andes groups while November 1987 marked the inclusion of FPMR. There has long been liaison among High Andes terrorist groups in addition to that provided by

OLAS—Peruvian Sendero weapons supply to FPMR for example—but whether or not this confederation has had serious practical effects is not obvious.

HL Narcoterrorism

DRUGS AND TERRORISM IN LATIN AMERICA (WKLY 1.4, 30 MAY 1996)

In the Colombian presidential runoff election of 19 July 1994 Liberal Party candidate Ernesto Samper Pizano won with 50.47 percent over his Conservative Party opponent Andres Pastrana Arango with 48.64 percent. Ten days later (29 June) a recording of a conversation, alleged to be "among Cali cocaine cartel chiefs," was reproduced in the Bogotá press. The conversation related to the alleged injection of narcotrafficking money into the Samper and Pastrana campaigns; it was described as the "fourth or fifth" such recording sent to the media by the unknown group, "Honorable Colombians." Two years later President Samper's campaign manager and defense minister, Botera Zea, is among his jailed associates, Samper in difficulty. In early May 1996 Bogotá Stock Exchange president Caballero Argaez remarked that "if President Samper must go to jail with 100 or 130 congressmen, so be it."

In April 1996 it was reported that Colombian coca production was up 15 percent from 1995, some 50,000 hectares (124,000 acres) now under cultivation. About the same time it was reported that, in the first quarter of 1996 in Peru, more than fourteen tons of drugs and 4,749 alleged narcotraffickers were taken in 3000 operations. The difference between narcotrafficking in Colombia and Peru is related to the difference between the treatment of the HL terrorists in the two nations since the MLs are largely narcoterroists. The remainder of this report will be concerned chiefly with FARC and ELN which have been covered in this chapter (see "Columbia").

Whether or not Khrushchev originally recruited Castro into narcotrafficking as Brian Crozier (*L'Express*, 26 December 1986) convincingly maintains, the headquarters for such activity has long been in Havana. Douglass,[123] the debriefer of the ranking Soviet Bloc defector, Czech general Jan Sejna, details most of the evidence relating to ML terrorist narcotrafficking in Latin America, pointing out that "Cuba and Czechoslovakia first established drug operations in the early 1960s." To Douglass's extensive evidence is here added (1) Apuleyo Mendoza's article (*El Tiempo* [Bogotá], 18 July 1989) on "new FARC fronts, narcos, labs, seas of coca," and (2) the *Semana* (Bogotá, 7 July 1992) coverage of the 1991 FARC and ELN budgets.

The departments of Boyaca, Mita, Vichada, and Vaupes encompass a sparsely populated 422,000 km² on the eastern slope of the Andes between the headwaters of the Orinoco and those of the Amazon. In 1992 FARC boss Luís Morantes (a.k.a. Jacobo Arenas) commanded the nine FARC fronts guarding coke production in the region, his headquarters at Uribe to the south of Bogotá. Nearby Front Twenty-six guarded the entry to the range (East Andes), Front Thirty-two near the Guayabero River watched the locals, Front Twenty-seven guarding the coca production upstream. The vast region of coca-producing fincas to the east was guarded by Front Sixteen, the military capturing a meticulous register of some of these fincas' production. Fronts Twenty-eight and Thirty-seven were to the northeast of the Meta River, Front Sixteen between the Meta and the Guaviare, and Front One to the south of Mitu.

At dawn on a February 1992 day authorities arrested a member of the ELN finance committee in Bucaramanga who called attention to a computer disk by trying to hide it. The disk contained data as valuable as any discovered during the attack on FARC headquarters at Casa Verde, interception of FARC Secretariat mail, and so forth, immense detail on ELN financial activity in the triangle of Santander, Arauca, and Casanare. There was kidnapping detail by name of victim, listing of extortion detail by enterprise, operational expense by front. *Semana* was able to use this data in conjunction with Colombian intelligence and military sources to arrive at the details of FARC and ELN incomes for 1991. (Exchange rate then: 625 pesos/US $1)

FARC income for 1991 was 98.8 billion pesos with 120 billion forecast for 1992, that for ELN 52.5 billion. FARC income broke down as (1) 14.8 billion for kidnappings (370 at 40 million each), (2) extortion from cattlemen per head 6 billion, (3) extortion on gold production 6 billion, (4) cocaine 50 billion, (5) poppy production 17 billion (estimated since effort new), (6) other 5 billion. ELN income was similar save for the absence of cocaine income; ELN moved into the coke trade later as illustrated by the July 1993 taking of a coke laboratory guarded by ELN front Luís Carlos Cárdenas, the lab producing three tons per week.

Colombia is in the forefront of narcoterrorism and deserves to be treated as an example. But Cuba remains the hub of such activities even though, as Enrique Gúzman recently reported (AFP, 1 May 1996), it now allegedly offers only safe haven rather than the logistical support of yesterday. Or does it?

DRUGS AND TERRORISM IN LATIN AMERICA, PART 2: OF PRESIDENTS AND
NARCOTRAFFICKERS (WKLY 2.12, 31 OCTOBER 1996)

In a period spanning the twenty-four years between 1972 and 1996 a common bond has apparently been established among three presidents, two of them U.S. and one Colombian through their alleged relationships with individuals who either were or would become narcotraffickers. (1) In the early 1970s U.S. president Richard Nixon is alleged to have received illegal financing for his presidential campaign from narcotrafficker Robert L. Vesco.[124] (2) In 1996 Colombian president Ernesto Samper was refused a visa for travel to the United States by the Clinton government on the basis that his campaign had received financing from the Colombian "cocaine cartels." (3) In 1996 U.S. president William Clinton is alleged to have received campaign financing for the U.S. General Elections of 5 November 1996 from narcotrafficker Jorge Cabrera.[125] In contradistinction to Latin American elections, LANS has no interest in U.S. elections save where they impinge on Latin American affairs; those of 5 November 1996 apparently do.

The link between President Nixon and President Clinton through their narcotrafficking is remarkable, the former's Robert Vesco now proving to have been the superior to the latter's Jorge Cabrera. Perhaps of even greater interest, however, is the additional evidence provided by these situations in proof of the fact that Fidel Castro is the narcotrafficking chief for the Western Hemisphere. Of lesser interest is the possibility that a serious investigation of Castro's drugs-for-guns could explain the Mena allegations (see chapter 4, "Target NACR"). In brief, the Vesco-Cabrera details are more important than appears to be generally realized.

Marxism-Leninism may be dead in Russia (Commonwealth of Independent States), but it is alive and well in Cuba and still active in narcotrafficking. This seems to have been illustrated by the article which appeared in *Izvestiya* (Moscow) on 30 July 1996. That daily reported that, according to the latest Customs Report, two emissaries from Havana had been arrested with 9.3 kilograms of cocaine, four from Panama with 8.9 kilograms. In its article *Izvestiya* reminded its readers that the Castro regime had been "accused" for decades of involvement in narcotrafficking. In reality, enough information has surfaced over the years to justify something more than an "accusation." Various authors have wondered why the U.S. government, under whichever political party, has taken no action against Castro's narcotics activities, it having reacted quite differently with the Panamanian caudillo, Noriega.

Some have answered themselves to the effect that such action against a Soviet protectorate such as Cuba, which would have apparently violated the Kennedy-Khrushchev Accords, would have been beyond U.S. resolve. Which, if true, still leaves open the question of U.S. behavior since the demise of the Soviet Union.

U.S. Impotence in the Face of Castroite Narcotrafficking

The impression which has been given by the U.S. government is one of timidity in the face of Castroite narcotrafficking. In May 1983 Under Secretary of State Lawrence Eagleburger commented that "it is difficult to believe that the Cuban government is not involved [in narcotrafficking]," then lapsed into silence as though instructed to do so. Attempts by U.S. agents to bring Castro and his government under court action for narcotrafficking, however sincerely pursued by lower-echelon agents, have sputtered into oblivion as happened with the Ruíz, father and son.

On 9 March 1988 U.S. agents in Miami detained Reinaldo Ruíz for transporting drugs from Colombia to the United States through Cuba. The agents later obtained a taped confession from Reinaldo and his son, Ruben, that on 10 April 1987 Ruben had flown 1000 pounds of cocaine from Colombia to Varadera, Cuba, where government personnel off-loaded it to a ship for transport to the United States. While speculative, the facts appear to indicate this evidence was the reason for the Castroite slaughter of the following year.

Major General Arnold Ochoa, nicknamed the "Rommel" of Castroite Cuba, was a much-decorated hero of Castro's African adventures. About the time of the 1989 Chicom-like purge, General Ochoa, Colonel Antonio de la Guardia, Major Amado Padrón Trujillo, Captain José Martínez Valdes, and ten others were arrested and tried for "narcotrafficking and high treason." On the court was Vice Admiral Aldo Santamaria who had been condemned in the United States on the Guillot narcotrafficking case.[126] This Vishinsky-like court condemned the accused, and Ochoa, de la Guardia, Padrón and Martínez were shot on 13 July 1989 in front of Minister of Justice Juan Escalona Reguero. As de la Guardia's aide explained, these executions "mató dos pajaros de un tiro" (killed two birds with one stone), and Caudillo Castro had demonstrated his "innocence" of the Ruíz charges.

There have been suggestions that "three birds" were actually involved, the third being U.S. responsibility to follow up evidence of

Castroite narcotrafficking. Various arcane theories may be evolved to explain U.S. inactivity, but the fact remains that such inactivity apparently continues to exist. Whatever the answer may be, during the course of the summer of 1996, enough additional information on Castroite narcotrafficking has come to light to justify further such questions after a repetition of certain key points from the treatment in Wkly 1.4 this chapter (see "Mexico").

Bryan Crosier (*L'Express* [Paris], 26 December 1996) convincingly maintains that Khrushchev originally recruited Castro into narcotrafficking. Douglass[127] details most of the evidence relating to ML terrorist narcotrafficking activity in Latin America, pointing out that "Cuba and Czechoslovakia first established drug operations in Colombia in the early 1960s." In Wkly 1.4 LANS specifically covered the narcotrafficking activities of the two still prominent Colombian terrorist organizations, FARC and ELN.

Robert L. Vesco

Robert L. Vesco fled the United States in 1973, soon to be pursued by what were probably well-founded charges of money laundering and narcotrafficking. He alighted first in the Bahamas, then in Costa Rica, and finally settled permanently in Castroite Cuba in what the *New York Times* (11 June 1995), following the lead of the *Miami Herald* (9 June 1995), described as "a splendid exile." In a land where the foreigner is not even allowed, Vesco had a villa in a glen overlooking the sea, this near one of Fidel Castro's many mansions, the one at Bone Key. He had two private jets, some half-dozen automobiles, two yachts. Even more unique than all this luxury in poverty-stricken Cuba was his personal staff of guards. Castro had made him dismiss his bodyguards in 1985. Then, as DGI (Cuban KGB) captain Enrique Garcia Díaz, a 1988 defector, told our colleague Ariel Remos (*Diario las Américas*), "Vesco is the only foreigner who has lived in Cuba with a personal security staff of ten men belonging to Castro's guard and headed by one of Fidel's aides-de-camp, Ramón Granda."

As Garcia pointed out, it would be naïve to suppose that such royal privileges would be granted to an individual who is not of considerable interest to Castro. As Vesco was. "Vesco advised the Cuban government," Garcia went on, "on all its illegal operations from violations of the U.S. embargo to narcotrafficking." Vesco became an intimate of Castro, a friend of José Abrahantes,[128] of Raul Castro and of de la Guardia who has been encountered. De la Guardia had directed narcotrafficking operations through CIMEX and Vesco was, according to Garcia, "the key piece. Washington wanted to extradite Vesco, but Vesco would never leave the island alive." The *modus operandi* for assuring that he never did was a "trial" even more bizarre than that of Ochoa, de la Guardia, and the rest.

Robert Vesco was arrested on 31 May 1995, tried in August 1996 and, of course, sentenced to thirteen years imprisonment, his Cuban wife, Lidia Alfons Llauger to nine. Press dispatches described the judicial proceeding as "complicated," as such a judicial farce usually is. It allegedly revolved around a pharmaceutical called Trixolane (TX), or Viroxan, invented by the U.S. citizen Stephen Herman and alleged to cure maladies from cancer to AIDS.

In addition to providing a method of preventing Vesco's departure from Cuba, the trial provided a forum for the gringo to distance himself from Castro as he was clearly instructed to do. This he did with a statement that he had never been acquainted with the Cuban caudillo. As has been attested by Garcia, this claim flew in the face of the facts with which he was personally familiar. Vesco, President Nixon's alleged donor and "the key piece" in Castro's narcotrafficking activities, was not leaving the island. But President Clinton's alleged donor, with whom Vesco had had extensive contact, was.

Jorge Cabrera

In the fall of 1996 the existence of a photograph of the "well-known narcotrafficker," Jorge Cabrera, with one or more of the occupants of the Presidential Palace in Washington, was reported. This had been taken in Miami, but it was also reported that Cabrera, as a substantial campaign contributor, had visited the Presidential Palace. Jorge, a Cuban-American resident in Miami, has been reported to have made various trips to Cuba and is one of Castro's contacts with potential investors.

In 1995 there was a meeting in Havana between certain of these investors, the Cuban caudillo, and Cabrera. Perhaps less efficient than Hitler's photographer, Castro's photographer ran out of film, borrowed a camera from an associate of Cabrera, shot the roll and returned the camera with the film still in it.

The film showed, among other things, a fulsome embrace of Cabrera by Fidel Castro; this piece of valuable evidence made its way into the hands of the Drug Enforcement Agency (DEA). It should be of interest to see if anything more is done with this evidence of Castroite involvement in narcotrafficking than has been done with that evidence gathered in the past.

Peruvian Terrorism

PERUVIAN TERRORISM (WKLY 2.2, 22 AUGUST 1996)

In late April 1996 representatives of the thirty-four Organization of American States (OAS) member states met in Lima in the First Specialized Inter-American Conference on Terrorism. The "Plan of Action" approved may or may not be effectively implemented, but the public classification of terrorism as a "delito comun grave" (serious common crime) was an important milestone in dealing with terrorist groups such as those in Peru.

The following month Peruvian president Alberto Kenyo Fujimori Fujimori was asked about "negotiating" the release of the U.S. terrorist, Lorene Helene Berenson. His reply was in much the same spirit: "I believe that terrorism cannot be treated as a business. Terrorism is very dangerous...we must be careful because terrorism is an international network." The reasons for what has been called a "recent resurgence of Peruvian terrorism" will be discussed after a review of the two main Peruvian terror groups, Sendero Luminoso and MRTA.

In 1964 the allegedly "Maoist" Bandera Roja emerged from the Peruvian CP, later fragmenting to yield a group which would provide the raw material for Latin America's most bloodthirsty terrorist organization, Sendero Luminoso. Formed by San Cristobal University professor Abímael Guzman Reynoso (b. 1932) in 1980, the group name was taken from the remark of the Peruvian communist, José Carlos Mariategui (d. 1930),[129] "el socialismo es el sendero luminoso que conduce al futuro" (socialism is the "shining path" that leads to the future). SL as the "avenging voice of the Incas" is largely the result of the interview with Manuel Gongora (*La República*, 12 March 1982) wherein Sendero "tactics" were claimed to be those of Atahualpa and Tupac Amaru.[130]

Sendero Luminoso "methods" were reputedly praised by Peruvian president Alan Garcia Pérez (1985–1990). These "methods" include mock "trials" and "executions " by throat slitting (cf. Victoria Fernández [UPI, 16 October 1986]), kidnap recruiting of children (cf. EFE, 24 March 1986), selection of villagers for mass slaughter (cf. Las Vegas [Huanaco Department] [UPI, 23 October 1986]), the "armed strike" where Peruvians not striking are murdered as "enemies of the people," poisoning a water supply (cf. Aguaytia [AFP, 16 November 1987]), beheading 1,000 llamas in Lachoc (Huancavelica Department [UPI, 16 August 1988]), and so on. As with the Colombian terrorists, Sendero is deeply involved in narcotrafficking. There has been some effort to portray Sendero as a "pariah" among Latin American terrorist groups, but this does not bear scrutiny. From 23 January 1986 Sendero belonged to the same international terror group, Batallón América, as did other terrorist groups in Colombia, Ecuador and Chile.

The other important Peruvian terrorist group, the Tupac Amaru Revolutionary Movement (MRTA) surfaced in September 1984 with its seizure of the UPI and Associated Press (AP) offices in Lima. This group has been called Tupac Amaru II, TA I having been formed in the Satipo region in May 1965 by Lobaton and Galvez and quickly dispersed by a government having no intention of putting up with it. Although the Tupas would extend their operations into the countryside in 1987—a car bomb in Arequipa, an attack on Juanjui and Yorongos (San Martin Department)—their "operations" have largely consisted of bombings in Lima beginning with the Avianca offices in 1985, and accelerating on Christmas eve. They offered to "liquidate," in a spirit of public service, the bankers and impresarios whom Pres. Garcia was harrying.

With his inauguration on 28 July 1990, President Fujimori assumed the leadership of a nation in which Sendero was wielding an influence out of all proportion to its importance. Perhaps this was because the avowed marxist, President Garcia, admired Senderista "principles," perhaps because a Garcia judge, for example, released Guzman's second-in-command (Osman Morote Barrionuevo) in July 1988 for "lack of evidence." Fujimori felt that more or less "peaceful" methods of dealing with the terrorists should be tried first, attempting to "neutralize" them by army-protected development in "vital" areas. The chaos only compounded. By October 1990, fourteen were dying daily in the terror. That fall Sendero penetration of the Peruvian Education Workers Union and the Armed Forces was detailed. And then came the Supreme Court decision exonerating Guzman from any blame in ten murders and ten terror attacks.

Two weeks later Fujimori acted: at 2300 local time on 5 April 1992 he announced that the Congress and the judiciary were dissolved and an "Emergency Government of National Construction," based on the Armed Forces with legislation by presidential decree, was inaugurated. On 11 April a private poll indicated that 91 percent of the Peruvians approved of this "autogolpe," a later report in *El Expreso* (Lima) giving him 82 percent.[131] But the most important poll was the 9 April 1995 election which President Fujimori won with 64.27 percent of the vote against 21.97 percent for his opponent, a Pérez de Cuellar who had conveniently appeared upon the scene from his position as OAS head in order to run.

After his autogolpe President Fujimori introduced his anti-terrorist program: (1) the National Anti-Terrorist Directorate (DINCOTE) and the Armed Forces were ordered to destroy terrorism and given the resources to do so; (2) Martial law was decreed against terrorism, legal action being taken out of the Garcia courts and put in military tribunals, life sentences being introduced; (3) Rural and urban civil-defense patrols, advised by the military, were introduced.[132]

Within the next year and a half unprecedented success was enjoyed by the Fujimori government in its battle against terrorism. In June 1992 Victor Polay Campos, the head of MRTA, was captured; twelve ranking Senderos were seized, and the central SL logistics apparatus destroyed that same month. But the telling blow was struck in September 1992 when a drunken Guzman and six of his top commanders were captured at the dance academy of ballerina Maritza Garrida Lecca. This coup was aided by the one million dollars which had been put on Guzmanm's head and which was duly shared by the forty DINCOTE agents making the arrest. In his address of 13 September 1992, Fujimori told the nation:

> All Peruvians know the significance of the capture of Abimael Guzman, alias "Cmdte. Gonzalo," because we know…[that] Sendero Luminoso…means destruction, death, and narcotics…the Peruvian…became acquainted with Abimael Guzman through the medium of a video…[and learned] that, instead of the revolutionary leader fabricated by the mythology, he was a drunken fellow, sluggishly performing a Greek dance…against a background…[of] the founders of Communism. Since then the intelligence services…have followed the trail of Guzman…[and] achieved…a transcendent success…

The successes continued; the terrorists were not released; and then came the surrender of the imprisoned Guzman. In a three-page letter of 6 October 1993 to Fujimori, Guzman surrendered telling the SL leadership to surrender and turn over their arms. An earlier letter (1 October) had asked for "peace negotiations" which Fujimori rejected, pointing out that Guzman knew that 90 percent of his command and staff had been captured and there was nothing left to negotiate. Whether the 90 percent figure was precise or otherwise, the Constitution and Society Institute (UCS) reported last year that terrorism in Peru had decreased

70 percent in 1994 from its level in 1993. But even though such is the case, the efforts on the part of the terrorists have continued: there is still an international network which is strongly supportive.

For example, last February MRTA propaganda head Nestor Cerpa Cartolini was found to be sending faxes to Paris-based International Tupa Line chief Hugo Avellaneda for re-faxing to Lima. Incidentally, this had to do with a plan to kidnap the Congress which led to Berenson's capture. Which leads to the question: Why is Peruvian terrorism so important to the International Left? One unsubstantiated answer of un-known value was provided by "a source in touch with Polish intelli-gence": Allegedly, "communications facilities have been installed in the High Andes which link, or linked, Sendero Luminoso and the re-gional command structure with Soviet submarines in the Pacific" (*Latin American Times* [London], vol. 11, no. 4, 1993]. For such to still be the case, however, there is a serious question of the Fujimori government's inability to locate these facilities by this time. Whatever the "why," it has recently been asserted that Peruvian terrorism is experiencing a resurgence in 1996.

It is not obvious that such is the case; rather, although the level of terrorist activity has been reduced, it has not been totally eliminated. In 1995 DINCOTE and the Military captured about 3,300 persons sus-pected of terrorist activity. Although 498 were soon released, this still left some 2,800 as the year's total bag. On 8 August 1996 the Attorney General announced that over 500 have been found guilty of the "crime of terrorism" this year. Further, on 18 August National Police director general Antonio Vidal Herrera said on the program "Contrapunto" that 700 terrorists have been captured so far this year, a decrease from the 1995 rate. Nor has the terrorist activity been as great.

The attack by Sendero in San Martín Department in February with grenades and rocket launchers, although killing ten military and two civilians, could have been the work of a very small group. One of the largest reported Sendero columns was operating against villages in the Amazon jungle on the weekend of 20–21 July, this terrorizing the vil-lagers with their "peoples assemblies." AFP reported this front to num-ber eighty, but such strength estimates are notoriously unreliable. A body count is routinely more trustworthy, however, and in early May a ten-day confrontation left a terrorist body count of thirty in Valle del Río Ene. It can probably be taken that a front-sized—usually company strength, or about 100 to 150—Sendero unit was involved. One front does not make a resurgence, however strenuously the terrorists and their international support networks may labor to present the appearance of one. A fresh blow was dealt the attempt by the 16 August capture of Camilo Santos Vera (a.k.a. Pedro Sánchez Flores), head of the northern Sendero command who had replaced the jailed Morote Barrionuevo (see above) and María Pantoja.

There have been two recent outrages in Lima, but, as Fujimori stated, these can be the work of isolated individuals or small groups and hardly indicate a meaningful "resurgence." Apropos of this is former DINCOTE director general John Caros's remark of 12 August, "In the silence any sound is alarming." Of greater importance is Fujimori's warning to the terrorists recently released from the prison sentences meted out by President Garcia's "soft-on-terrorism" judges. He warned them of his continuing "tough-on-terrorism" campaign.

And finally, whatever face President Fujimori might wish to put on a "terrorist resurgence," the countrymen displaced by terrorism are returning home. During the present year 2500 terrorist-displaced families have returned to their homes (AAN, 12 August 1996); on 15 August another 155 families returned to their homes in Barrio Huancas, Marcaraccay (Ayacucho Department).

PERUVIAN TUPAC AMARU TERRORISM (SPCL 2.17, 19 DECEMBER 1996)

The U.S. communications media does not "report the news"; it "makes the news" through its choice of those current events it judges worthy of reporting. Which might serve some purpose were these current events reported in that context necessary to render them coherent. But those events relating to Latin American terrorism—almost universally, narcoterrorism—are related out of context and then only when their bizarre sensationalism is sufficient to appeal to the most jaded tastes. In the last eleven years only two incidents have broken through the myopic disinterest of the U.S. media, the first in the Colombia of 1985, the second in the Peru of latter 1996.

Terrorist Attack on the Colombian Supreme Court, 1985

At 1140 local time on 6 November 1985, between thirty-five and fifty Nineteenth of April Movement (M-19) terrorists led by Andres Almarales got off a bus in the underground station at the Colombia Supreme Court Building in Bogotá. They then seized the building by murdering the concierge, two civilian guards and a secret service operative. Almarales had been released from prison on 21 June 1985 after the "amnesty" and "peace" of President Betancur. The Supreme Court Building is on the central plaza in Bogotá which it shares with the Nariño Presidential Palace, the National Capital, and the Mayoral Building. [When last viewed by the LANS editor some nine years later the Supreme Court Building had still not been rebuilt—Ed.]

By 1255 the Presidential Guard Battalion, three choppers, and nine "tanks"[133] had been concentrated in and above the plaza. At 1505 two armored vehicles followed by troops moved on the building, proceeding up the outside double staircase and breaking down the double steel doors into the entry salon. In the meantime (1420) M-19 had claimed "credit" for "capturing" the Supreme Court Building. The terrorists retreated to the third and fourth floors, seizing Supreme Court president Alfonso Reyes Echandia and 100 others as they did so. At about 2150 a fire broke out in that wing of the building fronting on Seventh Avenue, a fire which would destroy much of the structure. By 2320, 100 people had left the building, the nine magistrates remaining as hostages of the terrorists.

At some point during these activities a spokesman for the terrorists, identified as Eduardo Rodríguez, declared the seizure of the Supreme Court Building "the start of a war," a typically bombastic statement which would prove hollow. At about 1430 on 7 November 1985 military forces attacked and took the building which contained some 100 cadavers including those of the nine Supreme Court justices and the terrorists.

Batallón América had not then been officially inaugurated, but there is little doubt that this operation had been supported out of Havana, probably through the Latin American Solidarity Organization (OLAS) which had emerged from the 1966 TCC. It was not long before evidence of Nicaraguan FSLN participation began to emerge, for example.

The festivities hardly concluded, the English-language media again lapsed into lethargy toward more important terrorist developments, this indifference impervious to:

The Plot to Seize the Peruvian Legislature, 1995

Nor would the media awaken to the important prelude to the 1996–1997 Peruvian terrorist operation which would so delight it, the Japanese Embassy Operation (JEO). A word of background is necessary to a description of this terrorism.

On 28 July 1990 Alberto Kenyo Fujimori Fujimori succeeded avowed Marxist Alan Garcia as president of Peru. Young Garcia had roomed with a Victor Polay Campos (a.k.a. Rolando) when a student in Paris in the early 1970s; as president his coddling of Peruvian terrorists had resulted in perhaps the most vicious situation in Latin America. Some additional discussion of one of the two terrorist organizations—Sendero Luminoso and MRTA—is appropriate here.

A brief description of the MRTA has been given in the first article of this section. Here it is appropriate to add a further description of three of its chief terrorists, the jailed MRTA boss, Victor Polay Campos, the immediate JEO boss, Nestor Cerpa (also occasionally Serpa) Cartolini, and Cerpa's second-in-command, Roli Rojas Fernández (a.k.a. The Arab).

For a biography of Polay of which this terrorist himself should generally approve, cf. Strong.[134] Strong is apparently correct, however, that Polay was a roommate of the avowed Marxist and future Peruvian president, Alan Garcia, in Madrid. But whether Madrid or Paris, as has been reported in the press, this illuminates, first, a routine, if generally ignored characteristic of these ML chiefs allegedly devoted to the "poor," and, second, the relationship between this chief and the future Peruvian president.

Polay's presence in Madrid (or Paris) is once again proof of what LANS associate editor Emanuiloff-Max has emphasized: "The leaders and the majority of the integrants in the guerrilla (terrorist) movements originate in the layer of the semi-intelligentsia, from the university proletariat, from the 'bourgeoisie,' from various other of the resentful disclassed." A viewpoint to which Zack Kornfeder[135] attested long ago from his recruiting efforts in Peru's northern neighbors. Nor do "the poor" attend college in Spain or France. A roommate relationship is an intimate one; that between a future ML terrorist boss and a future Marxist president is worthy of note.

Nestor Cerpa (a.k.a. Evaristo) has much in common with the Brazilian Lula da Silva. Not only is MRTA associated with the São Paulo Forum formed by Castro and da Silva, both the Brazilian and the Peruvian terrorist began their careers as labor union chiefs. Cerpa first came to public attention in February 1979 when he led his union in the takeover of Cromotex, the firm for which the union worked. In the confrontation with the police which followed, four of his followers were killed. After that time he continued his "labor union" activities, working closely with Américo Gilvonio Conde (a.k.a. Juan Carlos) who was the "labor advisor" to the union. The pair soon migrated into MRTA as early and important members.

In that spirit of inflated self importance common to these terrorists, Cerpa was allegedly chief of the MRTA "Northeast Front" which was located in the jungle Department of San Martín, the southern boundary of which is roughly 200 miles north of Lima. Polay "escaped" from prison in 1990 to be recaptured by the Fujimori government in 1992. In the flurry of press reports appearing after the JEO began, Cerpa was described as boss of what remained of this terrorist group. Perhaps, but, again, perhaps not. In February 1996 Peruvian intelligence described him as MRTA's propaganda chief whom they discovered sending faxes to Paris-based International Tupa Line chief Hugo Avellandes in Paris.

Cerpa's second-in-command in the JEO is Roli Rojas Fernández (a.k.a. The Arab) who began his terrorist career with the MRTA in 1985. He was captured only to "escape" the following year with Polay Campos.

President Fujimori, "La Golconda" as Dr. Emanuiloff-Max calls him, took over from Polay Campos' roommate, President Garcia, initiated and carried out the most effective anti-terrorist campaign in contemporary Latin America where heads of state would soon be coddling the terrorists and trying to woo them to "peace." These ranged from President Zedillo in Mexico to a long series of Colombian presidents. In such a venue President Fujimori was soon a marked man to the MLs of the HL. Which calls for an aside.

In these last few days of 1996 various news services covering the JEO have been quick to point out that President Fujimori's popularity, the world now being run by polls, is falling. This is correct, but, taken out of context as it is, it confuses rather than enlightens. Led by Fidel Castro, his HL is waging an all-out propaganda war against "neoliberalism." In Peru, where Fujimori has been in the forefront of neoliberal efforts, this propaganda campaign was ineffective while the murderous threat from the Sendero and Tupa was still inescapably present. But, as the threat faded with La Golconda's effective anti-terrorism campaign, the HL propaganda against Fujimori began to sink into the always short attention span of the electorate. With results which are meaningless out of context. But to return to the Tupas.

Insofar as the Tupas were concerned, President Fujimori first caught their boss Polay Campos in 1992. In December 1995 his, until December 1996, efficient DINCOTE broke up an effort to take the National Legislature hostage, as had one of the ultimate double agents, Edén Pastora, almost 20 years before. In doing so DINCOTE nabbed Tupa second-in-command Miguel Rincón Rincón (a.k.a. Francisco) and "director of military operations" Jaime Ramírez. In the breakup of this kidnap operation three foreigners were caught, Lorene Helene Berenson (United States), Nancy Guiliana Conde (Bolivia), and Pacifico Castrejon (or Castrellon) Santamaria (Panama). Castro's HL was clearly at work against its prime target, President Fujimori's Peru. As the media dozed on, HL boss Castro was the featured speaker at an Iberian-American Summit in Chile, the honored speaker—and vice president—at the World Food Conference in Rome, and so on. But above all, he was chief of that HL which was preparing the next sensation for that somnolent media.

Tupa Terrorist Seizure of the Japanese Compound in Lima

At 2005[136] on 17 December 1996 twenty-odd Tupa terrorists, inside (garbed as waiters) and outside, blew an entry in the wall on the Guillermo Marconi Avenue side of the Japanese Embassy compound, taking over the residence area at which a reception was in progress. What followed should be familiar to the reader since, like Rip Van Winkle, the Fourth Estate again awakened. [LANS was originally told by the Peruvian embassy that the terrorists were holding "about 250"; other sources have varied substantially from this estimate. The numbers are not important *per se*—Ed.]

The *New York Times* (19 December 1996) called the affair a "stunning coup" for the terrorists, something of a *non sequitur*. A more realistic description would be "a stunning defeat" for DINCOTE. If, as the terrorists demand, their chiefs are freed and the entire pack is flown into the High Andes to renew its war against the people of Peru, it may mark the death knell of a uniquely successful war against terrorism. Coming after the FARC coup (see "Columbia," Wkly 2.15), it is not irrational to imagine this as turning the tide in favor of the HL.

Be this as it may, among the questions which may be asked are:

1. Was there a breakdown in Peruvian intelligence?
2. How many foreign (non-Peruvian) terrorists were involved?
3. What, if any, was the involvement of U.S. personnel?

1. Whether the breakdown was in DINCOTE or some other Peruvian intelligence organization, there was clearly a breakdown involving (a) background checks and (b) penetration of terrorist organizations.

There is no way in which a festivity to which several hundred people are invited can be kept classified. Therefore "everybody" knew of the affair, its location, the time it was to begin, etc. Perhaps even more important, "everybody" knew that the embassy in question shared an important relationship with President Fujimori—they are both of Japanese extraction.

Since "everybody" knew "everything," why did not intelligence perform background checks sufficient unto the needs, not only on the personnel working the affair—the "waiters"—but also on the personnel—chauffeurs, bodyguards, and so on—attending the invitees?

It is logical to suppose that, contrary to what happened in 1995, intelligence did not know that the terrorist operation was going to take place. What happened to that penetration of the terrorist organizations which assuredly made them privy to that information in 1995.

It appears not unreasonable to suppose that special efforts would have been warranted by the nature of this gala.

3. Since the demise of the Soviet Union various authors have stepped forward to join the long line of those stretching back to the secretary of Dzugashvili (a.k.a. Stalin), Boris Bajanov, who have testified to the espionage agents of the International Left. Among the more recent might be mentioned Koch (1994),[137] Sudoplatov (1994),[138] Klehr et al. (1995)[139] and any number of others published and to be published. And among those insufficiently discussed are the few thousand of the Venceremos Brigades who went to Cuba from the US to wallow in the ecstacy of Castro's "revolution."[140] That there has been and, from recent events, probably still is penetration of the U.S. government by Castroites is therefore not beyond the realm of possibility.[141]

The reception was scheduled for 1900. U.S. Ambassador Dennis Jet arrived at 1915 and left at 1945 for "another appointment," thus conveniently missing the initiation of the terrorist operation at 2005. Whether this has the significance which has been suggested to LANS cannot yet be established with any certainty.

The fulminations by some members of the U.S. government against the Fujimori government for failing to release the terrorist, Lorene Helene Berenson, has also been suggested as relevant to conjectured U.S. involvement.

CUI BONO? (WKLY 2.20, 26 DECEMBER 1996)

ALPHONSE EMANUILLOF-MAX, ASSOCIATE EDITOR, LANS

This is the question which in Roman Law[142] the investigator asks himself in seeking the solution of a crime. With the passage of time this question—"To the benefit of whom?"—reached out toward other criminal cases in attempts to explain them. Having said this, it is obvious that the subject which concerns us is the sad affair of last week at the Japanese embassy in Lima. Of course we are not going to chronicle the details. Instead, we will try to reflect on the motivations which could have led to the event.

One of the great universal lies, which has long held sway thanks to the fact that many people have believed it, is that "misery compels the poor to resort to arms and, through guerrilla movements, seek its liberation from the capitalist yoke," etcetera, etcetera. The falsity of such and similar asseverations consists in the simple fact that the leaders and the majority of the integrants in the guerrilla movements originate in the layer of the semi-intelligentsia, from the university proletariat, from the "bourgeoisie," and from various other of the resentful disclassed. The truly poor, the dispossessed and the unknown are precisely those who, of course, have no money and those whose pathetic priority consists in supporting their families and not in assaults in the name of pseudo-sociological theories which they do not understand for lack of education, those moreover having been proven to be tragic fallacies. See, for example, the cases of Russia in 1917, its satellites after 1945 and Cuba after 1959, where bad was supplanted by worst.

If the poor feel an imperious urgency to rebel against social injustice, which of course exists, they can advance the necessary structural changes through democratic elections. The others, the vitiated, are not valid and today are universally stigmatized. Precisely through democratic and transparent elections did Allende come to power in Chile, Miloshevich in Serbia, or Arana in Montevideo. Not so Lenin in Russia or Castro in Cuba.

But the criminals and the sociopaths do not wish to familiarize themselves with the perverse invention of the bourgeoisie which is democracy, and, therefore, do not recognize its rules of play for the simple reason that, temperamentally and by their idiosyncracies, they are not suited to social coexistence, nor is their worldview *eo ipso* suited to the tolerance which pluralism demands. The problem is, in many cases, more spiritual than political...But this particular subject is for psychiatrists and not for ignorant laymen such as the author.

Returning to the poor and socially unfortunate, it is obvious that, for lack of means, they are in no position to obtain the accoutrements of the guerrilla: the arms, munitions, adequate logistical infrastructure, specific guerrilla health services, rations, guerrilla uniforms, diversified camouflage, clandestine barracking facilities, and so forth.

Then the question is to be asked: Whence are provided all these poor Peruvians the means to bring to a head their "liberation war," to seize the Japanese embassy in Lima, threatening hundreds of innocents with death if their demands are not met? In the years before the 1989–1991 implosion in the U.S.S.R., the answer to this question was, based on obvious international conditions, easier to answer. Today an answer pregnant with discernment, although speculative, is required to answer it.

The power vacuum left by the disappearance of the Soviet Union with its specific methods of creating auxiliaries to its foreign policy, has caused the upsurge of new and distinct problems. This power vacuum left by the U.S.S.R. is being filled by other dissolvent forces. In order not to deal in further generalities we take the case of Colombia which suffers the enormous social and political power of the narcoindustry, its military apparatus, its penetration at the pinnacles of government, and so forth. It is practicable to assume, then, that the self-proclaimed Marxist guerrilla movements, now orphans of an economic support once provided by those governments which acted as guides, passed into the service of the drug magnates without whom their ideological patina would have had to change. It was more useful that the criminals declared themselves "battlers for anti-capitalist social justice and anti-imperialist national liberation" and other verbal weeds familiar for eighty years. This rhetoric reveals the true origin of their financial backers who will render them yet more vulnerable.

The objective is to weaken the political power, in this case, in Peru (tomorrow it could be in another country…), in order to put themselves in a position to dominate the state. And the Embassy of Japan was selected, given that Peru is prioritizing its relations with that country, being therefore more sensitive to any misfortune suffered by the Japanese.

It appears that, in view of the world reaction to the Colombian situation, the high cost of low morality is recognized in Lima as is the general premise that the will of the government cannot be dominated immediately after the economic elements. So the guerrillas have been brought in. While in the past the narcoindustry assured and strengthened its financial position, domesticating the political class through direct corruption, now it is trying to do so through reputedly ideological guerrilla action.

Rich fellows! They know how to adapt their methods with enviable rapidity and flexibility. And still there are people who do not believe in the imaginative and creative power of "savage capitalism"...The Peruvian guerrillas who committed their crimes in search of an amnesty for their imprisoned comrades (amnesty is not amnesia), in fact, never are going to pardon those who have been pardoned...

—Translated from the Spanish by the LANS editor

Notes

1. There is, of course, a rich literature on this subject: cf. William Z. Foster (*History of the Three Internationals*, International Publishers, 1955); Gustav A. Wetter, SJ (*Dialectical Materialism: A Historical and Systematic Survey of Philosophy in the Soviet Union*, Praeger, 1958]; E. R. Goodman (*The Soviet Design for a World State*, Columbia University Press, 1960); Günther Nollau (*International Communism and World Revolution: History and Methods*, Praeger, 1961); Leonard Schapiro (*The Communist Party of the Soviet Union*, Knopf, 1964); etc. Foster was head of the U.S. Communist Party (CPUSA), International Publishers its house organ.

2. In addition to the references given for the three Internationals, the documents edited by Jane Degras (*The Communist International: 1919–1943. Documents*, Cass, vol. 1, 1956; vol. 2, 1960; vol. 3 1971) are important here.

3. The "consensus," often a dubious aggregate, is convinced that the U.S.S.R. has transmogrified itself into a free-enterprise democracy. Whatever degree of truth this perhaps simplistic proposition may have, the genuine student of the subject should at least be aware of somewhat differing viewpoints such as that of Lev Timofeyev (*Russia's Secret Rulers: How the Government and the Criminal Mafia Exercises Their Powers*, Knopf, 1992), Yevgeni Albats (*The State within a State: The KGB and Its Hold on Russia—Past, Present and Future*, Farrar, Strauss, Giroux, 1994), the German journalist and legislator, Graf von Huyn, the former KGB officer, Anitoliy Golitsyn (*The Perestroika Deception*, Harle, 1995) and the British journalist, Christopher Story (editor, *Soviet Analyst*, London).

4. In a front-page piece in the *New York Times* (29 May 1943), Harold King begins his column "Premier Stalin, in a letter to the writer, said the winding up of the Communist International 'puts an end to the lie' that 'Moscow allegedly intends to intervene in the life of other nations and bolshevize them.'"

5. Leonard Schapiro ("The International Department of the CPSU: Key to Soviet Policy," *International Journal*, winter 1976–1977) states, inter alia, "By 1943...the stage had been reached when Soviet control over the world communist parties had become so firmly established that the continued existence of the Comintern was unnecessary...It was only after the Comintern had been dissolved that the Central Committee acquired a Foreign Affairs Department..." And Boris N. Ponomarev surfaced therein.

6. In the mid-1980s the LANS editor, in interviews with close relatives of Fonseca who knew him well during his formative years in Matagalpa, learned the details of his unfortunate childhood. The son of Fausto Amador, who handled financial details for the Nicaraguan caudillo Somoza Debayle, his stepmother early and understandably would not allow young Carlos into the bosom of the Amador family; it was the kitchen for the young, soon to be Borge-tutored Fonseca. Not long before his death, when his terrorist activities were in full swing, Carlos slipped into Managua. As his father left the theater one evening, Fonseca slipped out of the darkness and thrust a note into the father's hand.

"When I take over," the note said, "I am going to hang you from the highest tree in Managua." This for a father who had gotten Carlos out of well-deserved duress on five occasions.

7. Fidel Castro's Galician father Angel came to Cuba in 1898. Having fathered two children, Lidia and Pedro Emilio, by his wife, he fathered Fidel—and others—by the maid, Lina Ruz Gonzales. Unfortunately for Fidel, who according to all accounts bitterly resented his bastardy, Angel was unable to marry Ms. Ruz until the death of his wife. Bastardy is not necessarily stigmatic in Latin American society. For example, the illegitimate son of Somoza Garcia and half-brother of Somoza Debayle, José R. Somoza, appears to have been well adjusted and a member of the familial inner circle.

8. Of the Central Committee, CPSU.

9. Further testimony on this is provided by Pedro V. Domingo (pseud.), "Los Agentes Soviéticos en América Latina" (*Estudios sobre el comunismo*, April-June 1956) and Salvador Diaz Verson (*El Mundo*, 19 October 1960).

10. The renowned Cuban journalist, Salvador Diaz Verson, has, inter alia, testified to these matters (*Communist Threat to the U.S. through the Caribbean*, Senate Subcommittee on Internal Security [SISS], 1960, part 7, [Y4.J89/2:C73/27/pt.7]. Hereinafter, Threat 7).

11. Threat 7.

12. Juan Vives (pseud.), *Los Amos de Cuba*, Emecé Editores, 1982. The LANS editor has neither sought nor received permission to divulge Vives's name.

13. For this "financial angel" of the Institute of Pacific Relations (IPR), cf. *IPR* (Final Report, SISS, 1952) and Anthony Kubek (*How the Far East Was Lost: American Policy and the Creation of Communist China, 1941–1949*, Regnery, 1963).

14. Salvador Diaz Verson, *One Man, One Battle* (World Wide, 1980 [translated by Elena Diaz-Verson de Amos]).

15. Dr. Emanuiloff-Max is director of the Uruguayan Institute of International Studies.

16. While the argument of Dr. Emanuiloff-Max is not influenced by the fact, there are some differences of opinion on the question of the removal of the Soviet IRBMs from Cuba. The evidence that these missiles were not removed has perhaps been most generally provided by Néstor T. Carbonell (*And the Russians Stayed: The Sovietization of Cuba*, Morrow, 1989). This evidence is briefly treated in Wkly 1.2 of this chapter, "Fidel Ruz Castro."

17. Vargas Llosa, a Peruvian writer resident in England, ran against Alberto Fujimori in the presidential elections of 1990 and was soundly defeated. Since that time he has frequently applied his pen to attacks on his erstwhile opponent.

18. *Granma* is the official publication of the Central Committee of the Cuban Communist Party. *Granma* was originally the name of the ship which landed Castro and the eighty-one members of his "Twenty-sixth of July Movement" in Cuba on 25 November 1956.

19. China conducted what was allegedly its last nuclear test on 29 July 1996. The results were apparently to Mr. Jiang's liking, for, on 30 July 1996, the next day, the People's Republic joined the chorus demanding a ban on further such tests.

20. It is apparently PC in the United States to affirm that "communism is dead," thus soothing the egos of the U.S. Right which can then claim "victory in the cold war," and the U.S. Left which denied the existence of such a war. Several seldom-quoted sources of information hold this political "correctness" to be incorrect. Whether it is or is not, the maintenance of a geostrategic base in Cuba by Russia—or Germany, or Iraq, or the People's Republic of China—would appear to be a matter of interest to the United States.

21. The Piles of Rusty Junk (PRJ) Argument: Intelligence sources (bogus and authentic) have told LANS that: "Those missiles are just 'piles of rusty junk.'" This bizarre "argument" amounts to confirmation of non-removal, that the SS4s and SS5s would be PRJ now is an irrelevant truism.

22. Special Consultative Committee, OAS, *The "First Tricontinental Conference," Another Threat to the Security of the Inter-American System.* Pan American Union, 2 April 1966. (OEA/Series L/10/2.12)

23. This is often referred to as LASO, the acronym formed from the words in the English title.

24. "Communiqué on the Establishment of...[OLAS]," *Cuba Socialista,* Havana, February 1966.

25. Paul D. Bethel, *The Losers: The Definitive Report, by an Eyewitness, of the Communist Conquest of Cuba and the Soviet Penetration in Latin America* (Arlington House, 1969). Bethel had served in Cuba as Press Attache in the U.S. Embassy there before, during, and after the Castro takeover.

26. Pierre Broue, *Quand le Peuple Révoque le Président* (L'Harmattan, 1993).

27. Friar Beto, *Horizonte Perdido nos Bastidores do socialismo* (1993).

28. This was almost certainly Revolutionary Democratic Party (PRD) president Cuauhtémoc Cárdenas, now apparently EZLN liaison, who would figure prominently in future conferences.

29. This was one of the parties in President Caldera's victorious coalition.

30. This was originally the party of the deposed Noriega, now that of President Pérez Balladares. Pérez has not taken the sort of active FSP role that Cárdenas has taken.

31. See the first article (Spcl 2.1) in this chapter, "Umbrella Organizations and Activities."

32. The word, "ejido," derived from the Latin "exitus," is literally "the way out." In Spain before the conquest it was applied to common land attached to a village and used by the villagers primarily to pasture their cattle and gather firewood. In the Western Hemisphere the term was applied to the common land held by the Indian communities and used for agriculture.

33. Régis Debray, *Loués soient nos seigneurs: Une éducation politique* (Gallimard, 1996).

34. Régis Debray, *Revolution in the Revolution?* (Casa de las Américas, 1967). Casa de las Américas is Castro's Havana publishing house.

35. Leo Huberman and Paul M. Sweezy (eds), *Régis Debray and the Latin American Revolution*, Monthly Review (1969).

36. Bosch was one of the prime movers in the 1965 Dominican unpleasantness, he having long ago been described by a close associate of LANS, now deceased, as a prominent member of the "Caribbean Comintern." This was not meant to infer Ulianov's COMINTERN but referred to that loosely connected bevy of leftists which included Arevalo, Arbenz, Betancourt, Pepe Figueres et al. Blood feuds, however, often outweigh philosophical connections, particularly on the left, and the Castroite, José Antonio Peña Gómez, had absconded with Bosch's political party so that, in an amusing denouement, the latter has moved right to oppose Peña.

37. Daniel James, *The Complete Bolivian Diaries of Che Guevara and Other Captured Documents* (Stein and Day, 1968).

38. George Jacques Danton was the Old Cordelier (Camille Desmoulins) of the French Revolution—"toujours l'audace"—who was shortened by a head on 5 April 1794.

39. El Beni Department is on the eastern slope of the Andes.

40. Terry Reed and John Cummings, *Compromised: Clinton, Bush and the CIA* (Clandestine, 1995); Félix I. Rodríguez and John Weisman, *Shadow Warrior* (Pocket Books, 1989).
41. Elizabeth Burgos, *Me llamo Rigoberta Menchú y así me nació la conciencia* (Seix Barral, 1992).
42. The HL carries out its anti-neoliberal and AgRef programs "legally," its terrorist—almost entirely narcoterrorist—activities with unquestionable illegality. The terrorist activities will be treated later in this chapter (see "Columbia")Part III.C with the treatment of the terrorist groups themselves.
43. The Gallic sack of Rome rendered the city's founding date questionable, this ranging from the 813 B.C. of Timaeus to the mid-eighth century B.C. of Livy et al. At 3000 B.C., however, one is dealing only with the First Dynasty of the Egyptian Old Kingdom and King Narmer.
44. Plutarch, *Parallel Lives*, translated by John Dryden (various publishers); *Moralia, vol. 4: Roman Questions—Greek Questions—Greek and Roman Parallel Stories*, translated by Frank C. Babbitt (Loeb Classical Library, 1936).
45. [Heinrich] Karl Marx, *The Communist Manifesto*, translated by Samuel Moore, with an introduction by Stefan T. Possony, and a preface by Frederick Engels (Regnery, 1954).
46. Lazaro Cárdenas's son Cuauhtémoc, is quite active in the FSP.
47. See note 25.
48. The details on these Leagues were obtained in the LANS editor's 1963 interview with editor Carlos Todd. Also, Texas University professor of Latin American Studies J. W. F. Dulles very graciously furnished LANS with copies of the short-lived newspaper, *Liga*, published by Julião in 1962.
49. Threat 2 (see note 10).
50. Reproduced in the *New York Times*, 23 April 1948.
51. Cuban journalist Salvador Diaz Verson had been photographing Bashirov's house since 1943 when he and his associates caught Castro visiting there for his monthly stipend as a Kremlin agent.
52. Alberto Niño H., *Antecedentes y Secretos de 9 de abril* (Librería Siglo 20, 1949). Written after his retirement.
53. *Daily Mail* (Ireland), 13 April 1948.
54. *Daily Mail* (UK), 17 June 1948.
55. LANS files contain photos of Castro's arrival in Venezuela and Colombia.
56. Threat 10, p. 725 (see note 10).
57. James D. Henderson, *When Colombia Bled: A History of the Violence in Tolima.* (University of Alabama Press, 1985).
58. Carlos Lleros Restrepo, *De la República a la Dictadura* (ARGRA, 1955).
59. German Guzman Campos, Orlando Fals Borda and Eduardo Umana Lina, *La Violencia*, Tercer Mundo, 2 vols., 1962.
60. José María Nieto Rojas, *La batalla contra comunismo en Colombia* (Empresa Nacional, 1956).
61. But see the next article in this subsection.
62. These sub-classifications of basic ML groups are largely the product of (a) an obfuscation technique aimed at those who "study" these terrorist organizations or (b) a power struggle within the hierarchies. The (1) switching of chiefs from one category to another as they switch groups and the (2) coalition of such groups into unified groups belies the meaningfulness of such categorizations.
63. A FARC slaughter of campesinos in Uraba during the forty days before 20 August 1995 (EFE, 23 September 1995) offers certain points of interest. According to survivors, Katerina commanded the "wave of assassinations," the

methods of the seven separate slaughters, which left 100 dead, being to shoot the victims down, "tie their hands and finish them off with machetes." Katerina is allegedly the amante of Commandante Isaias Trujillo, he perhaps commanding Front Sixteen since located near Guaviare.

64. The pipeline-busting ELN, by 16 April 1995, had blown the Colombian oil pipeline, the Caño Limon-Covenas, 345 times spreading millions of barrels of crude over the country. This destruction continues.

65. Lehder was condemned to twenty-five years imprisonment by a Colombian court (December 1995), presumably to be served after he completes his life sentence in the United States.

66. From Eudocio Ravines (Peru) to Roger Miranda (Nicaragua) the true defectors from the ML cadres, who have come to realize the mistake they made in becoming involved, have been perhaps the most valuable source of information on these terror groups. But the testimony of "reintegratees," from the Ortega brothers (Nicaragua) to Handal (El Salvador) to lesser lights like "Sarney," should be accepted only insofar as it correlates with other, more reliable, information.

67. Nor does it mention the familiar practice of drafting young ladies as bed partners for the terrorist bosses, one more example of which also surfaced in October 1996. At that time two fifteen-year-old girls defected from FARC to the military, telling them that "we had to go to bed with the commandants when they wanted it." They further explained that there were "many minors" with these terrorists who have not defected "for fear of being tortured or killed."

68. Florencia and Caguán y Caquetá were originally the two administrative regions in the Special Comisaria of Caquetá. Caquetá contained 25,000 hectares, Caguán y Caquetá 22,500. What is now referred to as "the Caguán" is generally described by Caguán y Caquetá.

69. Plutarco Elias Calles was inaugurated president of Mexico on 30 November 1924. By article 83 of the Constitution of 1917, no one may serve more than one term as president so he formed the National Revolutionary Party (PNR) on 1 February 1928 in order to wield power through puppet presidents. By the time of the elections of 1940 the PNR had become the Mexican Revolutionary Party (PRM) which became the PRI after the elections of 1946.

70. Guillen will be discussed in the next section.

71. Ocosingo (Chiapas) mayor Romeo Suárez received a letter from Las Margaritas on 15 March 1993 relating to "barracks" where "insurgents were being trained" (*Diario de Juarez*, 7 January 1994). Andres Oppenheimer (*Bordering on Chaos: Guerrillas, Stockbrokers, Politicians, and Mexico's Road to Prosperity*, Little Brown, 1996) provides detail on the Mexican government's familiarity with the Zapatistas before 1 January 1994.

72. The Sandinista split, real or "theater," of which Sergio Ramírez leads the "moderate" faction, has resulted in certain dislocations within the Sandinistas yielding information which might otherwise have remained confidential. *Barricada* is a Sandinista daily.

73. Oppenheimer's account (*Chaos*, note 70) of an overall commander in Mexico City was apparently obtained from the terrorists themselves and hence, a priori, has no credence. If true, it is unique, and these terrorists seldom do anything unique. Even if true, however, Guillen has been in nominal command.

74. These will be recounted in connection with a similar incident in Guatemala (chapter 4, "Target Guatemala").

75. The fact that the National Executive Committee (CEN) of the PRD announced on 3 July 1996 that it had established a "formal relation" with the EZLN is relevant.

76. This was originally reported (*La Jornada*, 29 June 1996) as "about 100," but the "consensus" appears to have reduced this to the figure given.
77. Such claims by ML terrorists should never be accepted without independent proof.
78. Liga militant and PRD member Marcos Rascon surfaced in *La Jornada* on 4 January 1994 praising the "utopia of the Zapatista revolution."
79. The LANS editor's contact with the Mexican Ministry of Interior elicited essentially the same information.
80. This was the nickname for the call Netzahualcoyotl.
81. It should be kept in mind that many, if not all, of Latin America's "political prisoners" are in reality common criminals, guilty of such crimes as murder, kidnapping, extortion and so on.
82. Which brings to mind the statements by EPR chiefs to the press that their arms and supplies are the fruit of such activities, although the existence of "foreign aid" should certainly not be dismissed.
83. "Give me a machine gun and an ideology and applaud my crimes."
84. Daniel James, *Red Design for the Americas: Guatemala Prelude* (John Day, 1954). See also Ronald M. Schneider, *Communism in Guatemala: 1944–1954* (Praeger, 1958).
85. Stephen Schlesinger and Stephen Kinzer, *Bitter Fruit* (Doubleday, 1982).
86. Jean-François Ravel, *How Democracies Perish* (Doubleday, 1983).
87. Pp. 267–269, Threat 5.
88. U.S. House Select Committee on Communist Aggression, *Communist Aggression in Latin America: Guatemala* (1954), Y4.C73/5:L34/2.
89. José Lufs Garcia Aceituna, *El Movimiento armada de 13 de noviembre de 1960* (Tipográfica Nacional, 1962).
90. In the 1980s the LANS editor interviewed an individual who was closely related to Carlos Fonseca Amador, the founder of the FSLN in 1961. Here he learned the details of Fonseca's conversion of Turcios to ML when Fonseca was jailed in Guatemala, Turcios his jailer.
91. Mario Payera, *Days of the Jungle: The Testimony of a Guatemalan Guerrillero, 1972–1976* (Monthly Review [originally published by Casa de las Américas, Havana], 1983).
92. Anyone who doubts the ML character of the URNG should consult the formation documents for this organization which was put together in Sandinista Managua under the direction of "Barbaroja" (Redbeard) Piñiero Losada, Castro's chief of the Americas Department, Cuban CP. Formation documents appear, inter alia, in the report of the U.S. Senate Subcommittee on Security and Terrorism, 1982. Each document bears four different symbols—hammers and sickles, Che Guevara, and so on—at page top.
93. Davout (Marshal Louis Nicolas Davout, *Correspondance du maréchal Davout, Prince d'Eckmuhl*, 4 vols., Plon Nourrit, 1885) hardly considered the incident worth recounting, but Marshal Augereau's aide, le baron Henri Bro de Commères (*Mémoires de Général Bro, 1781–1844*, Plon Nourrit, n.d.), did: "The inhabitants of…Pressnitz [east of Auerstädt] had attacked…a munitions convoy. Several military who escorted it, belonging to the Third Corps, had been wounded, and some even killed. The marshal instantly gave orders to invest the village, to spare the women, children and old people, to have all those bearing arms shot and to burn the village…the old bailiff and principal inhabitants came to implore clemency…He pardoned them, saying, 'The French are conquerors, I will pardon you…The inhabitants expose themselves to these terrible vengeances when, violating the laws of war among civilized nations, they form themselves into bands of assassins.'"

94. LANS has been told by certain diplomatic sources that the Jennifer Harbury case (see chapter 4, "Target Guatemala"), has sparked extreme pressure from the United States for Guatemalan conclusion of these accords.

95. M-60 machine gun, 7.62mm NATO, Bridge Tool and Die.

96. Ambassador Curtin Winsor, Jr. was U.S. Ambassador to Costa Rica during the critical 1983–1985 period. He has extensive experience in Guatemala, recently returning from his latest fact-finding trip to that nation.

97. Four principal anti-communist groups emerged in the 1960s and are described, inter alia, by Louis S. Segesvary (*Guatemala: A Complex Scenario*, CSIS, Georgetown University, 1984), one of these being Mano Blanco or the National Organized Anti-Communist Movement (MANO). In April 1988 MANO announced its reactivation with the "red avalanche." In May 1988 it told the TASS and Prensa Latina (Castro's "news" agency) "journalists" to get out of Guatemala which they did without standing "on the order of their going."

98. *Acuerdos de Chapultepec*, Secretaria Nacional de Comunicaciones (SENCO) (San Salvador, n.d.). (The date of signing by the Government of El Salvador (16 January 1992) appears on p. 60.)

99. The CG will be encountered in the notes from the Turcios cadaver.

100. Practically speaking, this meant the elimination of any anti-MLs.

101. "Destacamento" is basically "detachment." During the course of the terrorist unpleasantness the term "Destacamento Militar"—as, for example, DM Four headquartered at San Francisco Gotera, Morazan Department—came to mean a reinforced infantry regiment, that is, an infantry regiment with attached armor, artillery, and choppers.

102. The five Anti-Terrorist Infantry Battalions (BIATs)—Arce, Atonal, Bracamonte, Bellosa, Atlacatl—were immediately demobbed.

103. This means there will be no anti-Marxism Leninism.

104. That is, FAES will not oppose "internal" subversion whether directed, supplied, and commanded from, say, Cuba or not.

105. The Latin American armies have been the only opposition to the well-armed HL. In El Salvador the opposition would now allegedly include only the National Police with Farabundi members.

106. 1987 interview with Rivas Leal by the LANS editor.

107. This order appears to be correct even though his disciples have reversed it in his *Obras* (Works).

108. Gewehr 3, a 7.62mm Heckler and Koch GmbH, later made in a series of models G3A1 through G3A4.

109. *San Francisco Chronicle* (17 January 1991) and in interviews with the LANS editor.

110. Further details are routine for such operations, having been encountered, for example, in 1954 Guatemala when the ML government of Arbenz was expelled. The document referenced in note 87 gives various examples of the Guatemalan situation. The LANS editor has gathered similar information on Pastora from other sources.

111. See note 109.

112. One of the commanders who furnished details to the LANS editor was at Bartola, four kilometers northwest.

113. While these holograph letters and diary entries could be forgeries by a Noriega newspaper, they could also be genuine, the result of a convoluted plot against Pastora by his alleged friend, Noriega.

114. There were some 275,000 inhabitants of the Atlantic Coast region of Nicaragua, 60 percent of them Miskito Indians, 5 percent Sumo Indians, 1 percent Rama Indians, 15 Percent Criollos (Afro-Caribs), and 14 percent ladinos. In

order to protect the region and to defend commnal lands and the natural resources the Alliance for the Progress of the Miskitos and sumos (ALPROMISO)
was formed in August 1973. By the Fall of 1979 the Sandinistas had taken over
and begun accusing ALPROMISO of "separatism." In an initial attempt to main
tain good relations with the Sandins the peoples of the coast changed the name
of their organization to MISURASATA. MISURA is from MIskito-SUmo-RAma,
SA from SAndinista, and "TA" the word for "get together." Sandinista mis-
treatment of the Indians worsened to the point where getting together was impossible, and MISURASATA was soon in the ranks of the enemy where it was
to be found when Spadafora was one of its important leaders.

115. The word in this century has principally been applied to individuals from the
US, but, as those familiar with the Spanish language are aware, it basically
means "foreigner." On the other hand, Ambassador Winsor was told by his
Mexican and Central American friends that the word originated during the
Mexican War of 1846 when the prisoners of war heard their American guards
singing "Green grow the lilies..."

116. This reference to Kolynos toothpaste would have required no footnote a half-
century ago, but perhaps it does now.

117. John William Cooke, *El peronismo y el golpe de estado (informe a las bases
del movimiento)* (Acción Revolucionario Peronista, 1966).

118. Bynum E. Weathers, Jr., *Guerrilla Warfare in Argentina and Colombia, 1974–
1982* (Air University Library, 1982).

119. Eudocio Ravines (*The Yenan Way*, Scribners, 1951) was born (1897) in the
"sleepy little highland city of Cajamarca, Peru." In 1917 he arrived in Lima
"hungry for some faith" and doubting his destiny. He found it temporarily
through José Carlos Mariategui: communism. Rising high in the COMINTERN
he served its "cause" in Spain during the Civil War and in the "Holy City of
Socialism." And saw too much. Choosing against further "pretending to a faith
that was not only dead in me but a decaying corpse," Ravines left the communists and devoted the rest of his life to opposing them.

120. LANS associate editor Alphonse Emanuiloff-Max has written extensively on
Latin America's guerrilla-terrorists, his *Guerrillas in Latin America* (Interdoc,
1971) being appropriate here.

121. The chief of Frente Ricardo Franco was José Fedor Rey (a.k.a. Javier Delgado).
He allegedly quit FARC as a dissident in 1984, his front some four times as
large as most such units. In 1986 he ordered the slaughter of 170 of his own
men as government spies or military, a doubtful reason. According to defectors
from his command in 1987 the number slaughtered was 260. Defectors also
accused him of deserting with $2 million.

122. From Sendero Luminoso to FARC, Latin American ML terrorists have inveighed
against "bloated capitalists and latifundists" but preyed upon the campesino. In
various countries Civil (Self) Defense Patrols have come into being to protect
him and have enjoyed considerable success in their efforts to do so. For example, in Colombia the local PAC cleared the Magdalena Media of a FARC
which had made campesino existence there impossible, a success which was
described in *El Tiempo* (Bogotá, 25 June 1989). This is the principal reason,
from Guatemala to Peru, for the fulmination against "paramilitary" groups.

123. Joseph D. Douglass, Jr., *Red Cocaine: The Drugging of America* (Clarion House,
1990). Dr. Douglass' book is now available from Book, Line and Thinker (Box
1878, Ft. Collins, CO 80522).

124. Vesco fled the US in 1973, accused of stealing $250,000 from Bernard Cornfeld's
Investors Overseas Service. That he was involved with narcotics peddling at

the time of his alleged campaign contributions has apparently not been demonstrated.

125. Cabrera appears to have been involved in narcotrafficking at the time of his campaign contributions and visit to the White House.

126. See note 123.

127. See note 123.

128. José Abrahantes Fernández, a "red-diaper baby," was once Castro's personal bodyguard, later vice minister of the Interior, then minister. With the 1989 show trial and execution of Ochoa et al., Abrahantes was sentenced to twenty years in prison where he mysteriously "died."

129. See note 119.

130. Atahualpa (1500–1533) had just won a civil war against his half-brother for the sovereignty of the Inca "Empire" when Francisco Pizarro arrived (1532) and dispatched this reigning Inca the following year after a reputedly sizable transaction in gold. There were two Peruvians called Tupac Amaru, the second of these the one the succession of terrorists have chosen as their namesake. José Gabriel Condorcanqui (Marqués of Oropesa, 1740–1781), a descendant of the last Inca, Tupac Amaru (d. 1571), chose the name Tupac Amaru II in beginning a revolution in 1780 which was put down in 1783.

131. The novelist, Vargas Llosa, was strident in his criticism of the president for this "un-democratic" action. That Vargas had been soundly defeated by Fujimori in the 1990 elections may have something to do with this criticism. After Fujimori reestablished "democracy," the people would elect him again.

132. The recently released *Las rondas Campesinas y la derrota Sendero Luminoso* by the Institute of Peruvian Studies (IEP) appears to dispute the relative importance of the Fujimori program and these Civilian Defense Patrols (CAPs), giving the major credit to the latter. It can be stated, however, without denigrating the importance of the CAPs, that the important advances against the terrorists were made *after* Fujimori introduced his program.

133. These were *not* treaded vehicles and hence armored cars of some sort rather than "tanks."

134. Simon Strong, *Shining Path: Terror and Revolution in Peru* (Times, 1992).

135. See note 49.

136. Subsequent to the distribution of this Report, additional available information indicated that the JEO initiation time was about one-half hour later.

137. Stevan Koch, *Double Lives: Spies and Writers in the Secret Soviet War Against the West* (Free Press, 1994).

138. Pavel Sudoplatov and Anatoli Sudoplatov (with Jerrold L. and Leona P. Schecter). *Special Tasks: The Memoirs of an Unwanted Witness—A Soviet Spymaster* (Little Brown, 1994).

139. Harvey Klehr, John Earl Haynes and Fridrikh Igorevich Firsov, *The Secret World of American Communism* (Yale University, 1995).

140. A former DGI (Cuban KGB) officer told the LANS editor two years ago that "several" of these occupy important positions in the U.S. government.

141. That the staffs of various important members of the U.S. government have been penetrated is likewise no secret. Which raises the specter of a LANS file photo wherein an important U.S. senator is portrayed on his arrival in Peru in the late 1980s embracing then President Alan Garcia, the roommate of the terrorist Polay Campos.

142. The term was introduced by Cicero in his discourse, *Pro Milone*, cited by Lucius Cassius Longinus Ravilla, Roman Consul, 127 B.C. (Cf. Loeb Classical Library, Cicero vol. 14, *Pro Milone—In Pisonem—Pro Sauro—Pro Fonteio Pro Rabiro*

Postumo—Pro Marcello—Pro Ligario—Pro Rege Deiotaro, translated by N. H. Watts, 1931.)

4

The Hemispheric Left Support

Introduction

The Hemispheric Left Support (HLS) is made of those allegedly "non-political" individuals and organizations who/which, wittingly or unwittingly, (a) furnish moral and material support to the Hemispheric Left (HL), (b) fabricate disinformation or exaggerate information in support of the MLs of the HL and (c) either fabricate or exaggerate accounts of "human rights" violations (HRV) by Latin American governments, their police and their armies.

In the next section the Liberation Theology (LibTheo) clerics, who roam Latin America from the Río Grande to Tierra del Fuego, are discussed. The contributions of these people to the objectives of the HL have been substantial. Examples are provided by Castro's "religious advisor," Friar Beto, the apologist for the Zapatistas, Bishop Ruíz, and a whole spectrum of terrorist support and militancy as is exemplified by the Colombian ELN.

A few samples of important disinformation operations will be given in the section "HLS Disinformation Operations," although these hardly scratch the surface of such immensely valuable contributions to the HL. It is therefore worthwhile to use this Introduction for three brief descriptions of such operations, these ranging from the childish ("Borge Castrated") to the vitally important ("The Robin-Hooding of Castro").

Borge Castrated

An example of a fabricated HRV tale was provided by the HLS accusation that the Somoza government of Nicaragua castrated the Sandinista terrorist, Tomás Borge. Borge's subsequent and well-known amorous activities rendered the charge nonsensical on the face of it, but this would become obvious only later. At the time the Somoza government called in a Red Cross official to inspect this FSLN terrorist, but few, if any, paid heed to this official's denial, and the desired effect had been created.

Bayonets and Babies

Within the last few years a naïve atrocity story was written by a well-known "journalist" and reproduced in one of the largest circulation newspapers in the United States. The tale had to do with a claim that Guatemalan soldiers amused themselves by tossing babies about on bayonets. This story originally came out of the China of the 1930s. The problem that the Guatemalan soldiers would encounter in tossing babies about on their bayonets is that the standard issue weapon in their army is the Galil (5.56mm assault rifle, Israel Military Industries) which does not take a bayonet; indeed, it does not even have a bayonet stud.

The Robin-Hooding of Fidel Castro

Herbert Lionel Matthews (b. 1900, New York, NY) joined the *New York Times* in July 1922. His coverage of Mussolini's Abyssinian adventure (1935–1936) was that of an admirer of Il Duce. His coverage of the Spanish Civil War (1936–1939) was that of an admirer of the Kremlin's International Brigades: these he describes as made up of "the finest group of men I ever knew or hope to know in my life."[1] He was a member of the League of American Writers, a Communist Front cited as such by the U.S. Attorney General and the House Committee on Un-American Activities and tracing its history back to the John Reed Clubs. Matthews's service to Fidel Castro was described by U.S. ambassador to Cuba, Earl E. T. Smith:

> Three front-page articles in the *New York Times* in early 1957 written by the editorialist Herbert Matthews, served to inflate Castro to world stature and world recognition. Until that time, Castro had been just another bandit in the Oriente Mountains of Cuba, with a handful of followers who had terrorized the campesinos, that is the peasants, throughout the countryside.[2]

Finally, the last section, "A Terrorist Operation in the United States," describes what remains the mysterious bombing of the Murrah Building in Oklahoma City, Oklahoma, United States. That this terrorist affair had any connection with matters Latin American remains seriously open to question. Even so, certain obvious experimental observations render it germane to terrorist operations in the region and hence worthy of inclusion here.

Liberation Theology and Liberation Theologians

"LIBERATION" THEOLOGY (SPCL 2.4, 5 SEPTEMBER 1996)

An article appeared in the *Dallas Morning News* (1 January 1996), shortly after the orchestrated Zapatista National Liberation Front (EZLN) "uprising" of 1 January 1994. In that article "Liberation Theology" (LibTheo) was defined as a "force...which teaches that priests have a religious duty to actively help the poor gain a share of society's bounty." Nor have such bizarre descriptions of LibTheo been restricted to the *Dallas Morning News*.[3] Indeed, this description of the LibTheo wolf in the sheeps-clothing of a Christian cleric is remarkably widespread. Since perhaps the most valuable allies of the HL are these clerics, as Fidel Castro attests with his Friar Beto, a more realistic specification of these Marxist theologians is demanded.

During the heyday of the Sandinista National Liberation Front (FSLN) a succinct, realistic description of LibTheo was given over Chilean television by the Nicaraguan Marxist cleric Ernesto Cardenal: "In order to be a good Christian it is primarily necessary to be a Marxist-Leninist." Nor does LibTheo appear to have changed appreciably in the intervening years.

In early 1996 Pope John Paul II was attacking LibTheo in his progress through Central America as Roman Catholic pontiffs have been doing, if at times somewhat diplomatically, since Pius X. Quick to the defense of LibTheo were former Friar Leonardo Boff, São Felix Bishop Pedro Casadaliga, and Nova Iguaçu Bishop Werner Siebenbrock (*Jornal do Brasil*, February 1996). While claiming Heinrich Karl Marx not to be the father of LibTheo, Boff described Marxism as "an effort to understand how the poor had been exploited," claimed "the Church never admitted this," then proceeded to align himself with the Marxist position. The Pope had told the Central Americans that LibTheo had fallen with the Berlin Wall which prompted the *non sequitur* from Bishop Siebenbrock: "The destruction of the Iron Curtain is a European political problem...but Liberation Theology was born in Latin America." As will be seen, LibTheo began in Protestant clerical circles in Europe, not among Catholics in Latin America.

Nor do the clerical practitioners of LibTheo stop at the theological waterline; they have been active in ML terrorist activities in many parts of Latin America. As Rev. Dr. Miguel Poradowsky (see below) has pointed out: (1) A few years ago all twenty of the "worker priests" in Santiago de Chile belonged to some Marxist party that included the CP; and (2) The terrorist group, Sendero Luminoso in Peru, arose from the Calama Group of clergy and laity in northern Chile. To which may be added that the Colombian People's Liberation Army (EPL) was formed in 1968 by the cleric Manuel Pérez, and an AFP dispatch (10 October 1989) reported this terrorist groups as led by twenty-nine clerics. Nor is this the size of it, the LibTheo situation in El Salvador[4] demanding individual treatment.

What has been said to this point relates to what the LibTheo clerics "say" and "do," and the layman should be quite capable of recording this, but a discussion of what LibTheo "is" requires the services of the theologian. In the latter 1980s the LANS editor worked closely with the Rev. Dr. Miguel Poradowsky in the translation of his *El Marxismo en la Teología*. The following review is intended to present Rev. Poradowsky's theological treatment of LibTheo.

El Marxismo en la Teología. Miguel Poradowsky. Imprenta LaHosa. Santiago de Chile. 1983. Second Edition. 292 pages. Reviewed by the editor, LANS.

Born in Poland in 1913, Poradowsky was ordained there in 1936, beginning his university studies in that country, to devote five years to their completion after World War II in Paris where he received doctorates in theology, law, and sociology. In 1950 he arrived under contract at the Catholic University of Santiago, Chile, remaining there until 1952 when, with a Spanish scholarship, he spent two years in Spain. In 1954 he joined the Theology Faculty of the Catholic University of Valparaiso where he remained.

In the Santiago of 1972 some 500 mostly Marxist clerics held the Latin American Congress of Christians for Socialism. Its final document, "The strategic friendship between the Christians and the Marxists," included a verbatim portion of Engels' description of early Christianity as "a party without a country, international...this party of revolt..." The Mexican delegation to the Congress was headed by the well-known Marxist Bishop of Cuernavaca, Sergio Méndez Arceo.

Poradowsky shows LibTheo to be the end result of a gradual marxization of a portion of the clergy, a marxization consistently opposed by the Vatican, Pope Paul IV remarking (10 October 1973) "against the multiple tendencies to secularize the sacerdotal service," other Pontiffs following suit. This gradual process consists of four phases: (1) Saduceeism; (2) horizontal Christianity; (3) demythologized Christianity; and (4) atheistic Christianity.

Sadduceeism, the term with which Poradowsky describes the first phase in the marxization of Christianity, is taken from the sect of the Sadducees in the time of Christ. The Sadducees did not believe in the resurrection, their religious life limited "to imploring God's blessing…to insure happiness in the earthly life…it is quite common in the works of Protestant theologians and from them has passed to Catholic theology in the thought of Bonhoeffer[5] and others."[6]

In the second phase, horizontal Christianity, the vertical dimension of the Cross, as symbol of man's love for God, is eliminated, leaving only the horizontal love of man for man. Bonhoeffer was among the first protagonists of this exclusive concern with mortal man. Through the process is skillfully woven the assertion of the alleged equality of the "perfect" socialist society of the future and the "eschatologically diffuse Kingdom of God on Earth." "One of the first…who began to construct bridges between Christianity and Marxism was…the Protestant theologian Karl Barth" for whom see his disciple Marquardt.[7] "There are points in which the position of Barth is almost identical with that of Marx." Bloch[8] had prepared the way for Barth.

In the third phase of this marxization of Christianity religion is detached from faith and destroyed. This may be illustrated by the remark of Julio Santa Ana, "Faith is the Christianity of the adult, mature person while religion is infantile Christianity."[9] The demythologized Christianity which follows is well illustrated by Porfirio Miranda[10] in his interpretation of the Bible from the Marxist point of view, an interpretation which was at least partly responsible for Pope Paul VI's warning (18 July 1973) "against… arbitrary ideologies…[seeking] to give to Christianity a new interpretation…"

The marxization of Christianity is completed with the fourth phase, atheistic Christianity, as perhaps most widely propagated in Latin America by Jordan Bishop McClave, cleric, Dominican and, after years of such "preaching," apostate. "Christ was neither a pious nor a religious man; this image of Christ worshipper of God and founder of a religion (Christianity) is the product of a legend.[11] As defender of the oppressed, Christ was the precursor of Marx and Lenin…" The French communist Roger Garaudy tells us this.

Leonardo Boff[12] is a Brazilian, a Franciscan monk, a perennial thorn in the Papal side. He was Castro's honored guest at the July 1993 São Paulo Forum. The "Marxist Mariology" of Boff[13] holds that the Marianist cult is but the "orchestration of Christianity by the bourgeoisie, classing the Blessed Virgin as "the revolutionary model of rebelling woman." "Virginity," Boff says, "is equivalent in Judaism to sterility," then proceeds to turn his marianist cult to the service of the Marxist revolution.

And that is the reality of LibTheo. As Poradowsky points out, "One truly helps the poor by working among them with the zeal invoked by Ozanam,[14] one kills and destroys to bring Marxism." The book, which has been reviewed, treats of related topics such as black theology and the theology of tribalism. While these are important, they are not as generally important to contemporary Latin America as "Liberation Theology."

HLS Disinformation Operations

Target NACR (Nicaraguan Anticommunist Resistance)

THE CONTRA-DRUG DISINFORMATION OPERATION
(WKLY 2.8, 3 OCTOBER 1996)

The most obvious mistake, which the U.S. CIA has made, may have been its attempt to ape its senior in intelligence, British MI5.[15] As a result, the CIA has stood aloof when attacked with various disinformation operations aimed at its destruction, refusing not only to attempt adequate answers, but even to obtain available information which would have demonstrated the anatomy of the operation. As will become clear, instead of "blowing over," such disinformation settles in as part of the landscape. As Emanuiloff-Max has remarked, "Nada mas tenaz que las leyendas, una vez echada a rodar el mundo. Los mitos son mas resistentes que las verdades, e impersonables a los hechos." (Nothing is more persevering than legends, once thrown out to roam the world. Myths are more enduring than truths and immune to facts.)

The policy has gone so far that a recent set of newspaper articles accusing the CIA of narcotrafficking has resulted in President Clinton and CIA director Deutsch declaring their intention of "investigating the charges." It is an observable fact that a portion of the citizenry and its political leadership are taking the charges seriously, charges making up one more roaming legend, a legend born twelve years ago.

Although attempts to destroy the CIA predate 1984, this particular operation began that year, primarily as a disinformation operation aimed at the Nicaraguan Anticommunist Resistance (NACR) but soon broadened to include the CIA. It may be divided into four phases: (1) the La Penca Bombing; (2) the Contra-Drug charges; (3) the Terry Reed book (*Compromised*, 1995); and (4) the three-article series which appeared in the *San Jose Mercury*, "Dark Alliance." This is not to say that each of the players in this series of events is intimately connected with all the others. But once the game began the deliciously scandalous nature of the charges would assure that it would be carried far and wide with open invitations to others to play.

The La Penca Bombing

In 1987 the LANS editor, because of his familiarity with the terrain, was commissioned to investigate the La Penca bombing and its aftermath, the contrived disinformation campaign from which the Contra drug charges have arisen.

It was 1915 on 30 May 1984 and full dark at La Penca, the stilted-shack headquarters of Democratic Revolutionary Alliance (ARDE) chief Edén Pastora (see chapter 3, "Nicaragua," Spcl 2.3) who was haranguing a group of journalists. An individual traveling with a passport identifying him as Per Anker Hansen had just set down a camera-case-looking object of cross section about ten-by-eighteen inches. A San José television Channel 7 camera, whose operator would not survive, has recorded his doing this and withdrawing from the shack. Just as Rosita, Pastora's radio operator, trips over the case on the floor the phony Anker Hansen detonates the bomb inside by remote control: Flames billow out through the roof and down through the floor, proving to various intelligence personnel whom the LANS editor has interviewed that the explosive was not the C4 which was claimed by the "CIA-did-it" theorists. This bombing was important enough so that it will be treated later in this chapter, (see "Target NACR", Spcl 2.9) but it is important here as the opening curtain in this disinformation operation.

"The Brains and the Horse"

Martha Spencer Honey (b. 9 March 1945, Orange, NJ) and Anthony Lance Avirgan (b. 30 November 1944, Philadelphia, PA) were a pair of "free lance 'journalists'" who had arrived in Costa Rica from Marxist Tanzania in 1983. They will be further discussed in Spcl 2.9 below. Although originally beaten to the punch by Fidel Castro's news agency (31 April 1984) in accusing the CIA of the bombing, Honey-Avirgan had soon taken up the cudgels of this accusation. That the accusation was contrived is ultimately demonstrated by the identity of the bomber, the Argentine Vital Roberto Gaguine (b. 23 June 1953).

Gaguine was identified as the bomber, inter alia, in the *Miami Herald* of 1 August 1993. That the *Herald* appears to have an anti-CIA bias was indicated in the same article, for example, by the equation of the CIA, the Cuban KGB (DGI) and the Nicaraguan KGB (DGSE)— ("an era when CIA, Sandinistas and Cuban spies fought a *nasty* little war" [*Herald*, 1 August 1993]). The bias was further emphasized by off-hand, unsupported anti-CIA remarks ("Given the CIA's history of *nasty* meddling in Latin America" [ibid.]). Thus, an admission by this source that the La Penca bombing was carried out by Gaguine, a member of the Argentine ML terrorist group People's Revolutionary Army (EPR),[16] should be convincing. The identification is based, first, on the match of a thumbprint on a Panamanian document filed by "Hansen" in 1982 and the fingerprints of Gaguine taken for his Argentine national identity card in 1972. Second, Gaguine's father and brother both identified him as the bomber from photographs taken at the time of the bombing.

The Pastora hit had been decided on by the Sandinista Politburo (Nine "Commanders," National Directorate) the year before (1983) so it appears probable, if unproven, that Honey-Avirgan, friends of the Sandinistas as has been attested, were aware of it. If not, Honey—the "Brains," Avirgan the "Horse"—demonstrated a superior talent for improvisation when her partner was brought back from the bombing to the hospital in Ciudad Quesada.

Transportation had been provided by canoe from Boca Tapada on the San Carlos River to and across the San Juan to La Penca. The first canoe to return contained the seriously injured Susan Morgan, the uninjured Gaguine, the uninjured Torgeson—Gaguine's "traveling companion"—and the uninjured Avirgan. On 28 November 1987 the LANS editor interviewed the man who had been chief of the emergency room at Ciudad Quesada Hospital that night, Dr. Max A. Pacheco Paniagua. At 2150, on receiving official notification of the terrorist bombing, Pacheco dispatched two medics, one paramedic, and four nurses to Boca Tapada to bring in the survivors. Memorable was the fire still in

Pacheco's eye when he spoke of the seriously wounded waiting for a boat-car trip to the hospital while the three healthy ones got away.

The physician adamantly maintained that Avirgan had no injuries save for some scratches and burns on his hands that Pacheco thought were self-inflicted. As he told the LANS editor, however, in such blasts there would be a shock wave which could have caused internal injuries, and he wanted tests. Apparently already thinking of the "hole in the side"[17] he would claim from the blast, Avirgan adamantly refused. U.S. Ambassador Curtin Winsor has told the editor that, when he visited Avirgan in a San José hospital, the latter had only "an injury to the middle finger of his left hand."

Finally, Honey herself admitted the fraud. "Martha called me two days later," San José USIS (U.S. Information Service) chief Mark Krischik told the LANS editor in a 1987 interview. "In reply to my 'How's Tony?', she answered, without thinking, 'The doctor says there's no big problem; it's mostly cosmetic.'"

Pacheco recalled that Honey arrived at the hospital about fifty minutes after Avirgan and began a scramble to get him out of the hospital and the country. [He would tell Ambassador Winsor that he wanted to "avoid being involved in the government investigation of La Penca."— Ed.] What happened to Torgeson and Gaguine is discussed in Spcl 2.9 below. Honey got her husband to Clinica Biblica in San José where Ambassador Winsor visited him and was told by Avirgan that he wanted to get out of the country "to prevent nerve damage" to his finger. This Winsor arranged, and Avirgan fled Costa Rica and detention as a material witness.

The next year Honey-Avirgan[18] began their anti-CIA campaign in earnest, blaming that organization for the La Penca bombing. John Hull would file a libel suit in a Costa Rican court as a result of this "report," which would be dismissed in a bizarre trial which gave Honey-Avirgan opening for another attack on the CIA,[19] this book dedicated to "David who gave his life." Honey-Avirgan alleged that Hull murdered David (Jarald David Mortera Cordoncillo) whom the LANS Editor later interviewed (15 November 1987) where Hull was hiding him from Pastora's "security chief."

The Contra-Drug Charges

The demonstrably false La Penca accusation against the Contras and the CIA would be amplified to include charges of Contra and CIA narcotrafficking. One of the first steps in the Contra-Drug disinformation operation was the Pocosol Gambit.

The Pocosol River empties into the San Juan about three miles upstream from El Castillo, Camp Pocosol three miles up the river from the San Juan on the left bank. On 25 May 1985 the Costa Rican Guardia Rural picked up the men at this camp, accused them of being Contras and imprisoned them in San José. There were thirteen men, some of whom claimed not to be Contras: one Frenchman, two Britishers, two North Americans, and eight Nicaraguans. Of these eleven furnished affidavits,[20] all of which correspond, *mutatis mutandis*, with the following sworn statement by the Britisher, John Howard Davies.

> After our arrest we were held incommunicado for eight days without being able to contact our embassy...during this time we were visited by...Honey-Avirgan...Honey-Avirgan made the offer of a quick release from prison if we would agree to make false statements that the Costa Rican Government, the US Embassy, the CIA, National Security Council, John Hull, etc., were actively involved in Contra activities, including linked and invented atrocities. Peter Glibbery [the other Britisher]...and Steve Carr [one of the U.S.] agreed to do so. Robert Thompson [the other U.S.], Claude Chaffard [the Frenchman], and myself [and the eight Nicaraguans] refused to say things that we knew to be false...we received offers of money for our bail from...Honey and Avirgan, providing we would...leave Costa Rica illegally and give false testimony before a U.S. congressional committee...Carr and Glibbery accepted and lived in the house of Honey and Avirgan...Carr and Glibbery also tried to get us to accept money that was being furnished by [U.S.] Senator John Kerry of Massachusetts...[if] we confirm...falsehoods of Carr and Glibbery in Washington.

West 57th Street

Cockburn's book of Honey allegations has been mentioned.[20] She also produced a program for CBS' *West 57th Street* (6 April 1987) entitled "Jane Wallace Reports on Charges That the CIA Funded the Contras through Illegal Drug Sales." Ms. Wallace opens the program with an intro capsuled in the statement "drug smuggling organized by the CIA to supply the Contras." The program claims the existence of various sources, but the only identified sources of the alleged Contra-Drug link are three convicted criminals dredged up out of the prisons of south Florida and dressed for television: Mike Tolliver, George Morales, and Gary Betzner. Unsupported testimony from such unreliable witnesses is the best that has been done in the ongoing attempt to destroy, first the Contras and now the CIA. Such suspect "testimony," when specific enough to be investigated, has proven fraudulent.

Betzner claims to have taken off from the Hull airstrip at Muelle (Costa Rica) with 500 kilograms of cocaine on two occasions. Which means he was never at the strip. This did not happen because it could not have happened as the LANS editor has demonstrated.

In the late 1940s the LANS editor was an experimental test pilot in the US Flight Test Division running single-engine takeoff tests on the (twin-engined) F-82E. These tests are appropriate to Betzner's alleged takeoff. Because (1) the Hull grass strip has an effective length of 1500 feet and (2) Betzner claims to have taken off a Cessna 402B with 1100 pounds of coke, the story is clearly fabricated. The LANS editor measured the Hull strip and found that it did not have the 2500-foot length indicated on the aeronautical chart.[21]

Such is the case because (a) the first (or last) 186 yards of the takeoff roll would be down (up) a hill constituting a taxi strip from the hangar and (b) the last (or first) 147 yards of roll would be along a dogleg left (or right). This nonsense shows that Betzner was never near the Hull strip. The LANS editor has used his FAA Approved Flight Manual, 1977 Model 402B, to calculate the takeoff roll which would be required to get this aircraft off the ground. Under the conditions obtaining at the Hull strip the 402B, *not overloaded*, would require 3070 feet of strip. The *700-pound overload* with 1100 pounds of coke would require substantially more.

This Contra-CIA-Drug disinformation operation was amateurishly prepared, but this hardly affected its success.

The Terry Reed Book

Terry Reed has written a book (*Compromised: Clinton, Bush and the CIA,* 1955) which will be reviewed in Spcl 1.8 below. It is allegedly an account of Reed's experiences at Mena, Arkansas, and in addition to claiming involvement in narcotrafficking by President Bush and President Clinton, again brings up the charge that the CIA was involved in bringing drugs into the United States in order to fund Contra activity in Central America.

A review of this book demonstrates this to be a simple extrapolation of the long lasting disinformation operation that has been discussed above.

There may or may not have been anything going on at Mena, but, if anything, it has not yet been demonstrated as having any connection with Central America. As observed in the field by the LANS editor, the Contras on the Northern Front (Honduran) were supplied largely with

Belgian FALs;[22] those on the Southern Front (Costa Rica) reported as supplied with AKs[23] and SKSs.[24]

Therefore, the M-16s described in *Compromised* were almost certainly not supplied to the Contras. FARC has been suggested to LANS as the destination for such weapons were any actually shipped. Until and unless further information is obtained *Compromised* warrants no further consideration.

LANS has been informed that Reed has withdrawn his lawsuit against the U.S. government.

The San Jose Mercury News Articles

Two articles involving CIA and Contra involvement in drug trafficking appeared in the *San Jose Mercury News* on 18 and 19 August 1996. The third article (20 August) discusses the impact of drugs on black Americans. At least until recently these articles appeared at the website of the *Mercury News* (http://www.sjmercury.com), and LANS subscribers are urged to peruse them carefully. [This was written in early October 1996 and ceased to be a viable suggestion shortly thereafter when the articles were removed from the website—Ed.]

The first article is entitled "America's 'Crack' Plague Has Roots in Nicaraguan War: Colombia-San Francisco Bay Area Drug Pipeline Helped Finance CIA-Backed Contras." The first paragraph of this article begins with "For the better part of a decade, a San Francisco Bay Area drug ring sold tons of cocaine…and funneled millions in drug profits to a Latin American guerrilla army run by the U.S. CIA…" This whammo opening statement is allegedly proven by the "testimony" of two known drug traffickers, Oscar Danilo Blandon Reyes and Juan Norwin Meneses Cantarero, and vague references to allegedly existent "documents."

The LANS editor spent time with the Nicaraguan Democratic Force, (Contras [FDN]) knew its military commander, Enrique Bermúdez, its overall leader, Adolfo Calero, and various other of its members, high and low. But he never heard of Blandon and Meneses nor has since found anyone who had. Roberto J. Arguelo, a prominent Nicaraguan banker and syndicated columnist, is particularly well acquainted with the Contras and had answered questions by the *Mercury News* author before publication. He had never heard of Blandon and Meneses either.

"These two were in the FDN," Arguello told LANS, "but they were PFCs [privates first class] that nobody ever heard of. That an army truck driver deals drugs on the side can hardly be used to condemn the commanding general for narcotrafficking." But, in understandable extrapolation of what has gone before, this appears to be what is happening here. In the first article Blandon is quoted as saying, "'There is a saying that the end justifies the means,' Blandon…testified…'And that's what Mr. Bermúdez told us in Honduras, OK? So we started raising money for the Contra revolution.'" In the second article the "means" statement of Blandon is repeated, but the following statement is added: "While Blandon says Bermúdez didn't know cocaine would be the fundraising device they used, the *presence* of the mysterious Mr. Meneses strongly *suggests* otherwise" [emphasis added].

In addition to this inconclusive "testimony" of the two narcotraffickers, there are various vague references to records of one sort and another. For example, in the first article it is stated that "The cash ['Freeway Rick'] Ross paid for cocaine, court records show, was then used to buy weapons and equipment for a guerrilla army…[the] FDN…" What "court records"?

THE CONTRA-DRUG DISINFORMATION OPERATION BEGINS: LA PENCA (SPCL 2.9, 3 OCTOBER 1996)

In Wkly 2.8 above the Contra-Drug Disinformation Operation has been discussed in general. Because of the importance of the La Penca bombing to this operation as its starting point, it will be discussed somewhat more extensively here. It was at La Penca that one more roaming legend was born twelve years ago. Although the NACR can be classified as the prime target, the operation was soon broadened to include the CIA.

The key players in the operation were two "freelance 'journalists.'" Martha Spencer Honey (b. 9 March 1945, Orange, NJ), the "Brains," and Anthony Lance Avirgan (b. 30 November 1944, Philadelphia, PA), the "Horse," who had arrived in Costa Rica the year before after a long stint in Marxist Tanzania. They would: (1) appear at Boca Tapada for departure for Pastora's news conference bringing the bomber and his "travelling companion" with them; (2) immediately begin propagating the fiction that Avirgan was wounded in the blast; (3) create a mythical "Amac Galil" as the CIA-hired bomber; (4) strive for years to use (2) and (3) to bring a RICO conspiracy charge against anyone they could conjure up who had any connection with the CIA and/or the Contras.

The La Penca Bombing

In 1987 the LANS Editor, because of his familiarity with the terrain, was commissioned to investigate the La Penca bombing and its aftermath, the contrived disinformation campaign from which the Contra-Drug charges have arisen.

Edén Pastora Gómez, the alleged Contra commander, had called a press conference for the evening of 30 May 1984. It was to be held at his La Penca "headquarters" on the north (left) bank of the San Juan River in Nicaraguan territory. On that 30 May three Democratic Revolutionary Alliance (ARDE) jeeps picked up all save three of the "journalists" who were to attend, taking them from San José to Boca Tapada. The bomber, travelling with the stolen passport of one Per Anker Hansen, his travelling companion, Torgeson, and Avirgan were taken to the landing in Honey's car. Boca Tapada is a few miles up the San Carlos River from the San Juan, the former emptying into the latter on its south (right) bank, La Penca on the left bank some two statute miles upstream. From its location it is about twenty-seven miles upstream to El Castillo.

It was 1915 and full dark at the stilted-shack headquarters of Pastora who was talking to the reporters when the blast occurred. As recorded by San José television Channel 6[25] camera whose operator would not survive, "Per Anker Hansen" put down a camera-case looking object (the bomb) of ten-by-eighteen inch cross section and withdrew from the shack. The bomber then took a position on the river side of some fuel drums setting off the charge by remote control. Two sketches of the shack and the personnel present were obtained by the LANS editor from La Nación (San José), one of which shows Avirgan against the east wall, about as far away from the explosive device as possible.

Pastora's radio operator, Rosita, had been pressed into service as a coffee server. On her way to deliver coffee to the counter around which Pastora and several journalists were gathered, she kicked the bomb over, the only hitch in the terrorist plan. In the act of stepping over the bomb again she was blown in half.

The explosive device was of "Claymore" type with bronze balls and steel rings (tori) imbedded horizontally around the explosive. As to the explosive, Fidel Castro's news agency began claiming it to be C4 the next morning, this probably based on the fact that the CIA supplied C4 to the Contras. Those experts with whom the LANS editor has talked maintain that the fiery nature of the blast indicates a phosphorous-based explosive, and, if Pastora suffered the burns alleged, this might be further verification.

The identity of the person who did the bombing was never in doubt; it was the man using the passport of Per Anker Hansen. The first canoe which arrived at Boca Tapada brought the seriously wounded Susan Morgan (*Newsweek*), the uninjured "Anker Hansen," the uninjured Torgeson, and the uninjured Avirgan. On 28 November 1987 the LANS editor interviewed the man who had been chief of the emergency room at Ciudad Quesada Hospital that night, Dr. Max A. Pacheco Paniagua. Only *one* other journalist did so. At 2150, on receiving official notification of the terrorist bombing, Pacheco dispatched two medics, one paramedic, and four nurses to Boca Tapada to bring in the survivors. Memorable was the fire still in Pacheco's eye when he spoke of the seriously wounded waiting for the boat-car trip to the hospital while the three healthy ones got away.

The physician adamantly maintained that Avirgan had no injuries save for some scratches and burns on his hands that Pacheco thought were self inflicted. As he told the LANS editor, however, in such blasts there would be a shock wave which could cause internal injuries, and he wanted tests. Apparently already thinking of the "hole in his side"[26] he would claim from the blast, Avirgan adamantly refused. U.S. Ambassador Curtin Winsor has told the LANS editor that, when he visited Avirgan in a San José hospital, the latter had only "an injury to the middle finger of his left hand."

Finally, Honey herself admitted the fraud. "Martha called me two days later," San José USIS chief Mark Krischik told the LANS editor in a 1987 interview. "In reply to my 'How's Tony?', she answered, without thinking, 'The doctor says there's no big problem; it's mostly cosmetic.'

"About that time," Krischik went on with a grin, "she realized her mistake, asked a trivial question or two, and rang off."

If Honey did not know beforehand that the bombing was to take place, she demonstrated a superior talent for improvisation when her partner was brought to the hospital in Ciudad Quesada. Pacheco recalled that Honey arrived at the hospital about fifty minutes after Avirgan and began a scramble to get him out of the hospital—which she did, not long after midnight—and the country. (He would tell Ambassador Winsor that he wanted to "avoid being involved in the government investigation of La Penca.") She got her husband to Clinica Biblica in San José where Ambassador Winsor visited him and was told by Avirgan that he wanted to get out of the country to "prevent nerve damage" to his finger. This Winsor arranged, and Avirgan fled Costa Rica and detention as a material witness.

About three o'clock in the morning Torgeson started raising hell, claiming that somebody had stolen $2000 from him. Dr. Pacheco thought that he was trying to draw attention away from the main issue by raising a phony one, but Torgeson carried on so that he called in Judicial Intelligence (OIJ). The pair, Torgeson, and "Anker Hansen," were in the waiting room until 0700 on the morning of 31 May, at which time they signed out of the hospital, never released.

Someone had arranged a taxi at the hospital for "Anker Hansen" and Torgeson, apparently the reason they left when they did. They taxied over the mountains to San José where the bomber registered at the Hotel Costa Rica, paying for his room in advance. He went to his room, then disappeared, not to be seen by the Costa Rican authorities again. The LANS editor encountered various rumors as to where "Anker Hansen" went and who he was, rumors now not worthy of repetition. Who Honey-Avirgan claimed him to be has proven to be fabulous, but, because of its importance to their disinformation operation, it should be repeated.

Amac Galil

Honey-Avirgan soon conjured up a "right wing"—meaning anti-ML—Arab in the pay of the CIA who was, according to them, the La Penca bomber. In the spring of 1988 the LANS editor appeared on a talk show with Avirgan and told him, inter alia, that he had no evidence of the existence of such an individual. To which Avirgan replied that "we have mountains of evidence, mountains." In reply to the host's request for just a piece of this evidence, Avirgan replied, "Jack Terrell." His inference was clear that, if Terrell was not their only piece of evidence on CIA-Contra involvement in La Penca, he was their best. Indeed, "Flaco" (Skinny) Jack had testified for the pair at the Hull suit against them as follows.

Terrel testified[27] that there was a "meeting in [Miami, FL]...and those present were Adolfo Calero [FDN head], Enrique Bermúdez [Contra military chief],..." He added various others who would probably be known to those intimately familiar with the Contras, then added "...and two other men who were sitting outside on Adolfo Calero's patio."

Terrell then "testified" that Calero said "...in the presence of these people that Pastora had to go...On this occasion I did not know that...we were conspiring to kill Pastora." Neither did the others of those, allegedly present, whom the LANS editor has since interviewed. There is some cross fire with Hull's lawyer before Honey's lawyer, Otto Castro Sánchez, takes up the questioning and soon gets to the identity of the two men he alleges were on Calero's patio. Terrell replied that "he [Felipe Vidal] told me that this man was an official with the Mosad [Israeli Intelligence] and that he used the name Amac Galil."

Honey-Avirgan then state[28] that Castro showed Terrell "a rather blurred photo" of the bomber which he could not identify, but he was later shown a "series of photos" by "judicial investigators" from which he did identify the bomber. But, when put under oath for a deposition in the United States, Terrell told a quite different story or, more accurately, no story at all.

The deposition was given in February 1988 and later reproduced in two parts totaling about 200 pages (in LANS files), much of which is reproduction of questions that the attorneys would have liked to ask the "witness." This was in the suit under the RICO Statute (Civil Action no. 86-1545-CIV-KING) brought by Honey-Avirgan (see Spcl 1.8 below). On page 12 he is asked about the documents he was directed to bring, and he begins pleading the Fifth Amendment and refusing to answer which he continues from this point. The questions about "Amac Galil" begin on page 49 of the first part, and his reticence continues. If any further proof of the non-existence of Amac Galil had been needed, it would have been furnished with the discovery of the real La Penca bomber.

Vital Roberto Gaguine

That the accusation against the CIA and the Contras was contrived is ultimately demonstrated by the identity of the bomber, the Argentine Vital Roberto Gaguine (b. 23 June 1953). Gaguine was identified as the bomber, inter alia, in the *Miami Herald* of 1 August 1993. That the *Herald* appears to have an anti-CIA bias is indicated in the same article. In one example of this, the CIA is equated to the Cuban KGB (DGI) and the Nicaraguan KGB (DGSE) with "an era when the CIA, Sandinista, and Cuban spies fought a *nasty* little war" (*Herald* 1 August 1993). Another is provided by off-hand anti-CIA remarks such as "Given the CIA's history of *nasty* meddling in Latin America..." (ibid.) [emphasis added]. Thus, an admission by this source that the La Penca bombing was carried out by a member of the Argentine ML terrorist group, People's Revolutionary Army (EPR),[29] Gaguine, should be convincing. The identification is based, first, on the match of a thumbprint on a Panamanian document filed by "Hansen" in 1982 and the fingerprints of Gaguine taken for his Argentine national identity card in 1972. Second, Gaguine's father and brother both identified him as the bomber from photographs taken at about the time of the bombing.

The Pastora hit had been decided upon by the Sandinista Politburo (Nine "Commanders," National Directorate) the year before (1983) so that it appears probable, if unproven, that Honey-Avirgan, friends of the Sandinistas as has been attested, were aware of it.

AMBASSADOR WINSOR ON THE LA PENCA BOMBING

(WKLY 2.9, 10 OCTOBER 1996)

LANS has received the following communication from Ambassador Winsor:

To the Editor:
   An additional note on Tony Avirgan's injuries, taken from my written recollections of the La Penca aftermath.
   He specifically had an injured upper left middle finger, for which he claimed "ligament damage requiring immediate evacuation on a waiting jet sent by a U.S. TV network." He claimed that his middle finger was important to his camera work. His appearance did suggest presence at a blast. There were dirt specks imbedded in all exposed portions of his skin. Unsightly, but doctors informed me that these were not injuries.
   To prevent ligament deterioration, a doctor had made a small incision in Avirgan's mid-abdomen in which his injured finger was inserted. This was the sum total of his injuries.
   I will always regret encouraging the Costa Ricans to let him go before interrogation. The improvised abdominal "wet" for his famous middle finger (Honey claimed lack of "consort" in her famous RICO lawsuit...) probably swayed my judgment by giving the injury an undo appearance of gravity.
   You might also have noted that the assassins, Avirgan and Morgan made it across the river and into Costa Rica ahead of my friend Linda Fraser, a reporter for the *Tico Times* (San José), whose legs were blown off. She died in agony with no medical care. She was a young mother of two and bitterly mourned in the *Tico Times*.
   Many, especially Honey, tried to blame the United States for not doing more. We had nothing available. The blast occurred in Sandinista Nicaragua. The evacuation, such as it was, crossed the San Juan River into one of Costa Rica's most remote areas. Pastora led the flight from the scene in his outboard, with a relatively minor knee injury and he took none of the wounded with him.
   The whole episode produced much tragedy, exposed gross cowardice, and enabled these vile assassins of character to have a field day.

Curtin Winsor, Jr.
U.S. Ambassador, San José, 1983–1985.

MENA, ARKANSAS: THE VIEW FROM CENTRAL AMERICA
(SPCL 1.8, 24 JULY 1996)

Compromised: Clinton, Bush and the CIA. Terry Reed and John Cummings. Clandestine Publishers. Woodacre, CA. 1995. 712 pp. (Revised and expanded edition of the 1994 book). Reviewed by the LANS editor.

Terry Reed is a Vietnam veteran who claims "knowledge of deep, dark, dirty government secrets that compromised individuals in positions of power" (p. x). His book, co-authored with the former *Newsday* writer, John Cummings, is allegedly "about the knowledge." Reed claims that "in Arkansas...I and others made our way carefully through the crack in the congressional compromise strategically built into the Boland amendments for the purpose of allowing secret aid to the Contras" (p. xi).

In this Preface to his second edition Reed tells us that "he sat in a dimly lit...bunker outside Little Rock...I observed the CIA compromise both major political parties, I can attest...[and] witnessed the creation of a counterfeit president" in a "CIA conspiracy to elevate 'proper candidates' to the [presidency]..." Finally, he tells us that he learned "firsthand...that our government's stated drug policy had been compromised by the CIA..." Later (p. 183) Reed asks "was there a secret alliance of agents worldwide" and is told by his alleged Agency superior, Sawahata: "Agency is the government."

Young Mr. Reed claims to have learned about the CIA "octopus," its involvement in drugs and laundered money for M-16s, in Mena, Arkansas, where he also uncovered the narcotrafficking activities of then Governor Bill Clinton and his retinue, of then President George Bush and of Lt. Col. Oliver North. Whatever part of his tale may be true, M-16s were not the weapons furnished the Nicaraguan Contras. As the LANS editor learned from time and contact with the Contras, these were largely Belgian FALs on the northern front, AK-47s, and SKSs on the southern.[30] More intriguing to this reviewer, anyone who operated in Central America during the 1980s has heard this tale before.

During the last ten years this reviewer was deeply involved, here and in Central America, in the investigation of a lawsuit brought against twenty-nine defendants under the RICO statute. The plaintiffs were two expatriate stringers, Martha Honey and Tony Avirgan, notorious for their sojourn in Hanoi at the height of the Vietnam War and their "From Hanoi With Love." "Hanoi" was a far-left propaganda piece which adumbrated their behavior in Marxist Tanzania from 1973 and in Costa Rica from 1983. Their intimate connection with the ML Sandinistas has been attested to the writer by various Central American intelligence and narcotics agents.

The lawsuit was the final phase of their attempt to destroy the Contras with fabricated disinformation, an effort in which they were strongly supported by Leslie Cockburn[31] and the Christic Institute. The reviewer has treated the Cockburn book in detail,[32] and Dr. Susan Huck[33] has dealt with the far-left Christics. The lawsuit was thrown out of court on 23 June 1988 as unsupported by a scintilla of evidence. Have Reed and Cummings taken up Honey-Avirgan's cudgels?

Reed-Cummings carry the CIA universal power "theory" a step further with Clinton and North in the Arkansas bunker plotting to run modified M-16s south and cocaine north, Contra-Drug again and an extrapolation of the efforts of Cockburn, the Christics and Honey-Avirgan, all of whom appear in *Compromised*. First, Reed tells us (p. 505) that Cockburn's book was the favorite of his lawyer, Steve Robison. Next the Christic investigator, Pierre, "decided...to help them [the Reed family]..., free of charge," which he, meaning the Christics, apparently did. Finally, Honey-Avirgan enter the scenario when Reed-Cummings claim a lawyer told them:

"...since the Christic ruling, no one in his right mind sues the government," a statement which is footnoted by an account of suit dismissal. The account describes allegations, which were exactly Reed's own, without telling us why these allegations, quite justifiably, were dropped. This was no Star Chamber hearing: In Case no. 86-1146-CIV-KING, U.S. District Judge James Lawrence King (Southern District of Florida) on 23 June 1988 ordered the case thrown out as backed by no evidence and justified his action in an opinion which may be obtained by writing to the Court (301 N. Miami Ave., Miami, FL 33128-7788).

It appears that Reed has extrapolated the disinformation operation of Honey-Avirgan, Cockburn, and the Christics with regard to the CIA and Contra-Drug. But his extensive detail may indicate that something was happening at Mena. Narcoterrorists, such as the ML FARC (see chapter 3, "Columbia"), have long paid top dollar or kilo of coke for the M-16. Is the "Mena secret" something akin to this?

However farfetched, these charges deserve an airing at some more cogent level than an occasional radio talk show, even should such an airing result in duress vile for sitting or retired presidents. But while giving presidents a vetting they may well deserve, let us finally reveal what a number of us have long known: The Honey-Avirgan-Christic-Cockburn-et al. disinformation, which may be in the process of extrapolation by Reed, should be described and ultimately exposed for what it was, one of the most vigorously pursued disinformation operations yet undertaken.

Target: Guatemala

THE ANATOMY OF A DISINFORMATION OPERATION: HARBURY IN GUATEMALA (WKLY 2.16, 28 NOVEMBER 1996)

[In November 1996 merchants in Coatepeque and Quezaltenango Departments of Guatemala report receiving extortion letters from the "Bamaca-Harbury Southern Front" of the self-styled Guatemalan People's Revolutionary Army (EPRG)— Ed.]

I do feel really, really pleased to finally, finally catch the CIA red-handed.
    — Jennifer Harbury in the *New York Times* (26 March 1995)

Jennifer Kristina Harbury burst upon the international scene in October 1994. Posed on a mattress in front of the National Palace in Guatemala City, Ms. Harbury held a photograph of an ORPA terrorist who she claimed to be her "disappeared husband." With this action she "went public" with what appears to be a carefully planned HRV campaign against the Guatemalan Army, the Guatemalan government and, ultimately, the U.S. CIA. Ms. Harbury's activities, as documented by LANS, are valuable not only as a case study of an HRV Campaign by the HLS but also as an example of the gullibility of the U.S. press and U.S. politicians.

Ms. Harbury is a U.S. citizen by birth, born in Baltimore, Maryland, on 27 October 1951. According to the account given to Ms. Manegold and Mr. DePalma by Ms. Harbury, the "New Hampshire woman" (NYT, 14 October 1994) spent her childhood in Baltimore (NYT, 27 July 1995) and "grew up in Connecticut" (NYT, 6 November 1994). She matriculated at Cornell, receiving a BA degree in Chinese from that university on 23 January 1974.[34]

She subsequently received a Doctor of Laws (JD) degree from Harvard Law School on 8 January 1978.[35]

On 6 November 1978 Ms. Harbury was licensed to practice law in the State of Texas having passed the Texas State Bar Examination.[36]

Interviews with Texas attorneys by LANS established that, to be admitted to the Texas Bar in November, her course of action had to be laid out well before she received her Harvard degree in January.

Ms. Harbury told Mr. Greenhouse (NYT, 14 October 1994) that "Guatemala first caught...[her] attention in the 1980s when she was a lawyer in Texas representing migrant farm workers." In her account to Ms. Manegold (NYT, 27 March 1995) this was more specifically described as "southern Texas where she worked with immigrants." The facts as obtained by LANS indicate these statements to be inaccurate, important because they relate to the crucial question as to when her contact with Guatemalan terrorism was established.

On 26 January 1996 LANS interviewed a co-worker of Ms. Harbury and the Director of Support Services for Texas Rural Legal Aid (TRLA). These interviews indicated that, while Harbury was a lawyer in south Texas "in the 1980s," it was only for a period of one year, a period which increases to 1.5 years if "the 1970s" are included. The personnel records in the border town of Weslaco, Texas, show that she worked in Weslaco from mid-1978—before she could legally practice law in Texas—until mid-1979 and again, from August 1986 to June 1987. She did work at the Weslaco Branch Office in Hereford, Texas, from mid-1979 to mid-1980, but Hereford is in *north* Texas some fifty miles from Amarillo.

During the one-and-a-half-year period, she told Greenhouse, "She encountered hundreds of immigrants from Guatemala..." (NYT, 14 October 1994). The Employer Relations Officer, U.S. Immigration and Naturalization Service (INS), told LANS (26 January 1996) that, while there are more Guatemalan immigrants now, at that time there were very few, most of the aliens being of Mexican nationality. Even now, only a few percent of the immigrants are Guatemalan.

These matters are of importance in demonstrating that Ms. Harbury's account of how her interest in Guatemalans was aroused is partially or totally contrived. And her alleged interest in the plight of the Guatemalans is what she claims led her to Mexico City and then "to the jungles of western Guatemala in her research" (NYT, 27 March 1995) on a book. She asserts that she met the terrorist, Efraín Bámaca Velásquez (a.k.a. Commandante Everardo) of Organization of the People in Arms (ORPA), in Guatemala.

Ms. Harbury claims that she met Bámaca "in 1990" (NYT, 27 March 1995). Whether or not she met him in 1990, if, indeed, she ever met the original Efraín Bámaca, this may indicate that she was with ORPA in

1990. If it is presumed that she was not associated with the terrorists before June 1987 when she terminated her association with TRLA, this date provides a lower limit on her "window of opportunity" for such a meeting. The window would have closed in 1993 with the publication of her book. Therefore, Ms. Harbury either (1) met Bámaca between 1987 and 1993 or (2) obtained the Bámaca name from the ORPA terrorists as useful for her purposes.

And she did write a book (*Bridge of Courage: Life Stories of the Guatemalan Compañeros and Compañeras*) or someone wrote one for her. It was first published by Common Courage (Morrow, Maine, 1993), then by A/C Press (Edinburgh, 1994) and Vehicle Presse (Montreal, 1994), republished (1994) and updated (1995) by Common.

Harbury Association with HLS

Ms. Harbury admitted to an association with the Hemispheric Left Support (HLS) on at least two occasions, to DePalma ("supported by a network of volunteers in Guatemala and...publicity in the [US]..." [NYT, 6 November 1994]) and to Manegold ("...they met in 1990. By then she had worked with the *underground* for years..." [NYT, 27 March 1995] [emphasis added]). Clearly these "years" fell within her 1987–1993 "window of opportunity" for Bámaca.

The Terrorist

José Leon Bámaca, the father of Efraín Bámaca Velásquez, appeared in a Guatemalan court in 1994 and attested to the existence of his son, Efraín, before 1976. The elder Bámaca then testified that he had heard nothing from his son since the latter had disappeared nineteen years before (1976). From this testimony alone it is possible that (1) Efraín Bámaca could have died at any time after 1976 or (2) is still alive. But a pillar of Ms. Harbury's HRV campaign *after its inception* is that he died during or after 1992. She maintains that she "married" him in 1991. The bizarre "proof" of this marriage is worthy of review.

Harbury "Marries" the Terrorist

Ms. Harbury told Ms. Manegold (NYT, 27 March 1995) that "they (Bámaca and Harbury) married on 25 September 1991. There was no priest or justice of the peace present...under Texas law it was a wedding," that is, it is supposed to have formalized their common-law marriage. But this statement is not precise, for such marriages are covered by subchapter "D" (Marriages without Formalities, Paragraphs 1.91–1.95 of the Texas Family Code.)

If Bámaca and Harbury were both in Texas on 25 September 1991 they could have "under Texas law…[had] a wedding" by following the requirements of Subchapter E. They would then have received "a declaration…[which] is *prima facie* evidence of the marriage…" In order to receive it they would have had to appear together before a County Clerk in any Texas county, furnish proof that they were of marriageable age, and execute and attest to a form largely concerned with their being married to no one else. Nor would there have been any reason for the happy couple not to follow this routine.

If Bámaca was in Texas in September 1991 as claimed by Ms. Harbury, he was in the United States illegally. This would, however, have posed no problem to the "marriage" since, as is assured by any county clerk, he would have been asked for *no* proof of legal entry. Therefore, it is a reasonable inference that (a) Bámaca was not in Texas in September 1991; or if he was in Texas at that time, then either (b) the pair had no thoughts of marriage or (c) the couple had no reason to legalize their relationship. As was made clear to LANS in interviews, a Texas County Clerk *under no conditions* would have issued a Declaration of Informal Marriage if only one of the parties appeared. It may therefore be inferred that:

Bámaca and Harbury had neither desire nor motivation for "informal marriage" in 1991 if indeed the "groom" was even in Texas at the time.

The Wedding Ceremony

Something happened prior to the Spring of 1993 which motivated Ms. Harbury to follow a procedure which declared her legally joined in informal marriage to Bámaca. She could, of course, have unilaterally applied to a county clerk, but she would, as LANS has been told, been laughed out of the office.[37]

But courts are more powerful than Clerks, and the 199th District Court of Texas provided the paperwork she required for her program.

The "proof" of the Harbury-Bámaca "marriage" is the "Declaration and Registration of Marriage, Travis County, Texas, USA" which was issued by the presiding judge of the court on 22 June 1993 declaring Harbury and Bámaca "legally married" on 25 September 1991. This decree was issued as a result of the "Original Petition for Declaratory Judgment" "In the matter of the Marriage of...Harbury and Bámaca..." in the District Court of the 199th Judicial District, Travis County, Texas. In this Petition, the "Supporting Affidavit" was filed on 21 May 1993. In this affidavit Harbury declared that "On or about September 25, 1991, Harbury and...Bámaca resided together in the State of Texas, agreed with each other to be married, exchanged vows with each other, cohabited and held themselves out as married..." Therefore, Ms. Harbury petitioned the court to declare her marriage to Bámaca to be "lawful under Texas law."

If this sworn statement is true, why did they not follow the simple procedure for legalizing "Informal Marriage" at the County Clerk's office which has been described above? The rational answer is that there was no need for such paperwork *before* her HRV campaign was laid out, whether or not Bámaca was in the United States in 1991 or, indeed, whether Harbury ever met him.

In order to assure "legality," Bámaca had to be notified of the action against him. This was done by posting the "Order for Service in lieu of Publication" (28 May 1993) in the Austin, Texas, Court House and appointing a lawyer for him ("Appointment of Attorney *ad litem*"). Bámaca not appearing to contest, the "registration of Marriage" was issued, all documents bearing the Case no. 93-06259. A final point with regard to this "marriage": If Bámaca was in Texas in 1991, he was in Texas illegally. LANS had checked with Guatemalan authorities and found that, since he had no passport, no visa to allow his legal entry would have been issued.

Disinformation Operation or True Love?

Ms. Harbury, in claiming "marriage" with a Guatemalan terrorist, may surely be presumed to be a supporter of Guatemalan terrorism. And Guatemalan terrorism has won its "victories," not with their murders of "hated landlords," but through their disinformation operations aimed at the destruction of the Guatemalan Army, the Guatemalan government, and the CIA. To this point, Ms. Harbury's porous account makes no sense at all, except perhaps to parts of the press and politicians, save as one more rather poorly contrived HRV Disinformation Operation:

If Ms. Harbury had met Bámaca in Guatemala, then later (1991) had him in Texas, all in the course of true love, why wait two years after his departure to generate a proof of "marriage"? The most logical answer to this is that the HRV Operation was not in the works until that time so that no such proof was needed. But with this proof in hand the Operation could go public.

And she appeared on the mattress. She would soon claim that two—
it would later be one—terrorists brought her "stunning news" (NYT, 14 October 1994) in early 1993 that Bámaca was alive in a "clandestine" prison. Based on this claim, she told EFE from her mattress in October 1994 that her "husband" "is being subjected [note present tense—Ed.] by Guatemalan military intelligence to physical and psychological tortures" and "they are trying to break him down mentally and win him as a collaborator." Ere long, "disappeared" turned to "killed," no more evidence of this being turned up than of "disappeared," although considerable digging (with shovels) would be done.

Ms. Harbury's appearance on the mattress was well received by a press which soon turned her claim of a "disappeared" husband into a *cause célèbre*. This in turn whisked her to Washington, DC,[38] where the real reason for her concern over her husband who "disappeared" in 1992 appears to have surfaced. She received a sympathetic ear from the Clinton administration and the Senate Intelligence Committee (April 1995), and her campaign blossomed into a booming anti-Guatemalan HRV operation which, by September 1995, had the United States virtually eliminating support to that country. Further, the campaign by the International Left against the CIA was to benefit substantially from "Señora" de Bámaca's efforts.

In Review

A Guatemalan terrorist support operation, Ms. Harbury's role as yet undelineated, was apparently in preparation before she arrived in Texas in mid 1978.

1. Her work with Guatemalan immigrants, according to LANS sources, could not have been as extensive as she has claimed. In all probability, this was little more than a cover for her subsequent work among the terrorists in the Guatemalan bush.
2. She allegedly spent some time with these terrorists, this of course "explainable" by her "book."
3. She may or may not have met Bámaca in the outback of Guatemala; he may or may not have slipped into Texas in 1991. (It has been suggested that Bámaca was already dead when Ms. Harbury got to Guatemala and hence even more useful.)
4. By claiming to have "married" him she drops the "author" cover and assumed at least the role of terrorist supporter.

5. It is by the terrorist supporters, as well as the terrorists, that the typical HRV Disinformation Operation is carried out, this one aimed at "victory through disinformation."

ANOTHER HL DISINFORMATION OPERATION?
(WKLY 2.6, 19 SEPTEMBER 1996)

That the Southern Sierra Campesino Organization (OCSS) is a front group for the Clandestine Revolutionary Worker's Party-Party of the Poor (PROCUP-PDLP) and, by simple extension, for the People's Revolutionary Army (EPR) appears to be established (cf. chapter 3, "Mexico," Wkly 2.5 and Spcl 2.5). Therefore, what is now being described as a "matanza" and a "masacre" of "innocent" OCSS campesinos by the tyrannical government of the State of Guerrero, Mexico, probably deserves more investigation than it has received. There are certain obvious holes in the theory of "innocent" campesinos:

1. The testimony as to the "innocence" of the campesinos and the "murderous brutality" of the police comes from OCSS members;

2. Four police were wounded in the confrontation according to immediate reports;

3. There were sixty people in two vehicles only thirty of whom were OCSS members, and yet the only casualties were among OCSS members; and

4. A second hand report by a PRD member claims the police planted guns on the OCSS personnel rather than finding them in a search.

In the final analysis: The government reports have been rejected, and the necessarily biased reports of the "victims" have been accepted. Although no final judgment can be made from these "facts," it is reminiscent of a situation which the LANS editor encountered in the Guatemala of 1993 when a confrontation took place between "activists' of the National Commission of Guatemalan Widows (CONAVIGUA)[39] and members of a Civilian Self Defense Patrol (PAC). Both sides agreed that the activists had been in Colotenango, Huehuetenango Department, for the purpose of "demonstrating" and demanding[40] that the PACs be abolished. Other "activist" groups were present in support of CONAVIGUA whose director, Rosalina Tuyuc, spoke at length on the incident. It appears that PSC members fired on the demonstrators, killing one and wounding two. Otherwise, the accounts of the PAC members and military personnel present contradict those of CONAVIGUA.

The official PAC report, through communique 321-92, and the statements of individuals in PAC assert that the patrol was guarding the bridge over the Selegua River when it was attacked with sticks and stones by the activists returning from their "demonstration." The PAC members claim that the demonstrators insulted them and tried to take their weapons. Although the number of demonstrators is not known exactly, PAC says that there were enough of them so that they had no choice but to fire on them.

CONAVIGUA claims that the PAC members were waiting to "ambush" them when they returned from their "peaceful" demonstration for the dissolution of the PACs. It says the PAC called them guerrillas, threatened to kill them, then fired on them. If the intent was to "ambush" them, the PAC people must be poor marksmen, sixty of them *only* to kill one and wound two at point blank range. Of the two wounded, one, interestingly enough, was shot through the hand. Certain sources in CONAVIGUA would claim that there were more dead whose families "spirited them off to their homes," leaving a great deal of "blood on the rocks" which was not found.

Which version is correct? On the one hand, provocation of the PAC people might be expected by an "activist" whose blood was up after demonstrating, "peacefully" or otherwise, against the PACs, one of which he now faced. On the other hand, there would not appear to be any reason for the PAC members suddenly to decide to "ambush" the returning demonstrators.

The demands of the URNG are routinely those of CONAVIGUA, an important such demand having been made the year before, this for the elimination of the PACs before the conclusion of a "peace" which has still not been finalized. The CONAVIGUA account of events in Los Naranjales, Guatemala, is exaggerated if only in claiming 150 PAC members involved, a PAC containing no more than 65, this one reported at 60. That 60 armed men set out to "ambush and massacre" a large crowd of civilians and only killed one, wounded one *in the hand* and another in the legs is bizarre. If on the other hand, the CONAVIGUA people did try to grab the PAC weapons, these three casualties would probably have been enough to stop them. And to furnish the HLS fodder for yet another disinformation operation.

A Terrorist Operation in the United States

THE BOMBING OF THE MURRAH BUILDING IN OKLAHOMA CITY
(SPCL 2.2, 22 AUGUST 1996)

On 19 April 1995 the Alfred P. Murrah Building in Oklahoma City, Oklahoma, was substantially damaged by explosive charges. "Who" was responsible for the bombing and "Why" the bombing was carried out are questions which have produced extensive speculation of dubious value.[41] The "How" on the other hand, is worthy of, and appropriate for, specific consideration here.

The U.S. government is apparently still taking the position that the only demolition charge involved in the operation was the ammonium nitrate-fuel oil (ANFO) vehicle bomb. However, available experimental and theoretical evidence indicates that a vehicle bomb could not have done the structural damage suffered by the Murrah Building. Since some of the experimental evidence comes from South America, the subject is relevant to LANS objectives.

Experimental Evidence

Two of the structures to be considered as experimental evidence are multi-storied and were constructed using reinforced-concrete vertical-strength members. The three buildings to be considered here were demonstrably subjected only to the blast effects of a vehicle bomb located outside their structure.

In all cases, the vehicle bomb wiped the facade off the building but left the vertical-strength members essentially unaffected.

1. In 1989 Colombian terrorists detonated a vehicle bomb near the entrance to the National Security Department (DAS) headquarters in Bogotá, which is housed in a building with which the LANS editor is familiar. The vehicle was parked next to the curb, the curb separated from the building by a one-meter sidewalk and a short set of stairs for a total separation of two to three meters from curb to facade. Thus, the bomb was much closer to the building than was the Oklahoma bomb. The blast wiped the face off the building, its vertical-support columns unaffected. Those who have access to *Revista DAS* (the official DAS publication) will find a before-and-after photograph of the building on the cover of issue no. 8, December 1990. (DAS address: Carrera 28, No. 17-50, Bogotá, D.E., Colombia.)

2. The recent bombing of the Saudi Arabian building housing U.S. Air Force personnel is the second example. The wirephotos clearly show that the damage is the result of a vehicle bomb, the face again wiped off the building, the vertical strength members essentially unaffected.

3. AFP carried a wirephoto on 31 July 1996 of the vehicle-bombed home of Peruvian General Manuel Varela Gamarra in Lima. There were apparently no reinforced-concrete vertical-strength members in this three-story home. Nevertheless, the façade-destroying effects of such a blast were evident in this brick structure.

These three examples suggest that the effect of a vehicle bomb is, not to demolish the vertical-strength members in a structure such as the Murrah Building but to wipe the facade off the building. The theory supports such a conclusion.

Theoretical Evidence

It is important to realize that an explosive charge, detonated at a distance from its target and, for all practical purposes, suspended above the ground, damages its target *only* by means of the air pressure in the blast wave created by the detonation. Such a blast is immensely less effective than that of a contact explosive strapped on—or otherwise effectively attached—or sunk into its target.

Brigadier General Benton K. Partin (USAF, Ret.) is a lifelong demolitions expert; on 13 July 1995 he released a twenty-three-page report entitled "Bomb Damage Analysis of Alfred P. Murrah Building, Oklahoma City, Oklahoma" which we synopsize.[42] He used the official estimate as to amount (4800 pounds) of explosive in the truck. From this he calculated that the resulting 4-1/2 foot explosive sphere would yield an over-pressure[43] of about one-half million pounds per square inch (psi) on explosion, this falling off to about 375 psi by the time the blast wave reached the first A-row column *which was collapsed*. (The A-row columns occupied the first row parallel to the building front, the B-row the second.) The yield strength of concrete is some 3,500 psi,[44] so that the vehicle bomb would have had to deliver ten times as much pressure as it did in order to destroy A-3. Further, the nearest A-row column (A-4) *was not collapsed*. One B-row column (B-3) was collapsed, and at its location the blast wave was down in strength to some 27 to 38 psi, the wave thus 100 times as weak as would have been required for column destruction. But how was the calculation carried out?

Gen. Partin used a simple inverse-cube dependence of the overpressure on separation from blast center.[45] This relation appears to have been generally supported by experimental testings of overpressure. A simple analysis may be introduced in favor of this relation. In the general case, an infinite series may be written for the overpressure as follows:

$$\ldots + ar^3 + br^2 + cr + d + er^{-1} + fr^{-2} + gr^{-3} + \ldots$$

The letters a, b, c,... are constants, the variable being "r," the separation from blast center. This series therefore includes all powers and inverse powers of the separation from blast center, the constants accompanying each of the terms in the series to be adjusted through experiment so as to portray precisely the overpressure as a function of separation from blast center.

The first point to be made about this series is that the terms in the powers of r—r , r^2, r^3, and so on—can be eliminated with a simple physical argument. These terms in the series will induce an increase in the overpressure with separation from blast center. The physics of the situation clearly demonstrates that such could only occur if there were additional energy sources—additional detonations—along the path from blast center. These powers of r may therefore be discarded. In the most general case, a constant term, d, would appear in the series separating the powers of r from the inverse powers of r, that is, there would be no attenuation of this term with distance. This may, from the boundary conditions of the problem, also be discarded, and only inverse powers of r remain. Ignoring the inverse r and r^2 terms for the moment, if the inverse r^3 term is kept, the higher powers—r^4, and so forth—become irrelevant at very short distances from blast center. Which leaves only the r^1, r^2 and r^3 terms.

The constants e, f, and g might be adjusted so that columns A-3, A-5, A-7 and B-3 could be destroyed as actually occurred. This would be a meaningless exercise, however, since such an equation would be certain to destroy columns A-4 and A-6—which were not destroyed—and probably others. There is no rational way to destroy the four columns, and only the four columns, with this ANFO vehicle bomb.

The ANFO vehicle bomb might have been utilized as a trigger in connection with, say, a pressure-sensitive detonator for contact explosives which were attached to the destroyed vertical-support members. Which is not to say that the ANFO explosive did act as a trigger, but it is to say that in this way only could it have been primarily responsible for the damage done to the Murrah Building.

General Partin's examination of photographs of the destroyed columns indicated to him that there were such contact charges used on these columns. Unfortunately, the surprising haste with which the building was demolished and removed rendered a thorough investigation of such allegations impossible. In keeping with the situation, considerable speculation has revolved around the reasons for the hurried building demolition after the bombing.

Notes

1. Herbert Lionel Matthews. *The Yoke and the Arrows: A Report on Spain*, George Braziller, 1957.

2. Threat 9. (See note 10, chapter 3.) See also Earl E. T. Smith (*The Fourth Floor: An Account of the Castro Communist Revolution*, Random House, 1962).

3. In a generally valuable book, Andres Oppenheimer (*Bordering on Chaos*, Little Brown, 1996) demonstrates an ignorance of the reality of LibTheo equivalent to that of the *Dallas Morning News*.

4. Monseñor Freddy Delgado (*La Iglesia Popular Nació en El Salvador, 1972– 1982*, n.d.) describes the "Base Communities" so important to this marxization in an El Salvador which was almost unique in its LibTheo problems.

5. Dietrich Bonhoeffer, *Résistance et Soumission,* Editions Labor et Fides, 1963.

6. Rosemary Reuther, *The Radical Kingdom*, Harper and Row, 1970; Paul van Buren, *The Secular Meaning of the Gospel*, MacMillan, 1963; J. A. T. Robinson, *Honest to God*, Westminster Press, 1963; Robert L. Richard, *Secularization Theology*, Burns and Oates, 1967; Jordan Bishop McClave, *Cristianismo radical y marxismo*, Editorial nuestro tiempo, 1970.

7. Friedrich-Wilhelm Marquardt, *Theologie und Socialismo: Das Beispiel Karl Barth*, Kaiser Grünwald, 1972.

8. Ernst Bloch, *Das Prinzip Hoffnung*, Suhrkamp, 1959.

9. Julio Santa Ana, *Cristianismo sin religión ensayo,* Editorial Alfa, 1969.

10. Porfirio Miranda, *Marx and the Bible,* Orbis, 1974.

11. "According to Prof. Jeanson…in his class…during the Week of Catholic Intellectuals, Paris, 1971."

12. Leonardo Boff, *Jesus Cristo, Liberador*, Vozes, 1972. As Dr. Alejandro Chafuen has cogently commented, "I predicted that few of them (liberation theologians) would embrace the new socialist myth: radical environmentalism. I thought that they would rather hug a child in poverty than a tree, and, except for a few exceptions (Boff), I was right."

13. Leonardo Boff, *María, mujer profetica y Liberadora*, Clar, 1978.

14. Antoine Ozanam (1813–1853), French scholar in the neo-Catholic movement in France, his works published in eleven volumes (Paris, 1862–1865).

15. While it is apparently not known to what extent the CIA has been infiltrated by the KGB, the Czech KGB (StB)—in 1958 the LANS editor learned that the Czech Cultural Attache was in charge of all Soviet Bloc espionage in the United States—and the DGI, much the same, if not more, can be said of MI5 for which cf. Peter Wright (*Spycatcher: The Candid Autobiography of a Senior Intelligence Officer*, Penguin, 1988).

16. This ML ("Trotskyite") terrorist group was active in Argentina in the 1970s until decapitated by the Argentine military when Roberto Santucho and its co-founder, Benito Urtega, were killed outside Buenos Aires. After this Enrique Haraldo Gorriaran Merlo was apparently chief. Gorriaran carried out the contract murder of Somoza Debayle in Asunción for the Sandinistas, subsequently moving to Managua where he was active in their terrorist operations, adding to his "luster" with the meaningless "attack" on the La Tablada Barracks in the Argentina of 1989. Among the terrorists killed there was Gaguine.

17. Leslie Cockburn, *Out of Control: The Story of the Reagan Administration's Secret War in Nicaragua, the Illegal Arms Pipeline, and the Contra Drug Connection*, Atlantic Monthly, 1987.

18. Martha Honey and Tony Avirgan. *La Penca: Reporte de una investigación*, El Gallo Roja, 1985.

19. Tony Avirgan and Martha Honey. *La Penca: On Trial in Costa Rica—The CIA vs. the Press*, Porvenir, 1987.

20. A long rambling rehash of events in Costa Rica recently appeared on the Internet, one quote relating to these affidavits: "The Justice Department ultimately con-

cluded that the affidavits had been forged." This statement is false, but false or true the LANS editor has interviewed Davies and Thompson by telephone and Chaffard in La Reforma Prison. There is no question as to the authenticity of the affidavits, xerox copies of all of which have been in the LANS files for years.

21. Cockburn makes the incredible statement that "the standard Costa Rica aviation map...noted a runway length of 3,301." The aeronautical chart shows no such thing. This nonsense appeared in the book which was the "favorite" of Mr. Terry Reed's attorney.

22. The FAL is the 7.62mm Fusil Automatique Léger manufactured by Fabrique Nationale d'Armes de Guerre, Herstal-lèz-Liège.

23. The AK-47 or simply AK (Avtomat Kalashnikov), a Soviet development, has been manufactured in various models and countries, all characterized by the permanent attachment of the gas piston to the bolt carrier.

24. The SKS (Samozaryadnyi Karabin Simonova) was a Soviet World War II development, but the ones used in Central America were of People's Republic of China manufacture.

25. This has been reported as Channel 7, but, since the Channel 6 reporter died in the blast, this is probably correct.

26. See note 17.

27. See note 19.

28. See note 19.

29. See note 16.

30. See notes 22–24.

31. See note 17.

32. R. G. Breene, Jr. *Ordeal by Perjury*, Faustian Publishers, 1989. *Ordeal* is now out of print.

33. Susan Huck. *Legal Terrorism: The Truth About the Christic Institute*, New World, 1989. This book is apparently still available from New World Publishing, 6819 El St., McLean, VA 22101-3831.

34. LANS interview with the Registrar, Cornell University, 29 January 1996.

35. LANS Interview Harvard.

36. LANS Interview Texas Bar.

37. Were this not the case women (men) would be popping up like weeds and claiming common law status with wealthy men (women), then waiting, or perhaps hastening, the demise of their "partners" in order to share the wealth.

38. A highly placed Washington source told LANS that Ms. Harbury's operation was immensely aided by a "policy vacuum" wherein a staffer to an important U.S. Congressman and a Guatemalan ambassador could wield immense influence on her behalf. The staffer, having "forced U.S. Ambassador to Guatemala McAfee to meet with Harbury," went on to bigger and better things in the Clinton Administration and is being charged with security violations in the case. The Guatemalan ambassador "was playing presidential politics...and did not use his credibility to refute her."

39. This organization included no widows of police and/or military personnel, only "widows" of Guatemalan National Revolutionary Union (URNG) and URNG support personnel.

40. The OCSS personnel involved in the incident at Aguas Blancas Ford were on their way to "demonstrate and demand" at Atoyac.

41. LANS has received some such information from Latin America, but it has been too nebulous to deserve repetition.

42. A LANS subscriber sent us the 20 March 1996 issue of *Strategic Investment* (Baltimore, MD) wherein (p. 3) it was reported that "A classified Pentagon study

determines the Oklahoma bombing was caused by...five separate bombs." If "bomb" is replaced by "explosive charge," this is what is being said here.

43. The "over-pressure" is the pressure at a given space point in the blast wave which is "over" the practically negligible ambient air pressure.

44. This is the figure used by General Partin. One of our readers having considerable experience with concrete informed LANS that this number was probably high. Practically speaking, however, the reduction of this number to what he considers a more reasonable one would have no effect on what follows.

45. An example of the "inverse cube" relationship may be helpful. For the overpressure at a distance "r," cube "r" and divide it into 1, take its inverse. Thus, if the overpressure is 500,000 at blast center, it is 500,000/(10)(10)(10) = 500 at 10 units of length from blast center. (Note that the units of the constants must be appropriate to the terms. For example if $P=gr^{-3}$, and P is in psi, then "r" must be in inches, "g" in units of pound-inches. Unless of course one prefers to use the month-ton-mile system.)

5

Latin American International Organizations

Introduction

This chapter collects the LANS articles which appeared during 1996 and which relate to certain of the hemispheric international organizations. Only a modest portion of the international Latin American organizations were treated by LANS in 1996. There has been no attempted equality of treatment of the many organizations which exist. Instead, only those organizations, the activities of which appeared more or less prominently in the news during the year, have been reviewed.

For order in presentation, the plethora of organizations has been divided into hemisphere-wide groups (see "Hemisphere-Wide Groupings") such as the OAS and the Iberian-American Summit. If contemporary rhetoric is to be accepted at face value, "free trade" is the "wave of the future," or at least it is considered such outside the confines of the Hemispheric Left. The proliferation of such groups has followed the rhetoric, perhaps more faithfully than have their accomplishments. A cross-section of the "summits" of these groups and certain necessary background material comprises "Trade and Tariff Associations."

There are a number of groupings of Latin American nations which, since concerned with technical matters such as regional power distribution, should be included in "Technical Groupings."

Associations of nations such as ODECA are regional by definition and as such appropriate for inclusion in "Regional Associations." Since there is an inherent urge to growth in such groupings, however, this category has demonstrated an interesting capacity for movement from regional to hemispheric status. Thus, what was regional in 1996, might transmogrify itself into hemispheric in 1997.

LATIN AMERICAN INTERNATIONAL ORGANIZATIONS (WKLY 1.5, 6 JUNE 1996)

A December 1991 Conference ("Improved Investment Climate in

Latin America and the Caribbean") was only one in a series (e.g., the Miami Summit of the Americas in December 1994) touting potential alleged returns of the region to foreign entrepreneurs. The realities have proven different for those who failed to take political verities and reasonable assessment of the production chains into consideration.

For example, in Costa Rica the Millicron misadventure and the debacle suffered by Alcoa and Martin Marietta could probably have been avoided by more realistic evaluation of the existing political situation. Exploration by Alcoa and Reynolds had demonstrated the existence of lateritic bauxite domain G (southwest of San Isidro) and H (along the Río Coto Brus). However, Alcoa and Martin Marietta were ultimately driven out with substantial losses by political-left demands.

While those considerations concerning the first four chapters of this *Annual* are crucial to such evaluation, the superficially more mundane aspects of the political situation is the proliferating crowd of Inter-American Organizations, the complex and more superficial activities of which may contain pitfalls for the eager but ignorant. Among those groups and agreements of which the potential investor-entrepreneur should be aware are the "Ecological" Summits and the "Sustainable Development" Agreements.

Hemisphere-Wide Groupings

Organization of American States

LATIN AMERICAN INTERNATIONAL ORGANIZATIONS (WKLY 1.5, 6 JUNE 1996)

The OAS is the successor to the Pan American Union (organized 1910) which in turn was the successor to the International Union of American Republics (organized 1889). The OAS was created at the Ninth Inter-American Congress in Bogotá in 1948 as a regional organization under the United Nations (UN) Charter, its organization revised in 1967.

The OAS General Assembly meets annually, each member having one vote. Its Permanent Council, seated in Washington, DC, is composed of one representative from each member state, its permanent central organ the General Secretariat headed by a Secretary General.

Castroite Cuba was ousted from the OAS in 1962. At the June 1994 meeting Secretary General Baena Soares was replaced by outgoing Colombian president César Gaviria Trujillo. Anti-Castro sources claim this to have been part of a plan for "normalization" of relations with Cuba while Costa Rican sources claim the Gaviria election to have been sponsored by the United States. Gaviria has admitted recently to being a "friend of Fidel."

The Twenty-sixth General Assembly of the OAS was initiated on 3 June 1996 in Panama.

[In early August "something new" occurred at the seat of the organization in Washington, the first approved appearance of the nongovernmental organizations (NGOs) to argue whatever position they have to argue. The position here was in support of the Summit on Sustainable Development—under another name below—which is to be held later in Bolivia. The new home of the International Left is, of course, the "environmental movement"—Gorbachev and Green Cross, etc.—and various "human rights" organizations are NGOs and involved with the Hemispheric Left Support. In early December Spain, together with France and Russia, sought to "improve and amplify" its observer status before the OAS to full diplomatic representation. There are presently "more than forty" permanent observers.]

Iberian-American Summits (Cumbre Iberoamérica)

SIX YEARS OF IBERIAN-AMERICAN SUMMITS
(WKLY 2.13, 7 NOVEMBER 1996)

On the weekend of 31 July 1996 a meeting of Iberian-American judicial officials and "experts" from the UN Development Program (PNUD) was held in Santiago de Chile, the meeting being in preparation for the Sixth Iberian-American Summit. The Summit is to be held in Santiago and Vino del Mar, Chile, on 10 and 11 November 1996. In May Foreign Minister José Miguel Insulza of Chile had produced a document on a subject allegedly proposed by President Frei and relating to "Governability by an efficient and participative democracy." This was proposed for "debate"—an idealized description of what will happen—at the Summit. It is interesting that Cuban caudillo Fidel Castro would allegedly engage in a debate on "participative democracy."

There would appear to be little doubt that the Cumbre Iberoamérica was largely developed to replace the OAS with a similar organization which does not include the United States. This was partly based on the view that the United States has little interest in the region, an opinion which is to some extent justified, for example, by the ignorance of the lands to the south routinely demonstrated by the English-language U.S. press. The opinion was of course heartily endorsed by the leader of the HL, Fidel Castro, who has a substantial following and who has of recent years been increasing his following with his war on "neoliberalism" and in support of AgRef.

But there is, or is supposed to be, more to the Iberian-American Summit than an association of Latin American nations. It is supposed to be an association of these nations and their "mother" nations, Portugal and Spain.

However well this "Summit" organization is developing, a certain faltering appeared at the Fourth Summit indicated by a desire to meet less frequently. A two-year interim between summits was suggested, this to begin with the Sixth Summit, and it will be of interest to see if this position will be supported.

The First Cumbre Iberoamérica

The First Summit was held at Guadalajara, Mexico, in July 1991 and hosted by President Carlos Salinas de Gortari of Mexico whom the *New York Times* (28 July 1991) accused of considering Castro a "stabilizing influence." Twenty-one Spanish- and Portuguese-speaking heads of state, to include President Felipe González of Spain and President Mario Soares of Portugal, assembled at this meeting which was perhaps typified by a photograph of a uniformed Castro seated centrally among the presidents of Spain, Ecuador, Colombia, and Argentina.

One observer dubbed the gathering "Ali Baba y los cuarenta ladrones" ("Ali Baba and the Forty Thieves") which, at least insofar as numbers are concerned, appears to be exaggerated. It is not clear that this summit had any effect more substantial than the scheduling of the Second Cumbre for the following year. It did give the Cuban caudillo the opportunity to fulminate about "blockades, dirty wars, mercenary invasions" and "illusions like the Alliance for Progress, the Baker Plan, the Brady Plan and the most recent of the fantasies, the Initiative for the Americas."

That Castro's fulminations did not fall on ears as deaf as were at the time reported will be seen by the effectively unanimous condemnation of the Cuban embargo which would issue from later summits.

The Second Cumbre Iberoamérica

In 1492 Columbus (Cristobal Colón) made his first journey to the Western Hemisphere which soon became, and largely remained, a Spanish- and Portuguese-speaking hemisphere. It was therefore appropriate that, on the Five Hundredth Anniversary of Columbus' feat, an Iberian-American Summit be celebrated in the symbolic seat of the Hispanic empire, Madrid. As was the Second Cumbre, timed to immediately precede the opening (25 July 1992) of the Summer Olympic Games in Barcelona, Spain.

The Spanish president was of course present, as were sixteen Latin American heads of state. President Soares pled ill health, although a conflict with Prime Minister Anibal Cavaco Silva of Portugal was said to be the problem. For reasons which would become clear the following year, President Carlos Andres Pérez of Portugal (see chapter 2, "Venezuela") was refused permission to travel. Colombian president Samper and Peruvian president Fujimori were unable to travel because of problems with HL narcoterrorism.

But the head of the HL, a Castro, if not "resplendent," at least unique in his ML caudillo uniform, stood out in the crowd. The resolutions which would be adopted were described the following year by the journalist Miguez. One of them would "commit" the Iberian-American nations to "democracy and respect for human rights."

The Third Cumbre Iberoamérica

Don Juan Carlos de Borbon, King of Spain, opened the Third Cumbre with a speech in which, as is routinely done by, say, Queen Elizabeth II of England, he spoke as he was directed to speak. He rejected "specific attempts to do violence to the democratic constitutional order freely established by the Iberian American peoples." It appears to be generally agreed that he was referring to the probably overrated and unsuccessful putsch in Venezuela, the short-lived buffoonery of Pres. Serrano in Guatemala, and the highly successful actions of Peruvian president Fujimori against the narcoterrorists of Sendero Luminoso, actions strongly supported by the Peruvians. The King then went on to support "democracy, development and human rights" and to oppose "hunger, sickness and 'underprivilege'" as socialists such as President González, who probably wrote the speech, have allegedly been for and against, respectively, for all of this and much of the last, century.

The Cumbre was held at Salvador de Bahía, Brazil, in July 1993. It was attended by nineteen American chiefs of state, the presidents of Spain and Portugal and twenty-one ministers of foreign affairs. The presidents of the Dominican Republic and Venezuela were absent.

One of the journalists covering this Cumbre, Alberto Miguez, wrote that "the great paradox of these conferences has been the immense distance between what is signed—bombastic utopian documents—and what is done." One action which, although not as specific as Cuban caudillo Castro would have wished, condemned *pro forma* the U.S. embargo of Cuba.

Thirteen of the presidents then flew from Salvador to São Paulo for the inauguration of the seat of PARLATINA (see below).

The Fourth Cumbre Iberoamérica

In April 1994 the Summit coordinating group met in Santa Fe de Bogotá, Colombia, and the Colombian vice minister of foreign affairs, Luís Guillermo Grillo, announced that the upcoming Cumbre would be chiefly concerned with "commerce and integration as elements for Iberian-American development." If this is interpreted to mean "commerce with, and integration [into the Latin American community of states of], Castroite Cuba," the statement proved accurate. This coordinating group was made up of representatives from the nations which had hosted or would host the First Summit (Mexico), Second (Spain), Third (Brazil), Fourth (Colombia), and Fifth (Argentina).

The Fourth Cumbre was held in the resort city of Cartagena de Indias, Colombia, on 14 and 15 June 1994. The affair was attended by nineteen Latin American heads of state and those of Spain and Portugal. Mexican president Salinas flew to Havana for a visit of a few hours before proceeding to Cartagena, leaving behind him in Cuba some thirty of Castro's political prisoners who had just declared a hunger strike. The coverage of the event by the *New York Times* (16 June 1994)— "Castro Dons Civvies"—was concerned with Castro's change from his ML caudillo uniform and the broad support which he was receiving from Latin America. Whether accurate or otherwise, this treatment described a "seventeen-fold" increase in Cuban exports to Colombia this year, this in the face of Castroite involvement in Colombian narcoterrorism. Needless to say, the embargo of Cuba was condemned. Although lip service continued to be given to "democracy in Cuba," Castro, lined up and waving with the other heads of state in front of the Cartagena Convention Center at the conclusion of the festivities, should have been satisfied with the summit.

The Fifth Cumbre Iberoamérica

The Fifth Cumbre concluded in San Carlos de Bariloche, Argentina, on 17 October 1995, some twenty-one Iberian-American nations having taken part. Particularly noteworthy among the statements emerging from this encounter was that of the Spanish secretary of state for cooperation, José Lupis Dicenta.

"After the first two summits," said Mr. Dicenta, "this type of meeting should restate its content and objectives. If we do not succeed in centering them and, above all, communicating [them] to Iberian-American public opinion so that they serve some purpose, their continuity is in serious danger." It had already been suggested in 1993 that, beginning in 1996, these summits be held every other year.

A thirty-nine-point declaration emerged from the Summit, most of which—anti-terrorism, anti-narcotrafficking, anti-corruption, etc.—were not particularly controversial, but the paragraph condemning the U.S. embargo against Cuba evoked a comment from President Carlos Menem of Argentina.

"That paragraph," Mr. Menem told a press conference, "was edited by Cuba, and we limited ourselves to adding something with relation to certain legislation which is in passage through the Congress of the United States." He was referring to the Helms-Burton Bill.

That there is an HL, as Miguez reports, is certainly true. If these summits have served any purpose save that of invigorating it by providing substantial favorable exposure for the Cuban caudillo, it is difficult to determine what that purpose may have been. This is apparently realized more widely than it is admitted, as will perhaps be demonstrated at the Sixth Cumbre if the two-year interval between summits is maintained there.

The Sixth Cumbre Iberoamérica

Before his defection (1988), Enrique Garcia was a captain in the Cuban KGB (DGI) and, with cover as vice consul in La Paz, Bolivia, he was second-in-command of the intelligence center there. In that capacity he was in charge, inter alia, of logistical support to the Special Operations Department (DOE) which directed support of subversive operations against Chile. These included the immense buildup of arms brought into the neighborhood of Vallenar, Atacama Province, Chile, on Soviet- and Cuban-flag vessels in 1986 which, if undiscovered, might have led to a "major East-West confrontation" (see chapter 3, "HL Terrorist Organizations: Monteneros, Coalitions").

As he told our colleague, Ariel Remos (*Diario las América*), Garcia was also privy to all the details of the assassination attempt against

General Augusto Pinochet Ugarte, its organization, development, and how it should be executed. "All the clandestine apparatus of military intelligence of the Cuban government, including the Americas Department and the DOE," Garcia said, "were created as arms of Fidel Castro, who always participated in any decisions on execution of important operations. As to the direction and execution of the assassination attempt against Pinochet, it is impossible that this would have been carried out without any consultation with, and approval by Castro..." And now Fidel Castro, personally in charge of Cuban "wetwork," is coming to Chile for the Sixth Cumbre.

Which inspired Garcia to make his statements and two Chilean Independent Democratic Union (UDI) deputies to present a judicial demand to the prosecutor that Castro be required to testify in this still open case. The only observable reaction by the Frei government has been a warning to anti-Castro groups not to demonstrate when Castro comes to Chile to discuss "participative democracy."

The background to the Sixth Cumbre may be concluded with a curious remark by Guatemalan foreign minister Eduardo Stein. Stein recently stated that Guatemalan president Alvaro Arzú hopes to get an "espalderazo" (pat on the back) at the summit for his "peace process" with the URNG.

THE SIXTH IBERIAN-AMERICAN SUMMIT
(WKLY 2.14, 14 NOVEMBER 1996)

In Santiago de Chile, at 0930 on 10 November 1996, the Sixth Iberian-American Summit was officially inaugurated by the foreign ministers and heads of state of some twenty-one nations. On the previous day these individuals had specified that a truly democratic regime requires "pluralism, human rights, free elections and freedom of expression," among other things, the Summit having been touted as devoted to a discussion of "participative democracy." Two days later this group all signed the Declaration of Vino del Mar, Castro "doing so with a flourish."

The summit host, Chilean president Frei, called the affair a "rousing success" while "analysts and diplomats" foresaw a "major opening in the Fidel Castro regime." Perhaps the most interesting part of the affair was a press conference held by Castro's foreign minister, Roberto Robaina. Said Mr. Robaina: "If you insist on asking me why we have only one candidate for president, I cannot explain clearly how our democratic system functions. In Cuba we have elections, which are not postulated by parties and are realized barrio by barrio." If this statement appears obfuscated, it is because it was meant so to appear. Other members of the Cuban delegation maintained the existence of "democracy" in Cuba with arguments similar to that of the foreign minister.

Armando Valladares is intimately familiar with Caudillo Castro's concern with "democracy and human rights" as his book[1] demonstrates. Valladares was invited to Santiago for the Sixth Summit but not by Chilean president Frei. He did not figure prominently in the festivities. Nor did those who sought to have the ML caudillo testify in the assassination attempt which he had ordered against Chilean president Pinochet.

Grupo de Río

LATIN AMERICAN INTERNATIONAL ORGANIZATIONS
(WKLY 1.5, 6 JUNE 1996)

This group had its origin in Contadora which was created in 1982 by Colombia, Panama, Mexico, and Venezuela specifically to counteract U.S. policy in Central America. In its First Presidential Summit it proposed, inter alia, to repudiate the foreign debt of any nation having a per capita income less than $1000 per year.

President Clinton sent the following message to its Seventh Summit:

> We are committed to work closely with all members of the Grupo de Río to strengthen...our collective defense of democracy in the hemisphere and assure the peaceful reestablishment of constitutional order wherever it has been interrupted. (Cf. sections on the Dominican Republic, Haiti, Paraguay.)

Twelve presidents and the prime minister of Trinidad and Tobago attended its Eighth Summit which took place at the Hotel Gloria in Río de Janeiro beginning on 8 September 1994. At this summit the group was describing itself as "the principal organization able to articulate the politic of Latin America." At this same meeting its "Troika"—the presidents of Brazil, Chile, and Ecuador—"presented" to the U.S. government an agenda for the then upcoming Miami Summit of the Americas at least part of which (e.g., hemispheric free market by 2005) was adopted unchanged.

The Sixth Meeting of Foreign Ministers of the European Union and the Grupo de Río ended in Cochabamba, Bolivia, on 16 April 1996, its labors bringing forth a statement against drugs.

THE TENTH SUMMIT OF GRUPO DE RÍO HEADS OF STATE
(WKLY 2.6, 19 SEPTEMBER 1996)

President Clinton sent a supportive message to the Eighth Grupo de Río Summit and accepted its agenda for his Miami Summit. This time he sent his UN ambassador, Madeleine Albright, in what may have been a clever maneuver, albeit, a clandestine one since the United States is excluded from membership in this organization. When the rhetoric at the foreign ministers meeting which preceded the summit is compared with the Declaration of Cochabamba (DC) issued by the heads of state on 4 September 1996, more caution, perhaps invoked by Madame Albright's behind-the-scenes operations, is found in the DC than might have been expected. Ambassador Albright had conducted a series of effectively clandestine "bilateral" meetings with various of the thirteen national delegations which may have ameliorated the DC. The theory advanced to account for this has Ambassador Albright telling the dignitaries to pay no heed to US support for the Helms-Burton Law and the proposed ouster of UN Secretary General Boutros Boutros-Ghali,[2] these positions mere "election-year politics."

On 2 February 1996 Bolivian foreign minister and Grupo de Río secretary pro tem Antonio Aranibar opened the Tenth Summit foreign minister session in the Simon I. Patino[3] Cultural Center in Cochabamba with: "The future of the...[Grupo de Río] is linked to its contribution to Latin American and Caribbean democracy, to continental integration processes and to a solid political role in our dialog with other regions of the world." He correctly predicted that the DC would refer to the "deepening of democracy," a "battle against poverty" and a condemnation of Helms-Burton.

Foreign Minister Alvaro Ramos of Uruguay reported unanimous rejection of the Helms-Burton Law by the Consultative Committee of the Latin American and Caribbean countries, to be followed by Panamanian foreign minister Arias with his "clear rejection of Helms-Burton." The refusal of the United States to grant a visa to President Samper of Colombia came in for its share of criticism—The Grupo de Río would "protest" (AFP, 17 July 1996)—although Colombian foreign minister Emma Mejia devoted her remarks to a plea for punishment of drug-related crimes such as money laundering, precursors—chemicals and other items necessary to drug production—and arms.

Foreign Minister Lampeia of Brazil discussed the pipeline for the transport of Bolivian gas to Brazil while President Fujimori of Peru discussed his tax incentives, port programs and duty-free zones. The attacks by, inter alia, Uruguayan vice president Hugo Batalla on "neoliberalism," the bogey of the HL, would not specifically appear in the DC, but echoes of them could be found in the "war on poverty" which, with wars on drugs, illiteracy and so on, would be declared.

In short, the support of Castroite Cuba was sustained only by the fourth point in the eight-point DC, this entitled "Extraterritoriality of National Laws," and stating, inter alia, "We reject any attempt to impose unilateral sanctions...We reaffirm...our energetic rejection...[of the] Helms Burton Law..."

The eighth point in the DC is entitled "Cultural Integration" and apparently relates to the creation of the Latin American Community of Nations (CLAN) proposed by PARLATINO president Adolfo Singer. Whether the ultimate integration, in support of which he invokes the Great Liberator, Simón Bolívar, is seriously advanced or whether this is one more attempt to replace the OAS with an organization such as the Grupo de Río which excludes North America is an interesting speculation.

The DC was signed by eleven presidents, one prime minister, one foreign minister, and one vice president.

Summit of the Americas

THE SECOND SUMMIT OF THE AMERICAS (WKLY 2.17, 5 DECEMBER 1996)

On 7–8 December 1996 what was originally billed as the Second Summit of the Americas will be held in Santa Cruz, Bolivia. By 1996, however, Bolivian deputy foreign minister Jaime Aparicio was claiming this to be the Hemispheric Summit on Sustainable Development, the U.S. State Department dubbing it a Conference on the Environment. This of course assured the presence of the "environmental" enthusiast, Vice President Albert Gore, but President Clinton is (at press time) not attending.[4] "Sustainable Development" (SD) is a present-day sacred cow and (1) frequently reflects the sometimes bizarre notions of some "environmentalists" while (2) providing the latterday home of the International Left.

Point 1 may be illustrated with the Honduran decree eliminating *all* harvesting of the renewable resource, timber; point 2 with Communist party of the Soviet Union (CPSU) chief Gorbachev's displacement from ruler of the Soviet Union to chief of the Green Cross environmental organization. Whatever this summit may prove to be, if anything, it began as the successor to the Summit of the Americas which was held in Miami, Florida, United States, in December 1994 and warrants review.

The Summit of the Americas concluded in Miami on 11 December 1994, thirty-four Western Hemisphere heads of state, all save Cuba's Castro, having converged there two days before. Castroite Cuba, having been excluded from the OAS some thirty years ago for inciting, directing, and supplying Latin American terrorism, was not included in this OAS meeting. In March 1994 President Clinton had first mentioned this summit and stated that Vice President Gore had gone to Mexico City "right after the approval of the North American Free Trade Alliance (NAFTA)" to announce it. He urged "us [to] think boldly and set forth a vision of progress...[and to] begin the work of building a genuine community for all of us in the hemisphere." By mid-November the Summit "Themes" had been enunciated by the Clinton administration as (1) Making Democracy Work: Reinventing Government; (2) Making Democracy Prosper: Hemispheric Economic Integration; and (3) Making Democracy Endure: SD.

The implementation of Summit Theme (3) had been initiated in Managua, Nicaragua, at the 12–13 October First Central American Ecological Summit (CAES) by Mr. Gore and the Clinton administration's allegedly hand-picked OAS secretary general,[5] former Colombian president Gaviria. This gathering of Central American heads of state formally agreed to a pre-scripted Alliance for SD (ASD) and concluded with a ceremonial signing of the ASD "declaration" at the Masaya Volcano which President De Leon Carpio of Guatemala and President Pérez Balladares of Panama were "unable to attend." Among serious environmentalists there is sharp divergence over the meaningfulness of SD. It does appear, however, that it presupposes a validity for the "global warming"[6] hypothesis which an increasing number of sober researchers are denying.

The Central American nations later trekked to the Miami Summit with an agenda calling for greater access to world markets, relief from their foreign debts and a twenty-three-point declaration which would have satisfied the most enthusiastic environmentalists. At about the same time the Grupo de Río nations, fresh from their Eighth Summit, were presenting an agenda to the U.S. government for the upcoming Miami Summit, at least a part of which, for example, hemispheric free market after 2005, was accepted without discussion. But what happened at the Miami Summit of 1994?

Chile joined NAFTA or it was agreed that it would do so. It is true that thirty-four heads of state agreed to begin talks in January 1995 aimed at establishing a free trade zone by 2005. These heads of state dutifully executed a twenty-eight-page "Action Plan" brimming with utopian projects among which may be remarked the following: (1) 2010 was set as the year when all hemispheric children will be completing primary school and when 75 percent of them will be completing high school; (2) By 2000 the child mortality of 1990, it is pledged, will be reduced by one-third, maternal mortality by one-half; (3) and so on.

Did any of these eminent statesmen believe that any of these goals would be approached? Was this elaborate, thirty-four-nation gala merely a public-relations gambit? Or was it something else?

Sources in Miami told LANS at the time that the real Miami agenda was the readmission of Castroite Cuba into the OAS. Whether or not this was accurate, the San Salvador meeting of Central American foreign ministers (23–25 November 1994) after the Ecology Summit in Nicaragua had this rehabilitation on its agenda for the Miami Summit. The Cuban community in Miami was convinced of the seriousness of the possibility and on 10 December some 200,000 to 300,000 of them demonstrated against it. However serious the danger of Castro readmission may have been, this demonstration strengthened the hand of President Menem of Argentina in opposing it.

* * *

Contemporary political documents are routinely written by statesmen using four guidelines:

a. An imminent disaster threatening the voting public looms.
b. Only these statesmen (politicians) are capable of protecting their constituents from this disaster and then only if they are given vast national and international powers and the perquisites which accompany such powers.
c. The document must be sufficiently vague so that the statesmen will be left "with room to maneuver" without awakening the suspicions of their constituents.
d. The scope of the document must be extensive enough to include any areas wherefrom power for the statesmen may now or in future be derived.

When such guidelines are considered in the context of SD it is not difficult to understand the ease with which Gorbachev migrated from the position of chief of one of the world's most totalitarian—and most "polluted"—states, the now defunct U.S.S.R., to that of chief of an "environmental" organization.

Just such a document was issued in June 1996 by the Bolivian Ministry of SD, this as a preliminary to what the Ministry's personnel then thought was to be a repeat of the 1994 Summit. In paragraph 1 of an all-encompassing Preamble, the Ministry clerks state:

> We, the Chiefs of State and elected governments of the Americas, have pledged ourselves to the achievement of sustainable development and we have agreed that the best way of achieving economic and social prosperity consists in offering opportunities to our citizens, providing them access to a productive and healthy environment which permits them to satisfy their needs and aspirations."

As Tocqueville's democracy carries within it the "seeds of its own destruction," so this first paragraph carries within it the whole panoply of that government control which is the only real measure of difference between "left " and "right." Paragraph 1 has been literally translated. Space not permitting, nor vitality justifying, further direct quotation, the subsequent paragraphs may be paraphrased as follows:

2. Extraction, production and consumption of resources are destructive and ruinous of natural riches. This will be "fixed."
3. Increasing exhaustion of natural resources demands immediate and specific action. [What action? Freedom of maneuver. In the early twentieth century "expert" opinion held that coal reserves were to have been exhausted long ago—Ed.]
4. Globalization of our economies demand coordinated efforts to reverse those processes which threaten...
5. The environment cannot be protected if the conditions of human existence are not improved with healthy and dynamic economies.
6. Sustainability embraces the human, social, economic and environmental dimensions of development.
7. Level all economic differences down to some common denominator, nationally and internationally.
8. Must accumulate capital in "its different dimensions": human, natural, financial, physical and institutional.
9. Conscious of differences in resources, this too will be regulated through methods of technical, *financial*, and other kinds of cooperation.
10. Firm support of the OAS and the UN.
11. Firmly committed to the Rio Earth Summit of January 1992.
12. This Summit is going to correct (a) increasing environmental deterioration, (b) increasing levels of poverty, (c) variations in demographics, migration and urbanization, and (d) decreasing creation of real wealth.
13. These imminent disasters will be fixed, how not relevant.

That this should be called the Second Summit of the Americas is borne out by the magnitude of the alleged "improvements" which are being "promised" by the Ministry clerks and which will largely or totally be endorsed by the heads of state. But not by as many heads of state as appeared in Miami.

As already noted, President Clinton is not attending. President Zedillo of Mexico and President Sanguinetti of Uruguay had "conflicts" which precluded their attendance while the Canadian chief of state tied his appearance to that of the U.S. president. By late November 1996 only twenty-six of the thirty-four nations represented in Miami had confirmed their attendance.

* * *

Although Mr. Clinton will be unable to attend the Bolivian Summit because of the press of cabinet appointments, Mrs. Clinton arrived in Bolivia on the afternoon of 3 December to attend the Sixth Conference of Wives of Hemispheric Presidents. In like manner, although Mr. Castro is unable to attend the Bolivian Summit having been expelled from the OAS, his representative, Cuban Women's Federation secretary general Yolando Ferrer, arrived in Bolivia on 30 November to attend the Sixth Conference of Wives.

Latin American Parliament (PARLATINO)

LATIN AMERICAN INTERNATIONAL ORGANIZATIONS (WKLY 1.5, 6 JUNE 1996)

PARLATINO was established in Lima, Peru, in 1964, its institutionalizing treaty signed in 1987. Thirteen presidents met in São Paulo, Brazil, for the inauguration of its permanent seat there in 1993. Its stated objective is the "integration of the nations of the zone." Run by a Junta Directiva, it sent a letter to the UN in August 1993 asking for observer status with that body.

In July 1994 its Special Commission on Social Debt issued the "Declaration of Caracas" after meeting in that Venezuelan city and effectively taking a Castroite anti-neoliberal position blaming the woes of the region on neoliberal (free-market) "microeconomic policies."

In 1996 it met in August to discuss methods of dealing with the $450 billion Latin American debt to include not paying it, another plank in the Cuban caudillo's platform. An observer at this "summit" asked why the economic policies of Fidel Castro, director of the hemisphere's ultimate economic disaster, should be so influential.

Latin American Integration Association (ALADI)
and Free Trade Organization of Latin America (ALCA)

LATIN AMERICAN INTERNATIONAL ORGANIZATIONS (WKLY 1.5, 6 JUNE 1996)

ALADI was founded in 1980, its enabling document the Treaty of Montevideo. It is made up of Argentina, Bolivia, Brazil, Colombia, Chile, Ecuador, Mexico, Paraguay, Peru, Uruguay, and Venezuela plus the Dominican Republic.

Its stated mission is to regulate commerce and seek necessary mechanisms to develop Latin American integration. It dutifully conducts summits from time to time.

ALCA was established with the avowed purpose of implementing the Hemispheric Free Trade Resolution of the December 1994 Miami Summit of the Americas.

Trade and Tariff Associations

COMMON MARKET OF THE SOUTHERN CONE
(WKLY 2.7, 26 SEPTEMBER 1996)

The Common Market of the Southern Cone (MERCOSUR) presently includes the South American nations of Argentina, Brazil, Paraguay, and Uruguay. In the Argentine city of San Luís, capital of San Luís province to the west of Buenos Aires, the Tenth Summit of MERCOSUR Presidents concluded on 25 June 1996 with the announcement that Chile will begin its official integration into their trading group next week (1 October 1996), to be followed next year by Bolivia. Which renders this an appropriate time to discuss this free-trade association which is similar, if hardly identical, to NAFTA or the Free Commerce Treaty (TLC).

On 26 March 1991 in Asunción, Paraguay, the presidents of Argentina, Carlos Menem; Brazil, Fernando Collor de Mello; Paraguay, Andres Rodríguez; and Uruguay, Luís Lacalle, signed an agreement creating MERCOSUR, a regional trading organization. Although all save one of the presidents (Menem) has been replaced,[7] this agreement was preliminarily implemented by its original target date of 1 January 1994. This trading bloc contains some 190 million citizens producing somewhere between one-half and three-quarters of the Latin American gross domestic product (GDP). When fully implemented there will allegedly be no tariff barriers and no restrictions on the movement of people, capital, and products among the four nations.

If there is any truth to the current rhetoric on one "global economy," common markets would appear to be the "wave of the future." The arguments in favor of such economic groupings include expanded markets, elimination of duplication and efficiency of cooperative production for the included economies. The argument against is primarily the protectionist one. The tariff which excludes the products of the nations with lower wage scales, protects the wage scales of the excluding nation. Insofar as MERCOSUR is concerned the same arguments are encountered, an example of the protectionist position being that of Barton (*Christianity and Crisis*, 1993) who adds a curious protectionist concern for "small business" to the usual notions of wages. A 1992 *Business Week* assessment of the already observed effects of MERCOSUR included an increase in trade within the bloc from $2.2 billion in 1987 to $4.9 billion in 1991. Later evaluations appear generally to support a continuing favorable assessment.

One question about such agreements is seldom mentioned. Laws establishing minimum wages apparently exist in all the nations involved. A check with various sources by LANS has verified that the subject of minimum wage differentials between the nations in such trading agreements has not arisen; minimum wage is not mentioned in these agreements. It would therefore appear that whatever nation has the highest minimum wage, if there is a differential, will soon collect the greatest number of the most unskilled in the bloc.

Frenkel et al.[8] have attempted a "theoretical" treatment of the question, "Is world trade becoming more regionalized as a result of preferential agreements such as...MERCOSUR?" They then ask if this is a "good thing" or a "bad thing," concluding it to be the former. However inconclusive such treatments may be, MERCOSUR appears so far to have been a good thing insofar as the member nations are concerned.

Last spring, for example, Jeff Ryser (*Global Finances*, May 1996) reported trade among the four nations doubling to almost $16 billion annually, Dallas and Katz (*Business Week*, 22 April 1996) reporting Brazilian and Argentine trucking up 450 percent. All this was in spite of the temporary setbacks brought on by the collapse of the Mexican peso (Hinchberger, *International Busines*, June 1995). Interestingly enough, Hinchberger had reported such intra-pact trade in mid-1995 as having doubled to over $10 billion, Ryser in 1996 as having "doubled" to over $16 billion. Assuming the correctness of both figures puts the latter (1996) at 60 percent more than the former (1995). For the trading partners it would appear to be a "good thing."

Perhaps the most familiar of MERCOSUR's progenitors is the 1960s creation, the Central American Common Market which Frankel et al. described with apparent accuracy as not having initially "come to much." The Latin American Integration Association (ALADI) is another and perhaps more important such organization. But the most immediate ancestor of MERCOSUR would seem to be the agreement of May 1990. At that time Argentine secretary of Latin American affairs Raul Carignano announced the creation of a "free commerce zone" among Argentina, Brazil, and Chile, something, he said, "we must do today." The shifting sands of politics had molded this into MERCOSUR by the following Spring.

In June 1991, in what was described as a reply to U.S. president George Bush's "Initiative for the Americas," Four Plus One (Cuatro Mas Uno) was created with the signing of an agreement between the United States and the MERCOSUR nations creating a council on commerce and investment. Mr. Bush had made the creation of a "zone of free commerce from Alaska to Tierra del Fuego" a centerpiece of his "Initiative for the Americas," a cry which would be taken up by Mr. Clinton at the Miami Summit of the Americas. The Bush-Clinton proposal would move more slowly, however, than would the one made at Asunción.

On 5 August 1994, the ministers of finance and foreign policy having paved the way, the MERCOSUR presidents met in Buenos Aires to decide on the details of the "foreign" tariffs for the bloc. "Foreign" tariffs are the common Tariff charged on trade goods and services from and to the bloc. The presidents were also to decide on the reduction of the internal tariffs. The target figure for "foreign" duties had been set as 20 percent, but there was considerable haggling to be done here. By the agreement reached, however, duty on industrial machinery and equipment (capital goods) (1) would be 14 percent until 2001 in the case of Argentina and Brazil, Uruguay and Paraguay, who had asked for much lower rates, being given until 2006 to adjust their tariffs on such products. Data processing (2) and electronics equipment (3) would have a foreign tariff which will rise from 12 percent to 16 percent in 2006. All told, capital goods, data processing, and electronics equipment represented 15 percent of the listed products. For the other 85 percent of products foreign duties would rise from 0 percent to 20 percent with the initiation of the trading bloc on 1 January 1995.

And the agreement, apparently modified to suit the taste of the various pacting nations, did go into effect on 1 January 1994, in time to be buffeted by the "tequila effect" of the Mexican peso debacle but apparently not too seriously damaged. Certain South American nations have been seeking admission to MERCOSUR, most prominent among which were Chile and Bolivia.

On 25 June 1996 President Frei of Chile, at the San Luís, Argentina, summit meeting, signed an agreement which, with the ratification of the Chilean Congress, will enlarge MERCOSUR into a truly "Southern Cone" trading bloc on 1 October 1996. Chilean economic staff ministers Eduard Aninat and Alvaro Garcia described this as "a great triumph for Chile." It was initially reported that Chile's membership in ALADI, another trading group, would interfere with its entry into MERCOSUR. As Minister Councilor Carmen Domínguez of the Chilean embassy told LANS, however, a waiver, which eliminated this impasse, was possible under the ALADI 1980 Treaty of Montevideo. If affairs proceed on schedule, as they have to this time, Bolivia will join the Southern Cone group in 1997.

ON THE ORIGINS OF MERCOSUR (SPCL 2.14, 24 NOVEMBER 1996)
ALPHONSE EMANUILOFF-MAX, ASSOCIATE EDITOR, LANS

The subject of MERCOSUR has risen above the regional reference for which it was originally developed and, in the short time since 1995, it has been transformed into an integral part of the economic, and therefore political, systems on the international scene. In addition to the many commentaries, articles, essays, monographs, and even books devoted to MERCOSUR, it appears to us opportune to mention something about the genesis of the South American Common Market, which generally, in the clamor of dispassionate oratory or technical discussion, is passed over and perhaps even ignored. On the fringe of its other antecedents, in origin very close to MERCOSUR, is to be included the clearly Uruguayan initiative, strongly and immediately supported by Buenos Aires, which began with the Treaty of La Plata between Uruguay and Argentina and which led, twenty years later, to the South American Common Market.

* * *

One must take into account that MERCOSUR was not possible under the mechanisms of ALALC. Under its methods of operation, the dismantling of tariffs was effected through negotiations the results of which automatically encompassed all the members through the most favored nation clause. At the 1974 conference of Buenos Aires, Uruguay proposed the following twofold plan of action:

1. To transform the basin of the Plata (encompassing Argentina, Bolivia, Brazil, Paraguay, and Uruguay) into a more profoundly integrated association which included matters of commerce and economy. It would advance toward an arrangement using accords between pairs of countries in accordance with the needs of each. Later development of this concept materialized in the reality of accords such as Argentine Uruguayan Economic Cooperation Convention (CAUSE), Commercial Expansion Protocol (PEC) and that with Paraguay. (See *ut infra*).

2. In order to render these accords viable, especially for Brazil and Argentina, it was proposed that the ALALC system be modified, transforming it into ALADI. And within the framework of this, it was possible to create MERCOSUR.

In this sense, and looking retrospectively from the panorama of today, what appears to us remarkable is the thrust of Uruguayan political intentions at that time. And in this cold and objective verification of the facts there is no other evaluation which expresses it. We emphasize it again prophylactically in order to forewarn some reader, as suspicious as he is wrong thinking, against ignoring the simple truth that the integration processes need solid political and economic bases, something far from the circumstantially imperious regime.

* * *

Of course, the technobureaucratic difficulties, typical of all attempts at innovation in these latitudes where any change leaves damage in its wake, were not few. And the great change that Uruguay made in its foreign policy in the seventies was the precursor of the regional exchange alliances with Argentina and Brazil which used to be called "political oscillation." This type of democracy, which is manifested in constant vacillations because of momentary and circumstantial factors, made possible, in practice, the consolidation of stable relations with nobody. And without stable interstate relations, it is impossible to seek the creation of realistic economic fundamentals. In place of oscillation, parallelism was sought in the development of political and economic relations with Brazil and Argentina. Thus, between 1972 and 1976 was born first CAUSE, with Argentinian and Brazilian participation in Palmar; bridges over the River Uruguay and the improvement of Routes 5,

8, and 9, the lateral maritime limit with Brazil and the Treaty of La Plata and its Maritime Front with Argentina. Some of those common projects were terminated later. However, with Argentina were approved the statutes of the Rivers Uruguay and La Plata.

Here it must be noted, as concerns the treaties of CAUSE and PEC, that conceptually and in practical application they signaled, with their "by pairs of countries" style, a significantly evolutionary event. While the mechanisms of ALALC consisted in collective negotiations, the results of which affected all parties, PEC and CAUSE allowed the arrival at solutions more appropriate to the possibilities and interests of the countries involved. It is obvious that bilateral negotiations are *eo ipso* more efficient and more procedurally amenable to implementations than multilateral negotiations. The latter require a full consensus and frequently collide with specific interest of the various participants whose compatibility demands much more capacity for negotiation and the predisposition toward the conclusions. Uruguay demonstrated as much successful tenacity as flexibility, advancing the modification of the morphological structure of ALALC, the accords were extended to the Cuena del Plata. At the same time Uruguay signed the accords with La Paz and Asunción, offered port facilities to Bolivia and Paraguay, based on navigation through Hidrovia.

The Argentinian-Uruguayan decision to construct the Colonia-Buenos Aires Bridge, was manifested for the first time more than twenty years ago in a September 1976 document. The installation of the gas pipeline was prepared by the construction of the Fray Bentos-Unzue Bridge. The joint exploitation and export of Bolivian iron from Mutin to Nueva Palmira was considered a part of the integration process. And the possibilities of bringing the Pacific closer demanded the accords with Chile, pacting reciprocal port facilities.

* * *

The activities carried out at the beginning of the 1970s by Uruguay in conjunction with Argentina can, then, be considered as the prefiguration of MERCOSUR over which hangs the threat of historical forgetfulness. From this viewpoint there is also the need to mention the role of two of the principal protagonists in this grand undertaking. Juan Carlos Blanco, minister of foreign relations during the period and later senior in the restored democracy, knew how to reduce the problematical whole that faced him from economic abstractions to the level of tangible realities. In doing so he converged with the ebullient Argentine ambassador, Guillermo de la Plaza, who arrived in Montevideo sent by the Perón government with full powers. Through the Rioplato Commercial Days and other multiple initiatives, de la Plaza created a climate very propitious for the completion of the treaties. Both, coinciding in their objectives but with different manners and styles, established the cornerstone of MERCOSUR.

—Translated from the Spanish by the LANS editor

Technical Groupings

Latin American Energy Organization (OLADE)

TWENTY-EIGHTH OLADE MEETING (WKLY 2.17, 5 DECEMBER 1996)

The Twenty-eighth OLADE meeting took place in Guatemala City on 21–22 November 1996 and brought together the ministers of energy from twenty-five Latin American countries. The meeting was preceded by the Twenty-sixth Junta of OLADE Experts which set the agenda.

The OLADE secretary general, the Venezuelan Francisco Gutiérrez, reported that the objective of the meeting was the establishment of a "Latin American Energy Network." This network will extend from Mexico through Central America and down the Andes to Chile, there to swing north again through Argentina, Uruguay, Brazil, Venezuela, and Colombia.

For a number of years OLADE has participated in the establishment of such a network in Central America. Another plan for a similar network to encompass the Caribbean islands was presented to a meeting of the Association of Caribbean States (AEC) Ministers of Energy in San José, Costa Rica, on 24 November. Mr. Gutiérrez stated that the island situation is different in various ways, for example, Santa Lucia has "enormous" geothermal potential due to volcanoes, Barbados and Jamaica suited to wind generation of power.

OLADE, which will be taken over by new officers in January 1997, is "hoping" for the physical completion of the project in two years.

Latin American Economic System (SELA) and Economic Commission for Latin America and the Caribbean (CEPAL)

LATIN AMERICAN INTERNATIONAL ORGANIZATIONS (WKLY 1.5, 6 JUNE 1996)

SELA has twenty-seven member countries, the organization's technical banking personnel devoting themselves largely to technical banking problems.

CEPAL is a "technical organ" of the UN having its seat in Santiago de Chile, its permanent executive secretary the Guatemalan Gert Rosenthal. CEPAL, founded in 1951, held its twenty-fifth session in the resort city of Cartagena de Indios in April 1994. At that time its findings were upbeat, reporting control of inflation and 3 percent increase in GDP. By April 1996, perhaps due to the continuing antineoliberal campaign of the HL, gloom had descended on the twenty-sixth session in San José, Latin America there being cited as having had "a 7 to 8 percent drop in per capita GDP." Which, more than anything else, probably indicates the replacement of free-market with anti-free-market personnel among the representatives serving on the Commission.

Regional Associations

LATIN AMERICAN INTERNATIONAL ASSOCIATIONS (WKLY 1.5, 6 JUNE 1996)

The Organization of Central American States (ODECA) was formed in 1951 to establish the regional unity of Central America, its members Costa Rica, Nicaragua, Honduras, El Salvador, and Guatemala. ODECA has executive, legislative (PARLACEN), and judicial (Central American Court of Justice) branches, it having established the Central American Common Market in 1960. Its Twenty-eighth Summit was held in May 1996 in Montelimar, Nicaragua, its First Summit in Esquipulas, Guatemala, in 1986. The 1996 Summit finished with glowing promises of integration, the centuries old cry in the region.

The Central American Parliament (PARLACEN) numbers only three of the five ODECA states among its members, the Costa Rican and Nicaraguan legislatures not having approved the PARLACEN constitution adopted by a presidential summit in 1987. PARLACEN Political Commission president Danilo Roca told the Conference of Political Parties (Managua, 20–22 May 1996) that "we would be citizens in each [Central American] country" with the same rights under the Central American Nationality Treaty recently approved by a plenary session of PARLACEN.

Andes Pact (PA) had its Eighth Summit in early March which was attended by five Andean nation presidents. At this Summit the "sustainable development" theme played a major role.

G-3 is the three-nation group consisting of Mexico, Colombia, and Venezuela.

The Caribbean Community (CARICOM) and Central America held the Third Central America-CARICOM Ministerial Meeting in San José, Costa Rica in late 1996. This grouping now claims twenty votes in forums such as the OAS and expressed a desire to flex its political muscles.

First Cumbre de Misses [sic] de Centroamérica
(First Summit of Central American Misses)

Various Central American *reinas de belleza* (beauty queens) will assemble in Managua, Nicaragua, from 5 to 10 March 1997 in order to coordinate support actions for social, tourism, and "ecological" problems. The Summit will be hosted by Miss Luz Marina Herdocia, Señorita Nicaragua, who assured the local press that the ladies will sign a document promising benefits to *la niñez* (childhood) as well as tourism and ecological development.

Notes

1. Armando Valladares, *Against All Hope: The Prison Memoirs of Armando Valladares*, Knopf, 1986.
2. The Grupo de Río proceedings contain no reference to this alleged U.S. policy although press reports of the bilateral meeting between Ambassador Albright have the ambassador in Cochabamba to support such a move.
3. Simon I. Patino (b. 1860, Cochabamaba Valley) bought his first share in an Oruro tin mine in 1894, bought full control by 1897, and in 1900 his La Salvadora struck the richest veins ever found in Bolivia. Buying out British and Chilean mining operations and, by 1916, taking over the world's largest smelter of Bolivian tin in Liverpool, he remained Bolivia's dominant miner and chief private banker until his death in the 1940s.
4. Of the various speculations as to the reason for the non-appearance of the U.S. chief of state, President Clinton's own reason—his concern with appointments to his new cabinet prevents his attendance—appears to be least generally accepted.
5. Various sources were convinced that the well known Costa Rican foreign minister was in line to be head of the OAS, only to be overruled by U.S. insistence on an individual who could "deal with Castro." OAS secretary general Gaviria's ability to deal with the Cuban caudillo was illustrated earlier this year by his pilgrimage to Havana to secure the release of his brother from Colombian terrorists.
6. Any sophomore physicist should be familiar with the "greenhouse effect." Therein the electronic-vibrational bands of the atmospheric molecules absorb more strongly from the incoming 6000°K solar black body curve than do their vibration-rotation bands from the 300°K outgoing terrestrial black body curve. The result is of course a warming. But something more than such sophomoric knowledge should be applied to the problem.

7. Fernando Henrique Cardosa is now president of Brazil, Juan Carlos Wasmosy president of Paraguay, and Julio María Sanguinetti president of Uruguay.
8. U. Frankel, E. Stein and, W. Shang-jin, *Journal of Development Economics* 47 (1995).

Contributors

José Carlos Graça Wagner, a native of São Paulo, Brazil, graduated from São Paulo University Law School in the mid-1950s. He was professor of tax and economy law for fifteen years, in 1957 founding his own law offices in São Paulo which now have a branch office in Brasilia and associated offices in six important Brazilian cities. A counselor to various Brazilian legal associations to include the Brazilian Bar Association, and other professional and educational organizations to include the University of São Paulo, he has authored many juridical and economic articles for prominent Brazilian newspapers and periodicals, and he is now serving as president of the Board of the Casper Libero University Foundation. His *Point and Counterpoint* publication and his widely broadcast Opinion on the Air cover various aspects of Brazilian political and social life. He is the president of the Brazilian Foundation for Economic Freedom and Social Development, and his expertise on the São Paulo Forum brought him the accolade of an unsuccessful 1994 lawsuit from da Silva's Workers Party (PT) for "election crime."

Alphonse Emanuiloff-Max is an Uruguayan political scientist, writer, journalist, and honorary consul. Dr. Alphonse Emanuiloff-Max, a native of Bulgaria, received his doctorate in political science in the 1950s in England, then moved to Uruguay and continued his career as a foreign correspondent for various publications in South America, the United States, Africa, and Australia from 1955 to the present. He published an English-language weekly during the 1960s and 1970s, served on various international committees, acted as Uruguayan consul for various Latin American nations and has held posts in the Montevideo city government. He has been the director of the Uruguayan Institute for International Studies and of its publication, *Revista Uruguaya de Estudios Internacionales,* since 1982. He is now president of the POLO publishing and printing company and editor of the daily, *Ultimas Noticias,* and the Uruguayan edition of the Pan American weekly, *Tiempos del Mundo.*

Mario Rosenthal has roots in both the United States and Central America. Born in Guatemala City in 1916 of an American father and a

Salvadoran mother, he grew up in San Francisco, California, attending San Matteo College during the depths of the Depression. He arrived in El Salvador for a brief visit in 1933 when the country was still recovering from the communist-organized uprising of the year before. During the 1936–1951 period he watched U.S. enterprise transform jungles into productive farms, working for seven years for the United Fruit Company, later associated with El Salvador's leading commercial enterprises while familiarizing himself with the economics and politics of the nation. The opportunity to enter his true vocation, journalism, arose after he became a correspondent for the Associated Press reporting from Guatemala and El Salvador. He moved to New York, published *Guatemala* (Twayne, 1961), a review of that country's history to the time of publication, and in collaboration with former President Miguel Ydigoras Fuentes of Guatemala, published the latter's *My War with Communism* (Prentice-Hall, 1962). The book detailed Fidel Castro's support of the leftist movement in Guatemala, a movement which still exists under the same leadership. He was editorial page editor of the most important Spanish-language daily in the United States, *El Diario-La Prensa* of New York. He retired to El Salvador in 1979 as the twelve years of the Marxist-Leninist insurrection was catching fire. He was editor and publisher of the bilingual *El Salvador News-Gazette* until it was sold. Today he continues bravely to express his opinions in his weekly column for *Diario de Hoy*, El Salvador's leading newspaper.

Robert G. Breene, Jr., received a bachelor's degree in military science and engineering from the United States Military Academy (West Point) in 1945, and a doctor of philosophy degree in theoretical physics from Ohio State University in 1953. His career during the succeeding years was succinctly described by *Soldier of Fortune* in 1987:

> **Renaissance Writer**: Robert G. Breene, Jr. has never had to worry much about boredom. In the last forty years he has been a fighter pilot, a test pilot for the Air Force [Flight Test Division, 1947–50], an engineering consultant in the Near East, Far East, and South America [Transportation Consultants, Inc.], a professor of physics, and a newspaper correspondent in Central America for the *Union Leader*. And in his spare time he owned and operated a 600-head cattle ranch in Nevada.
>
> Dr. Breene has also found time to write about his work along the way. In addition to many scientific papers and books, he has authored articles on Nicaragua, El Salvador, Cuba, and Guatemala, and two soon-to-be-published works on military history..."

During the latter 1980s and early 1990s, Breene has carried out investigations in Latin America for various organizations and publications.

Key to Index Abbreviations

A
acct—account
aka—also known as
amb—ambassador
Arg—Argentina

B
BA—Buenos Aires
Bat Amer—Battalon America
bio—biography
Bol—Bolivia
Braz—Brazil
Brit—British

C
cand—candidate
capt—captain
CC—Central Committee
cmd—command
cmdr—commander
Col—Colombia, colonel
cong—congress(ional)
const—constitution(al)
coord—coordinator
corp—corporation
CP—Communist Party
CR—Costa Rica
ct—court

D
dept—department
dir—director
disinfo—disinformation
dpty—deputy
DR—Dominican Republic

E
Ecuad—Ecuador
elect—election(s), elected
ES—El Salvador
est—established, estimated
exec—executive

F
fdr—founder
forgn—foreign
Fr—French
frndshp—friendship

G
Gen—General (title)
gen—general
govt—government
gp—group
Guat—Guatemala

H
hd—head
Hond—Honduras
hq—headquarters

I
imp—important
inaug—inauguration
info—information
intl—international
intro—introduction

K
km—kilometer

L
ldr—leader
LibTheo—Liberation Theology

M
maj—major
Mex—Mexico, Mexican
mgr—manager
muni—municipality

N
narco(traff)—narcotraffick(er, ing)
Nica—Nicaragua

O
ofc—office
ofcly—officially
opn—operation
org—organization

P
Pan—Panama
Paramil—Paramilitary
Parg—Paraguay
pol—political
prob—probably
prof—professor

R
R—River
rd—round
reln—relation
rept—report
Res—Resolution

retd—retired

S
secy—secretary
Sov—Soviet
Span—Spanish
spcl-special

T
terr-terrorist
trnd—trained
trng—training

U
UN—United Nations
Urug—Uruguay

Y
yr—year

Name Index

Abrahantes, José
  friend of Vesco, 167
  died in prison, 188, n.128
Acevedo, Hector Luís
  PPD PR pres. cand. 1996, 26
Acosta, Luz Marian
  assistant to Cardenal, attests to
    Guillen in Nica, 125
Adan Garcia, Abelardo
  Castro letter to, 87
Alemán, José Manuel
  bankrolled Caribbean Legion, 86
Alemán Lacayo, Arnoldo
  elected mayor Managua, bio, 1995
    nominated pres by AL, 29
  wins 1st rd victory over Ortega,
    says no "protocols of transi-
    tion," 37
Alessandri, Jorge
  voter to (1970) from Frei Montalvo
    (1964), 12
Alessandri Besa, Arturo
  UPC pres cand 1993, 13
Alfaro, Eloy
  Ecuad caudillo, his "thought" and
    Alfaro Vive, 162
Alfonsín, Raul
  agreed support const changes of
    UCR, 10
  to decide on pres run in 1998, 11
  turns over pres early to Menem, his
    Primavera Plan, 48
Alfonso, Almino
  Goulart keeps this advocate of a
    "Cuban regime" as PTB ldr in
    Braz House, 57
Allende Gossens, Salvador
  "Marxist physician," 12
  more votes in defeat (1964) than in
    victory (1970), 12
Almarales, Andres

and M-19 attack on Col Supreme Ct,
  amnestied that year by Betancur,
  173
Alsogary, Alvaro
  Arg Min Economy (1956–8); on
    Menem economic plan, 48
Alvarez, Carlos (Chacho)
  ldr of FREPASO, seeks alliance with
    UCR, 10–11
Ana María, major
  at 1996 Chiapas encounter, 102
Andrade, Fernando
  FDNG pres candidate, 5
Arana, Mariana
  in near 3-way tie for Urug pres, 15
Aranibar, Antonio
  MBL 1993 pres cand, 17
Arbenz Guzmán, Jacobo
  Guat pres 1945, "flirted with the
    communists," 135
  directs Guat uprising-invasion from
    Cuba 1960, 136
Arce Castaño, Bayardo
  FSLN Politburo, at URNG forma-
    tion in 1980 Managua, 137
Ardon, René
  Callejas minister, charges against, 7
Arévalo Bermejo, Juan José
  Guat pres 1951, "became one with
    them," ousted by Castillo Armas,
    135
  directs Guat uprising-invasion from
    Cuba, 136
Arguello, Roberto J.
  columnist and banker, H. Ortega in-
    terview, 100
Arias, Celea
  his *My Ideas* & PLH doctrine, 6
Arias, Oscar
  CR pres, credited with Esquipulas
    Accords, 28

255

captured in attempt on Peru legislature, 171

Bermúdez, Enrique
FDN military cmdr, in 1st "Dark Alliance" art narco claims he knew of narcotraff,
in 2nd he did not, 203
in CR court Terrell testifies present at meet with "Amac Galil," in Florida court takes Fifth, 206–207

Bertrand, Francisco
PNH emerges under 1915, 7

Betancourt, Romulo
hd CR CP 1930s, 3
C. A. Pérez his protégée, bio, US Sen Johnston calls "communist ldr of LA," 74

Betancourt de Lisker, Regina
MUM pres cand 1994 Col elects, 19

Betancur Cuartas, Belisario
Col pres 1982, his "peace" an armed camp, 117–118
offers "white flag" to terrorists, "peace of," 161
amnestied Almarales yr of Supreme Ct attack, 173

Beto, Friar
Castro's cleric, introduces Castro and Lula, 98, 191, 193
his periodical, at IV FSP, 99
his works in Rainha home, 108

Biehl, John
Arias advisor, and Esquipulas Accords, 28

Bigotes, Julio
aka Miguel Urroz, Pastora lieutenant, 153
Pastora security chief, 155

Black, George
apologist for Guat terrorists, intro to Payeras book, on new FAR, 137

Blades, Ruben
Salsa singer and MPE Pan pres cand, 9

Bodán, Oliver
Nica journalist, on Guillen-Cerna relationship, 125

Boff, Leonardo
ex friar, LibTheo, on Marxism, 193
his marxist mariology, 196

Bogarev, Basily
Castro intermediary, 87

pres Soviet Youth Society, 110

Bolaños Geyer, Enrique
COSEP hd, potential UNO pres cand, 28
Nica AL vice pres cand 1996, 29

Bolívar, Simón
Great Liberator, Bol named after, 53

Bonhoeffer, Dietrich
LibTheo cleric, LibTheo passed from Protestant to Catholic by him, 195

Bonilla, Policarpo
and PLH doctrine, 6

Borge, Tomás
surviving FSLN fdr, tells TV D. Ortega "now believes in God," 35
represents FSLN at FCPR, 142
frequent visitor to Havana, 150
Pastora enemy, puts price on Hull, 151
deputy minister of defense, 152
his castration claimed, 191

Bordón, José Otavio
FREPASO cand for Arg pres 1995, 10
senator, 10

Borja, Rodrigo
Ecuad pres, of ID, arrange Alfaro peace, 162

Bosch, Juan
in book on Debray, 104

Botero, Fernando
Samper's camp mgr and Min Def, jailed on narco charges, 20
on narco charges, 20, 163

Boutros Ghali, Boutros
UN secy gel, reelection, 92

Braden Spruille
US amb, on Robin Hooding of Castro, 103
on Castillo Armas' revolt, 135

Branco, Humberto Castello
Braz army ofcr, counter coup ousts Goulart, 57–58

Brezhnev, Leonard
Sov chief of state, at XXIII CPSU Cong, 97

Brizola, Leonel
PDT pres cand 1994, 11
orchestrates navy rebellion, 58

Bucaram Ortiz, Abdala
PRE pres cand 1996, wins in runoff, bio, 21

independent Nica Assembly deputy, 30

MAR pres cand, challenges various cand, 30

Hernández Chavarria, Carlos
secy genl of UABJO, murdered by ORCUP, 132

Higuchi, Susana
wife of Fujimori 1990, left Peru pres palace, into politics, 23–24

Hirschfeld Almada, J.
Mex dir genl of airports, kidnapped, 129

Hoenigsberg, Guillermo
overhears Castro and del Pino discuss Bogotazo, 111

Honey, Martha Spencer
in La Penca and Contra Drug disinfo opns, 197–199, 203–207
offer Pocosol captives money and freedom for "false testimony" according to affidavits, 200
"From Hanoi With Love," 209–210

Hull, John
Borge price on head 1995, 151
sues Honey-Avirgan in CR court, H-A allege he murdered David (see Mortera), 199
accused of shipping drugs out of his strip, demonstrably impossible, 201

Ibañez, Bernardo
pres IAWC, report on Bogotazo, 109

Illia, Arturo
Arg pres, amnesty frees Cooke, 159

Imbassay, Antonio
wins mayor Salvador (Braz), 12

Jackson, Jesse
invited by Pérez B. as Pan elect observer 1994, 9

Jaramillo, Cecilia
psychologist, attests to Bucaram normality, 22

Jet, Dennis
US amb to Peru, leaves Jap emb shortly before MRTA attack, 178

Jiang Zemin
pres Peoples Rep China, with Zedillo, 92
Castro visits, 92

Jiménez Sarmiento, D.
director Mex Liga de Septiembre, dead in kidnap attempt, 129

John Paul II
RC pope, on LibTheo, 193

Jorge, Antonio
prof of Economics and Intl Relns, on Cuban economy, 91–92

Jovel, Ernesto
aka Roberto Roca, a FARN chief, 147

Julião, Francisco
honorary pres Braz Peasant Leagues, 107

Keiko, Sofia
eldest Fujimori daughter, Peru 1st Lady, 23

Khrushchev, Nikita
allegedly recruited Castro to narco-trafficking, 163

King, James Lawrence
US district court judge, heard Honey-Avirgan RICO suit, dismissed as with no evidence, 210

Kornfeder, Joseph Zack
ML recruiter, defector, on whom left recruits, 175

Krischik, Mark
USIS chief in San José, interview on Honey, 199, 205

Lacayo Oyanguren, Antonio
de Chamorro's son in law, power behiund throne, 28
restructures Nica Assembly, 30
challenged for pres run as president's son in law, 31

Lacerda, Carlos
politician and journalist, Vargas security hd orders murder, 57

Laina, Domingo
secy of Cuban Peoples' Power Assembly, visits Parg, 14

Laro, Juan
vice pres IAWC, confirms Ibañez on Bogatazo, 109

La Violencia
grows out of Col Bogotazo, FARC formed during, 111

Lechín Oquendo, Juan
hd of Bol POR and FSTMB, repre-

US amb, hears Castro on radio during Bogotazo, 111
Paz, Rodrigo
Ecuad DP pres cand 1996, 21
Paz Ballivian, Ricardo
expelled from Ecuad CONDEPA, supported by Monica Medina, 18
Paz Estensorro, Victor
fdr ("godfather") of Bol MNR, 51
put into pres 1952, aucceeded Siles 1964, to exile 1964, supports Banzer 1971,
pres 1985, 52
Paz Tejeda, Carlos A.
Guat army col, overall military command 1960 revolt-invasion, 136
Paz Zamora, Jaime
accused Bol narco activities, retires, returns, 18
nephew of Paz E., Banzer drew toward free mkt, pres 1989, 53–54
visits Echeverria in prison, retires, visits Eid in prison, out of retire, 55
Peña Gómez, Francisco
in 1996 DR elects, Castroite, at Sandin rally Managua, 25
"race card" in runoff elect, support from IV FSP, 100
Peñaranda, Enrique
Bol genl ofcr, elected pres 1940, 51
Pérez, Carlos Andres
Figueres felicitates, 3
Ven pres, removed for malversion 1993, 24, 73
oil deal with Nica, 41
biography, pres (1973–9), pres (1988–93), 74–75
secret meeting with Castro et al, 75
Pérez, Manuel
current Col ELN chief, cleric, aka Poliarco, with Alonso Ajeda formed EPL, 113, 194
Pérez Baladares, Ernesto
aka Toro (Bull), won Pan pres 1994 with 33.3%, 9
Pérez de Cuellar, Javier
OAS hd, Peru pres cand 1995, 23, 170
Pérez Jímenez, Marcos
Ven caudillo, ousted by Betancourt coup, 74
Pérez Paz, Oswaldo Alvarez

COPEI Ven pres cand , 24
Perón, Juan Domingo
biography, elected Arg pres 1946, asylum 1955, ret 1973, 46–47
death leaves Isabel Arg pres, 158
leaves Cooke as head his resistance, 159
Petronius Arbiter
1st century AD Roman satirist, 22
Peynado, Lacinto
on PRSC ticket in 1996 DR elects, 25
Piñera, José
independent Chile pres cand 1993, 12
Piñiera Losado, Manuel
head Cuba Americas Dept, courses for Guillen, 126
at URNG formation in 1980 Managua, 137
at FMLN formation in 1980 Managua, 146–147
Pinochet Ugarte, Augusto
produces Chile "economic miracle," 13
Castro assassination attempt against, 232
Pipes, Richard
Baird Prof of History, on nazi-communist equivalence, 2
Pius X
RC pope, on LibTheo, 193
Pizarro, Eugenio
MIDA Chile pres cand 1993, 13
Pizarro, Gonzalo
arrived Peru early XVI Century, 50
Pizarro, Hernando
arrived in Peru early XVI Century, 50
Pizarro Leon-Gómez, Carlos
hd Col M-19, negotiated peace, killed, 116
Plutarch
1st Century AD Greek historian, biographer of Tiberius G., 107
Polay Campos, Victor
MRTA chief, captured Jun 92, 171
brief bio, 174–175
college roommate of Alan Garcia, 175
Pombo
diarist with Guevara in Bol, 105
Pont, Raul

Subject Index

in 1996 pres elects, 21
AR-15 [Armalite Rifle]
    carried by EPR at Aguas Blancas,
        127
ARDE [Democratic Revolutionary Alliance]
    Pastora military chief of, 152–153
    La Penca bombing at hq of, 197
ARENA [National Republican Alliance] (ES)
    In 1994 elects gets pres & 39 legislative seats, 4
Argentina
    illustration of 3 left ideologies, 2
    political divisions, 10
Argentine Constitution of 1853
    allegedly modeled on US Const, 46
Argentine Constitution of 1994
    Constituent Assembly replaced 1853 Const with, 10
Argentine Legislature
    Bicameral; Senate & Chamber of Deputies under 1994 Const, 10
Argentine Economy
    roots of problems; Menem and recovery, 46–50
    Chafuen on, 48
    battle for neoliberalism, 48–50
    Tagliavinni & Edwards on, 49–50
Argentine Stock Exchange
    fell 3% 4/1/95; fell 3% 4/2/95; Tequila Effect, 45
    [Nuestra Señora de] Asunción capital of Parg; founded 1537 by Juan de Salazar y Espinoza, 72
ATE [Assopciation of State Workers] (Arg)
    opposing privatization, 49

Babies and bayonets
    disinformation on tale, 127
Bandera Roja
    "Maoist," emerged from Peru CP 1964, 169
Barricada (Managua)
    reported Guillen immediate superior Cerna, trained in Brigade 3–68, 125
Batallón América
    intl terror org formed 1986, brief bio, 162
    Sendero member with other gps, 169

Bogotazo
    Castro's participation in, 85, 111
    genl. Discussion of, 109–112
    La Violencia arose from, 111–112
Bolivia
    illustration of 3 left ideologies, 2, 57
    cocaleros in, 17
    landlocked by War of the Pacific; disastrous Chaco War; named for Bolívar, 53
    legal and illegal coca-leaf production, 54
    entry into MERCOSUR, 55–56
BOS [Southern Opposition Bloc] (Nica)
    financed by C. A. Pérez; A. Cesar emerged from, 75
Brady Bonds
    dollar denominated on sale in Caracas (1995), 77
Brazil
    as empire until 1889; the Vargas period (1930–1955); the Goulart crisis ended by 1963 counter coup; Sarney, Collor de Mello & democracy, 56–59
Brigade 3–68
    responsible for Jinotega, Nica, Guillen trained in, 125–126
Broad Front [Urug]
    defined, 42, n.13
[Santa María de] Buenos Aires
    est 1590 by Juan de Garay, 46
    first constitution 1996, 11

C-4
    Plastic explosive, Castro news claims used at La Penca, 204
Cambio 94 (Pan)
    Carles pres candidate 1994, 9
CAP [Peoples Armed Commandos]
    dissolved by Mex govt 1971, 129
CAP [Civil Defense Patrols], various countries
    in Peru, 189
Caribbean Legion
    brings Pepe Figueres to power in CR, 3
Carter Center
    35 observers of Nica elects from include ex US Pres Carter, ex CR Pres Arias & ex Ecuad Pres Hurtado, 36

wins 35 deputies 1994, 12

PPD [Party for Democracy] (Chile)
  won 2 Senate and 15 deputy seats
    1993, in council race 1996, 13–
    14

PPD [Popular Democratic Party] (PR)
  in pres. race, won 6 Senate and 16
    House seats 1992, 26

PPR [Reformed Progressive Party]
    (Braz)
  won 52 deputies 1994, 12

PPUA [American United Proletarian
    Party]
  Mex group arose about 1971, 129

PPV [Prisoners' Party] (CR)
  in 1998 elects., 4

Prague (Czechoslovakia), 84

PRAP [Public Administration Reform
    Program] (Hond)
  Reina's agency for neoliberalism, 71

PRD [Revolutionary Democratic Party]
    (Mex)
  wins 14 muni races State of Mex,
    59 deputies 1994, 27
  in FSP encounters, 98–99
  est "formal reln" with EZLN, 185,
    n.75

PRD [Revolutionary Democratic Party]
    (Pan)
  wins pres. and 31 seats 1994, 9
  at FSP, 99
  at Aguas Blancas 1996, 127

PRE [Ecuad Roldosista Party] (Ecuad)
  Bucaram won pres. under 1996, won
    19 congress seats, 21

Prensa Libre (Guat)
  Reina remarks on "Chicago boys," 5

PRI [Institutional Revolutionary Party]
    (Mex)
  won 62 muni races, State of Mex,
    300 deputies in 1994 elects.,
    throws out accords, 27
  ambivalence on Castro in, 124
  predecessors, 185, n.69

PRIN [National Left Revolutionary
    Party] (Bol)
  Porcel Salazar represents at TCC,
    104

PRJ [Piles of Rusty Junk] argument on
    missiles in Cuba, 182, n.21

PRN [Nica Resistance Party] (Nica)
  Contra organization, 29

est. win 1 Assembly seat, 40

Proceso
  Mex periodical further info on
    groups leading to EPR, 129

PROCUP [Clandestine Revolutionary
    Workers Party]
  allegedly arose from 1965 Madera
    Barracks attack, 129

PROCUP-PDLP
  PROCUP and PDLP joined by 1992,
    129
  EPR armed branch of, 131
  militants seized on arms charges,
    organization of, 134
  OCSS front group for, 217

Progressive Encounter (Urug)
  in near tie for 1994 pres. elect., 15

PRONA [National Order Rebuilding
    Party] (Braz)
  in pres. race 1995, 11

PRONAL [National Project] (Nica)
  Lacayo org. for pres. race, 30
  est. won 2 seats, 40

Protoocols of Transition (Nica)
  set stage for Sandins to "govern
    from below," 30

PRS [Radical Social Democrat] (Chile)
  1996 councilmanic elects., 14

PRSC [Social Christian Reform Party]
    (DR)
  in 1996 elects., 25

PRTC [Central American Workers
    Party] (ES)
  remains in FMLN, 4
  one of five terrorist gps in FMLN,
    147

PS [Socialist Party] (Chile)
  won 5 Senate, 15 deputy seats, 13

PSB [Braz Socialist Party] (Braz)
  won 14 deputies 1994, 12

PSC [Social Chritian Party] (Chile)
  in 1996 councilmanic race, 14

PSC [Social Conservative Party] (Col)
  2nd in pres. race, wins 40 Senate and
    40 deputy seats 1994, 19–20, 163

PSC [Social Christian Party] (Ecuad)
  won 26 Congress seats 1996, 21

PSDB [Braz Social Democrat Party]
    (Braz)
  Cardosa pres. cand of 1994, 11
  won 22 Senate and 108 deputy seats
    1994, 12